CW00923239

THE FABULOUS FRANCES FARQUHARSON

THE COLOURFUL LIFE OF AN AMERICAN IN THE HIGHLANDS

THE FABULOUS FRANCES FARQUHARSON

THE COLOURFUL LIFE OF AN AMERICAN IN THE HIGHLANDS

CAROLINE YOUNG

First published 2023

The History Press
97 St George's Place, Cheltenham,
Gloucestershire, GL50 3QB
www.thehistorypress.co.uk

© Caroline Young, 2023

The right of Caroline Young to be identified as the Author
of this work has been asserted in accordance with the
Copyright, Designs and Patents Act 1988.

All rights reserved. No part of this book may be reprinted
or reproduced or utilised in any form or by any electronic,
mechanical or other means, now known or hereafter invented,
including photocopying and recording, or in any information
storage or retrieval system, without the permission in writing
from the Publishers.

British Library Cataloguing in Publication Data.
A catalogue record for this book is available from the British Library.

ISBN 978 1 80399 253 2

Typesetting and origination by The History Press
Printed and bound in Great Britain by TJ Books Limited, Padstow, Cornwall.

Trees for LYfe

Contents

Foreword

Some years after my mother's death, when going through her papers, I found a considerable amount of handwritten and undated chapters in her unique handwriting. It was the beginning of a book which she obviously never wrote.

A great deal of what she had written about was her life in Seattle and the beginning of her travels in Europe, which was new to me and I found it incredibly fascinating. It was groundbreaking, especially for the early 1900s, and I felt it would be nice to share her life story with you.

She really lived four completely different lives, beginning in Seattle via Europe and England, and culminating in the wilds of Northern Scotland.

Shorty afterwards I was approached by Caroline Young, who asked permission to write about my mother. She sent me her book about Coco Chanel and having read it I decided to let her take on the task. Together we have pieced together her life like a jigsaw puzzle – much enjoyable! I hope you will enjoy it. I am very grateful to Caroline for all her work.

There is no doubt my mother was a truly remarkable person and I feel very fortunate to have had her as my mother. She is much missed.

Marybelle Drummond

Acknowledgements

Firstly, thank you Marybelle for allowing me to tell the story of your mother, and for providing her partially written memoir, which helped me piece it all together. I'm eternally grateful! Over the last couple of years, I've loved exploring Frances' colourful life and I only hope that I have done her justice. Hearing Marybelle describe her mother so vividly, insisting that there was absolutely no one like her – she was so incredibly unique, flamboyant and charming – stayed with me as I worked to complete this biography. Marybelle also put me in touch with her second cousin in Seattle, Heidi Narte, who shared photos of Frances and her father, and provided some of her knowledge and research into her early life in Washington.

I also owe gratitude to Georgina Ripley, curator of modern and contemporary design at the National Museum of Scotland, who first told me about the American in the Highlands and her fabulous wardrobe. I was researching my 2017 book *Tartan and Tweed* and Georgina mentioned that Frances Farquharson was a wonderful example of someone who put her own stamp on tartan, combining the traditions of the fabric with an eccentric flair. It was at that moment I made a mental note to find out more about Frances, and it was during the Covid pandemic, as I explored new writing opportunities, that I was able to begin delving into her life.

Thanks also to Lisa Mason, assistant curator of modern and contemporary design at the National Museum of Scotland, who shared photos and details of the museum's collection of pieces from Frances' wardrobe, and who showed me the Schiaparelli dresses and suits, and a natty rainbow-coloured bag and matching peep-toe shoes from Saks Fifth Avenue.

As part of this research, I visited the collection centre at Aberdeen Art Gallery and Museum and viewing the items in its collection, including the famous tartan cape, tweed suits and colourful evening gowns, gave me further insight into her fabulous wardrobe. Thanks to Morna Annandale, Madeline Ward and Jenna Rose at the galleries, who arranged this and were helpful with my questions.

I'm really grateful to Norma Sudworth, who spoke so wonderfully about her father Norman Meldrum, who was Captain Farquharson's personal piper. And to David Geddes, president of the Braemar Royal Highland Centre, and Doreen Wood, who sat down with me in the visitor centre to discuss their memories of Frances. Doreen opened up the doors of Braemar Castle for me so that I could take a look around and explore. It was the day before it was set to close for an extended refurbishment, so it felt very fortuitous.

Charlotte and Catherine Drummond, thank you for sharing your memories of assisting Frances at Invercauld, and of her kindness and wisdom; and to Hugh Cantlie for granting me some time to talk about how Frances was such an encouraging force of nature. I'm also grateful to Marcia Brocklebank, who spoke of her friend Francie so beautifully, describing her colour, dynamism, warmth and kindness.

Thanks to Justine Picardie, who kindly shared her knowledge of being a *Harper's Bazaar* editor, as well as some of her discoveries when she had looked into Frances' life.

I'm also very grateful to Annie Stewart of the Scottish textile company Anta. We met for coffee in Edinburgh, and her impressions of Frances from that time were invaluable. She kindly gave permission to use her beautiful Anta Frances Farquharson tartan on the cover of this book, which she was inspired to design after meeting her in 1990. The beauty of this fabric is a perfect representation of Frances Farquharson and her distinctive and impressively inimitable life.

Finally, thanks to my agent Isabel Atherton at Creative Authors, and Mark Beynon and Rebecca Newton at The History Press for their encouragement and support.

Introduction

On the outskirts of Aberdeen, in a purpose-built modern construction, is the archive of the Aberdeen Art Gallery and Museum, a temperature-controlled storage space with rows that unfold like butterflies to reveal countless treasures. Within this vast collection is the extensive, perfectly preserved wardrobe of Frances Farquharson.

As the beautiful American-born editor of the British edition of *Harper's Bazaar* in the thirties and forties, you'd expect that Mrs Farquharson would possess the fabulous wardrobe to match. There are hundreds of items in the archive, from delicate silk dresses and blouses by Schiaparelli and Mainbocher to sturdy but smooth-to-the-touch tweeds from local weavers, polished leather shoes and gleaming brooches, and the bright powder-puff tam-o'-shanters that were her signature in the Highlands of Scotland. Indeed, this collection not only reveals the rich and varied life of a fashion dynamo but also provides an insight into what made her so attractive to all who knew her.

She was the vivacious American who charmed aristocracy when she arrived in Europe from Seattle in the roaring twenties. Glowing with enthusiasm, she was an energetic counterpoint to Old-World tradition, and whenever she arrived in a room, all eyes were drawn to her. As a fashion journalist in the thirties, she lived a whirl of exclusive parties, fashion shows and debutante balls, where she introduced Elsa Schiaparelli's daughter at the 1938 season. Her patrician image regularly featured in the society columns, a regal sculpted eyebrow, sharp cheekbones and a halo of fur accentuating her dark-haired beauty.

Alongside the black wool dress by Edward Molyneaux and the cream blouse by Elsa Schiaparelli, both of whom were personal friends, there are vintage pieces from Marks & Spencer, including a black pleated day dress from the 1940s, which wouldn't look out of place in department stores today.

She wasn't particular about labels – if an item was well made and flattering, she would embrace it. Evening mules decorated with hearts were worn to a New York Valentine's Day ball; there's a summer dress bought on a trip to Palm Beach in 1930; yellow espadrilles from Majorca; a tartan two-piece swimsuit to champion Scotland when on beach holidays in the 1950s; a printed Hermès silk turban from the 1940s; pairs of glitzy peep-toed Delman shoes; and a selection of mohair skirts and tops from Scottish manufacturers in an array of brilliant hues.

Also included in the collection is a pair of brown shoes which were part of the government's utility scheme, introduced in 1942. Following the outbreak of war in 1939, Frances earned plaudits for her wartime leadership of British *Harper's Bazaar*, under her business name, The Hon. Mrs James Rodney, from her late first husband. Not only did she print morale-boosting messages and practical advice to the women of Britain, who were suffering under bombing raids and rationing, but she delivered an ambitious campaign in the United States to encourage American department stores to buy British. As the only woman in the boardroom, she actively persuaded the Ministry of Trade and reluctant textile manufacturers, who were sceptical of her feminine energy, that British exports could deliver much-needed dollars to help win the war.

A red leather Elsa Schiaparelli travel bag still has a brown cardboard transport tag attached to it, handwritten with the words 'Invercauld'. The bag may have been from the 1930s, but Frances was carrying it with her more than a decade later, when she first visited Royal Deeside with her third husband, Captain Alwyne Farquharson, the 16th Laird of Invercauld. After the war, she spent the second half of her life in Invercauld, in the heart of the Cairngorms on Royal Deeside.

The item in the collection that sums up Frances the most is the dramatic Farquharson tartan wool cloak, worn with a matching jacket, skirt and cap, which was custom-made for her by Aberdeen tailors Christie & Gregor. It was once she married Alwyne, Chief of Clan Farquharson, in 1949, that she fully embraced Scottish traditions to affirm her new position as lady of one of the largest estates in Scotland and owner of two castles – Invercauld and Braemar, and Torloisk House on the Isle of Mull. She wholeheartedly embraced the Highlands, where she was tireless in promoting the culture – its history, music, cottage-industry arts and its textiles.

With her flamboyant glamour and the tartan capes punctuating every sweeping gesture, she became one of the most recognisable figures in the village of Braemar, and her indomitable and persuasive persona helped to bring much-needed business to the area. For almost fifty years she appeared side-by-side with the royal family in their pavilion at the annual Braemar Gathering, where she ensured she was always cheerleading Scotland, and its textiles, in her eye-catching tartan outfits.

If you wish to follow in her footsteps, Braemar is an hour's drive from Aberdeen. The further west you travel, the road becomes windier and the gentle green farmland turns craggy and rough, with endless hills covered in smatterings of gorse and heather. The grouse moors resemble a piece of tweed fabric, in their rusty browns, oranges and greens, like the leaves that blaze in autumn. Eventually, you come to the immense Invercauld Estate, which edges onto the deep forests of Deeside. Invercauld is only a short drive to Balmoral Castle, reached along a narrow road which clings to the River Dee and is flanked by deep forests of soaring pine trees.

In the village, there are faint whispers in the air, and in the babble of the Cluny Waters that cuts through it, of a remarkable woman and her unique spirit. Her influence is evident in the yellow and pink interiors of the turreted fairy-tale castle, Braemar. In the disused local church, where she ran a theatre, she designed pink murals which told the story of the Farquharson family, but these have long been hidden away when the building was converted to flats. The fashion boutique, men's sporting clothes shop and the antique shop she founded in the village closed soon after her death, and the colourful embellishments to the grey granite of Invercauld, such as the yellow window frames and pink game larder, have been painted over.

Still, you can imagine her draped in the green and blue Farquharson tartan, resplendent against the grey stone of Invercauld Castle, and with the outdoor larder like a rose petal against a layer of fresh snow. As her daughter Marybelle Drummond said, 'Like most Americans, she didn't do things by halves. She didn't paint, but she was an artist, expressing herself through clothes and colour.'

I came across one of her elaborate tartan costumes in the National Museum of Scotland in Edinburgh, which also holds an extensive collection of pieces from her wardrobe, while researching a book on tartan, and the story of a true fashion original living in Scotland captivated me. I made enquiries at the offices of Invercauld as to whether I could be put in touch with her family, so that I could delve a little deeper into her life. Her much younger husband, Captain Alwyne Farquharson, who had celebrated his centenary year in 2019, had been namechecked in an episode of Netflix's *The Crown* in Season One, for leasing some of his moors to the queen. A couple of weeks later, I received a phone call from Marybelle and a handwritten letter from Captain Alwyne, from the Farquharson seat in Norfolk, where the captain now lived with his second wife:

> I should begin by telling you I am now aged 101 years old, exceptionally deaf, and don't see as well as I once did, but I will try to help you as best I can. My darling wife Francie was indeed remarkable in many ways, and enjoyed helping people develop their talents.

Over the course of several more phone calls with Marybelle, we chatted about Frances' life and how best to tell her story in a biography. As I learnt more about her, the more intriguing she became. She possessed a completely unique and intuitive sense of style, a natural warmth and charm that drew people to her, and a contagious *joie de vivre*. She was larger than life; a force of nature who threw herself into every new adventure with gusto and held a lifelong passion for helping others achieve their best. All those who received a letter from her could attest to her distinctive and effervescent looped handwriting in black marker. As a journalist, she had an impeccable memory, never taking notes and never forgetting the details about the people she interviewed.

She came of age at the dawn of a new era for women's liberation, yet it was still incredibly unusual for an American woman to live her life so independently. She chose to travel the world, rather than settle down to raise a family in her hometown. She crossed the Atlantic with her eyes wide open, relishing each new experience, and in turn, Old Europe was receptive to charming American girls like her, who were beyond the restrictions of the established class system.

The upper echelons tended to be off limits to those who hadn't been born into it, but Frances was welcomed into the most exclusive spaces, from London's Marlborough House to a Romanian royal palace in the Carpathian Mountains. She used her own talents and magnetism to forge a path into the top rungs of society, where she met some of the most interesting figures of the day and was witness to some of the major events of the twentieth century.

Her life may have resembled that of an American character in a Henry James novel, who is both intrigued by and intriguing to Europeans. Perhaps she could be considered a real-life Isabel Archer from *The Portrait of a Lady*, a New-World beauty who moves to Europe to stay with her aunt, mixes with old money and is determined to see all she can and maintain her freedom, before choosing a husband and settling down. At a time when women rarely found independent success, Frances transcended boundaries as a working woman of her own means, and unlike Isabel Archer, she wasn't constrained by her husband when she did decide to settle.

I discovered that she'd gone by several different names throughout her life, with each one defining the next chapter in her journey. She was Frances Lovell Oldham, the Hon. Mrs James Rodney, Mrs Charles Gordon, Mrs Frances Farquharson of Invercauld. She was a Seattle Gibson Girl in the first decades of the twentieth century, a jazz-loving American in Europe in the twenties, a fashion editor for one of the most influential magazines in the thirties, and a rallying force during the Second World War to make a difference to the war effort. By the fifties, she used her persuasiveness and influence to boost the fortunes of Invercauld Estate and to help put the tiny village of Braemar on the map. Throughout her life, she created different worlds for herself, as if they were distinct chapters in her book, moving on to another incarnation when one was closed.

Many aspects of her life could be defined by that eye-catching costume on display in the fashion galleries of the National Museum of Scotland. Among the eighteenth-century panniers, corseted Victorian gowns and sixties mini-dresses is a feast of tartan extravagance: a Turkish harem trouser suit and turban in vivid green-and-blue checks, cut with narrow stripes of red and yellow. It's a rare and kitsch combination of Scottish heritage and Middle Eastern style, and it was the type of suit that could be mistaken for a punky Vivienne Westwood or Jean Paul Gaultier. But rather than being created and worn by an *enfant terrible* of the seventies and eighties or shipped to the Highlands by a Paris atelier, it was of course conjured up by Frances herself.

As well as showcasing her family tartan, the suit represented her career as a prominent fashion editor, and her fascination with other cultures. After sketching it out, she gave her design to a local tailor, who constructed it from silk fabric in the Farquharson tartan. I found out, through conversations with Marybelle, that her mother wore it to one of the famous ghillies balls at Balmoral Castle in the late fifties, hosted by Queen Elizabeth and Prince Philip. Held every September to mark the end of the summer season at Balmoral, the dance was a tradition begun by Queen Victoria and Prince Albert in their first year in the castle in 1852, as a way of thanking their staff and servants.

As the sun set over the turrets of Balmoral Castle, the guests waited to be greeted by the Queen and Prince Philip in the drawing room. It was a custom of the ball for ladies to wear long ballgowns, and for gentlemen to be in black-tie Highland dress, with a kilt in their family tartan. But here was Frances, dressed in tartan by way of the Middle East, and wowing the room with her warm, magnetic personality. As the guests took to the ballroom floor to dance the Eightsome Reel, we can only imagine the comment Prince Philip would have made about such a striking outfit.

The eccentricity of this outfit perfectly encapsulated her sense of fun, her confidence and her innate affection for Scotland. Hers is a remarkable story, and through the eyes of the Fabulous Frances Farquharson, we can experience the life of a very modern twentieth-century woman.

9 December 1933, Hampshire

The fire broke out in the early hours of an icy December morning, when the crackling of flames cut through the stillness of the night and the corridors of the country home choked with acrid smoke. Frances and James Rodney had only retired to bed a few hours before, having spent an evening being entertained by their host, famed Chicago architect Leander J. McCormick, and his wife, Renée, the Countess de Fleurieu, in the comforts of their antique-filled drawing room, warmed by a roaring fire.

They were awakened by the sound of Mrs McCormick's panicked French lilt calling out in the night to rouse her sleeping guests and servants. Mid-slumber confusion was followed by the realisation that the house was on fire. They pulled back the covers of the four-poster bed and rushed out the bedroom door into the hallway. With smoke clouding their view, they felt their way to the staircase, but just as they reached their escape route, flames shot out over it, engulfing the main exit point in the house. Frances and her husband of five years, Captain James Rodney, had been invited for a weekend retreat at McCormick's newly renovated historic country spread, known as the Heronry. McCormick, originally from Chicago, was the son of the author and inventor L. Hamilton McCormick, and grandson of one of the founders of the International Harvester Company. He may have been of rich American stock, but he was raised and educated in England, having attended Eton and Cambridge. He had recently wed the Countess de Fleurieu, herself an author of several novels set in France, including *Dangerous Apple*, and had adopted her two children from her first marriage. With his architect's eye, having worked on some of Chicago's most prestigious buildings as part of a wave of modernist construction in the first decades of the century, he used his trust fund to purchase an idyllic English country manor in need of renovations.

The Heronry, an old mill house with an irregular shape from the adaptations and extensions carried out over the years, was 2 miles from the picturesque Hampshire village of Whitchurch, and positioned by the River Test, which was renowned for its trout fishing. After moving in the year before, the McCormicks spent £3,000 modernising it, with electricity powered by the mill in the river and central heating installed to take the edge off the cold and bring it into line with an American's expectation of comfort. Renée had decorated it in the French style, with crisp white walls, heavy curtains and antiques to complement the oak panelling. Leander had recently received a shipment of some of his paintings from his home in the United States, which he hung proudly on the walls of his retreat.

Typically, after breakfast, McCormick would go down to the bottom of his garden to fish for fat trout and would encourage his guests to do the same. On news of the fire, a society columnist at the *Daily Mail* recounted how they, too, had stayed at the Heronry just a few months before, in a room close to where the Rodneys had been sleeping:

> That week-end I had caught a large basket of trout in a neighbour's stream, and coming in late for dinner had told my hostess that I had brought the basket into the hall. She cried out in mock alarm, in her delightful broken English. 'Why you bring those nasty fish inside my lovely white house?'[1]

To celebrate the remodelling of the home and bring in the Christmas season, the McCormicks hosted a weekend for a select group of guests, including Frances and husband James, who had visited previously. As a writer for several publications, including *Vogue*, *Harper's Bazaar*, and the *Daily Mail*, Frances' authoritative voice offered insights into the sailing season on the Isle of Wight, the best country retreats to visit for the weekend and advice on finding harmony in marriage. She spoke from first-hand experience; her marriage to James was considered one of the most loving in London's top circles. They adored one another, both respecting each other's needs, and with James fully supportive of her career as a writer.

James, the son of Lady Corisande Evelyn Vere Guest and the late George Rodney, the 7th Baron Rodney, was tall and chiselled and sported a dashing moustache that made him look every inch the flying hero of the First World War. He was now working as an insurance broker for his uncle, Ivor Guest's firm, while also fuelling his love of aviation as the trainer for Britain's first auxiliary flying squadron. They'd married in 1928, settling into a life of domestic bliss in their cosy house in Marylebone, which she'd painted in bold yellows, reds and purples and decorated with treasures gleaned on her extensive travels.

In one of her regular *Seattle Daily Times* columns, which recounted her trips around Europe, Frances spoke of the effects of being an American overseas and she was 'always seeking in every face a familiar one from home'. McCormick was one of these familiar faces, not only through the recognition of his accent, but his way of conducting business; the Americans just had a different way about them.

Another guest at the weekend party was Louis Jean Marie, the 12th Duke de la Trémoille, the 23-year-old heir to one of France's oldest families. Having succeeded to the title at the age of 11, following the death of his father, he was the last male of his direct line, as the title couldn't be passed down via his four sisters, who had all married into branches of European nobility. The duke had completed his military service in the French crack cavalry regiment, Chasseurs d'Afrique, and was looking forward to some relaxation in the English countryside. He arrived at Croydon Airfield from Paris on the Friday afternoon and was driven to meet his hosts at the Heronry.[2]

Following dinner at 8 p.m., the McCormicks and their guests had spent a quiet evening by the fireside, with the duke entertaining them with his array of card tricks. They retired to bed just after 11 p.m., drifting into hazy sleep. What started out as a small fire in an unoccupied bedroom soon spread out across the carpets, licking its way up the wood panelling and around the door frames.[3]

After rushing to wake her husband, Renée McCormick ran through the corridors in her nightgown, shouting warnings to their guests and servants. With the smoke thick in the air, they felt their way along the halls to the duke's room, and Renée called out to him, instructing him to find his way to the stairs. To their relief, they heard him shout out a reply that he was making his way out. With no time to grab an overcoat over her nightwear, and trapped on the first floor, Renée climbed out of the window, lowered herself down and ran across the lawn to the garage, where the chauffeur, Frank Jackson, and his wife, slept in a room above. He immediately rang the fire brigade at Andover, which was 6 miles away.[4]

The servants of the house gathered outside, still in their nightclothes, desperately trying to do what they could by throwing buckets of water on the flames and searching for ladders to reach the upper windows. The heat from the blaze radiated into the ice-cold atmosphere, and smoke billowed from the windows and into the air.

Unable to find the staircase through the smoke, Frances and James retreated into the bedroom, closing the door tightly behind them, in the hope that they could escape through the window. But there was no ladder available and it was a 20ft drop to the ground. James was recipient of the Distinguished Service Order, the Star of 1915 and the Military Cross for his service in the war, which was cut short when he was wounded in action in France. These experiences may have helped him keep a cool head with the awful realisation that the only way out was through the window.[5] Frances looked down at the ground below and recoiled at the thought of jumping so far to the ground.

The flames were crackling outside the door, and smoke crept underneath the gap. Soon it would infiltrate the room, making it impossible to breathe.

James gathered up sheets and towels to make a rope they could climb down, and he smashed the windowpane with his fists. He helped Frances clamber out of the window and on to the narrow sill, holding onto the rope. She lowered herself down, aiming for the flower beds directly below in the hopes it would cushion the fall. She slipped, landed awkwardly, with a thud, and cried out as the pain radiated through her back. Seeing her distress, James jumped after her onto the flower beds and rushed to Frances, who was struggling to move. The *Seattle Times* later described Captain Rodney's heroism; even though he was suffering cuts and burns, he thought only of his wife.

When the ambulance arrived from Andover, the Rodneys were taken to Royal Hants Hospital at Winchester and Frank Jackson organised a roll-call of the guests and servants. An older German maid, Louisa Krug, had similarly been trapped in her room but had managed to escape by clambering down the drainpipe. As Jackson called out the names, it became apparent that the Duke de La Trémoille was missing. After Leander tried throwing pebbles at the duke's bedroom window, Jackson took hold of a ladder and climbed up it to take a closer look. He broke the glass in the window to see better, but through the smoke there was no sign of him.

Renée was adamant that she had heard the duke calling out that he was heading for the staircase, and in the confusion, no one had noticed that he wasn't outside. It was only once the fire was extinguished after dawn that the charred body of the duke was discovered in the ash. It was later thought that he had become disorientated in a house he was unfamiliar with and found himself trapped in the upstairs bathroom when he had seen the stairs alight.

The fire was so severe that the floor caved in, sending him plummeting into the pantry on the ground floor, and he was engulfed in flames. Frances would later recount a story she'd heard that there had been a curse placed on his ancient family, where the eldest son was destined to die by fire.

At the hospital, Frances was taken for an X-ray, which revealed that she had fractured a vertebrae in her spine. She underwent an operation to repair some of the damage, and the hospital released a bulletin that she was 'seriously ill, but there is no reason why she should not pull through'.

Before being taken into surgery, Frances insisted to her nurses that her husband should be kept informed of her condition. She hadn't seen him since their ride in the ambulance, and she was concerned that he would be fretting at not knowing how she was doing. No one had the heart at this point to tell her that, despite having seemed fine, her beloved husband had died soon after his arrival at hospital.

Summer 1985, Invercauld

Except for the splash of yellow on the window frames and the pink of the outdoor games larder, popping like cherry blossom, the solid granite towers and gables of Invercauld were a sober presence in the Dee Valley, set against a stirring backdrop of mountains and pine forest and with the rush of the river Dee flowing through. The sixteenth-century castle had been extended and reinvented in the last century as a romantic Highland confection in the Scots Baronial style, and over the last decades, had been brightened by the colourful touches introduced by the chatelaine, Frances Farquharson. Sometimes described as 'eccentric' in her wearing of tartan, head to foot, she laughed it off and declared herself 'more Scottish than the Scots'. As her husband, Alwyne, who was seventeen years younger, dryly stated, 'If my wife's eccentric then I must be eccentric'.[6]

Inside the fourteen-bedroom mansion, with its maze of staircases and passageways, Frances was sitting on her tartan sofa in one of the most relaxing rooms in the house, with the veteran British journalist Joy Billington, who was writing for the *Washington Post*. On Joy's arrival, Frances, dressed in a tartan skirt and Shetland wool sweater, greeted her warmly. She led the reporter up the mighty stairwell lined with portraits of the family's Farquharson ancestors and along the warren of passageways to show her into the Tartan Room, which offered a more intimate space for entertaining her guests. For one thing, it was often the warmest room in the house.

The light streamed through the window as she offered tea and shortbread, served on delicate china, to the ash-blonde reporter, and Frances gave no sign that her back was aching. It had been fifty years since she'd fractured her spine in the terrible fire. She was now 82 years old, still sprightly and with enthusiasm sparkling in her eyes, but increasingly, she'd been struggling with her health, not just with her mobility, but with kidney issues and rheumatism. Yet she was always stoical, never complaining, and typically chose not to reveal much about her past, rarely talking about the night of the fire or the years spent in recovery.

She preferred to concentrate on the present, rather than events in previous incarnations, as that was when she was the Hon. Mrs James Rodney, and she was now Mrs Frances Farquharson, and had been for four decades.

She had fully embraced Highland living after marrying the laird in 1949, and in the years since, she had become entwined with the land. Arriving in Braemar like a cannonball of energy, she had immediately injected vitality into the sleepy village which, like Brigadoon, only seemed to come alive once a year for the Braemar Gathering. She fought to boost its fortunes by bringing culture and business to the region and did all she could to keep Invercauld Estate afloat, as there were hundreds of people whose livelihood depended on it. 'It's just as well you didn't marry a dolly bird,' she told her husband, 'as the estate would never have survived.'[7]

Joy Billington had moved to Scotland with her chaplain husband, and as part of her fondness for interviewing women of renown, she had approached Frances to talk about her life as the lady of a vast Highland estate. She was interested in the reasons why she had opened her home to paying guests, particularly very rich American ones, and she was also curious about her life before, one Billington described as 'pure Henry James' – leaving her Seattle home at a young age and being initiated into European society with help from 'two aristocratic Russian godmothers in Paris and London'.

'There are quite a number of reasons,' Frances told her, as she answered the first question:

One is tax. Our taxes here on the land are crippling and if you do a certain amount of open house, you get certain concessions on maintenance. And of course, maintenance in this part of the world is a very costly thing. Your rooms, your doon spoots, everything to do with the maintenance of a big property.

Joy was momentarily confused by the expression, 'doon spoots'.
'That's down spouts?'
Frances nodded. She spoke rapidly, as she recounted the fabulous dinners and entertainments that attracted paying guests and the week-long shooting

parties, even though she was averse to killing anything herself. They would draw in incredibly wealthy Americans – the Rockefellers, the du Ponts, international celebrities like Eva Gabor and a group of Swedes who were relaxed about which husband and wife slept in the same bed with whom. Invercauld came alive during these events, where the bejewelled guests were led into a candlelit dining hall by the piper, who also served as plumber during the day, and where the table was set with beautiful silver and vases of flowers.

As she took in her surroundings, with views over the tree-covered valley to the river, Joy couldn't help but comment on all the tartan furnishings, from the settees to the tables to the screens. 'You obviously love tartan,' she said.

'Well, it's called the Tartan Room,' Frances wryly replied.

'Could you have ever guessed as a girl in Seattle that you'd own 300,000 acres?' Joy asked, as she tried to find out more about her life before.

'I don't feel I own it even now,' Frances replied. 'I feel I belong to it. As I belong to the laird, my husband.'

This remote Scottish estate was thousands of miles from the American city where she was born and was almost a world apart. As colourful as her life had been, it was an extraordinary leap for a girl from the Pacific Northwest to now be the caretaker of spectacular heather- covered hills, grouse moors and a 24-mile stretch of the River Dee, crystal clear and teaming with salmon. No doubt the fast-growing city of her youth would be barely recognisable to her, yet the Highland landscape must have reminded her of the vast mountains and lakes of Washington. Because it was in turn-of-the-century Seattle that Frances' remarkable story begins.

Part One

Miss Frances Oldham

Chapter One

'Although I was born in Seattle, I always felt, from the very beginning, that I was destined to live my life on the other side of the Atlantic,' Frances reflected in the draft pages of an unpublished memoir, written in the 1940s. 'I was American born, of American parents, but for some odd reason I never felt that the United States was my real home.'

As a child she was enveloped in the beauty of America's Pacific Northwest, where the clouds clung to forest-clad mountains and lingered over Puget Sound. Spending the second half of her life in the Scottish Highlands, it was as if she'd nurtured a lifelong spiritual connection to an awe-inspiring, rugged landscape. Yet growing up among such expansive beauty, she felt a deep desire to see beyond sleepy Seattle and Lake Washington to the vibrant capitals of Europe. Her father had, as he told his daughter, travelled west 'to get away' from his relations, and later, she was desperate to rediscover them. 'My father loved the West and succeeded in transferring his love of the wild open spaces to my younger brother and sister, but I was his black swan,' she recalled. 'I dreamed of the capitals of Europe at night, and it never even occurred to me that I might never see them.'

Her father, Robert Pollard Oldham, was just out of Harvard University law school when he arrived in Seattle at the turn of the century. Following his graduation, his father, a renowned Ohioan judge, Francis Fox Oldham (who went to the Treasury Department in Washington, DC as legal adviser in 1903) offered to pay for a voyage around the world as a 'final fling' before he settled down in a law office. Robert planned out a trip that would take him the breadth of the United States to the west coast and then across the Pacific to the Far East.

Yet landing in Seattle as an idealistic 25-year-old, his travels were side-lined when he was introduced to a young beauty named Mary Bell Strickland, of a grand Bostonian family, whose ancestors were the historian Agnes Strickland and the American engineer and inventor of the steamboat, Robert Fulton. Born in Pendleton, Oregon, in 1882, and going by the name Bell, she arrived in Seattle in 1901 following schooling on the east coast.[1]

Robert fell in love with both the majesty of the Pacific Northwest and with dark-haired Bell, and they married on New Year's Day, 1902. Instead of continuing with his plans for travelling, Robert opened a law office in Seattle. The city would be his home for the rest of his life. As Frances noted, 'I obviously did not inherit my desire to travel from him.'

Frances Strickland Lovell Oldham, their first child, came into the world on 19 November 1902. She was named Frances in honour of her father's younger sister, and her middle names referenced her mother's maiden name and the Lovell lineage of her grandmother, Betty. Frances' younger brother, Robert Pollard Oldham Junior, was born a year and a half later on 18 March 1904.

The family lived in comfort in a large home at 1234 Eighth Avenue West, which rested high above Elliott Bay and offered spectacular views across Puget Sound. Young Frances loved being able to play in a garden that looked out over the sparkling bay and where the scent of pine was carried on the wind.

After being introduced to horse riding from the age of 3, she was given her own pony, which she kept tied up in the back garden. She frequently practised riding on him and this skill would stand her in good stead when it came to mixing with Europe's aristocracy when she was in her twenties.

The family home was also well placed for experiencing the Pacific Northwest's lakes and mountains, and Frances threw herself into sports, embracing canoe paddling and fishing on the lakes in summer, and skating and skiing in winter. 'All these sports I took in my stride as the seasons came and went,' she said.

Despite her childhood dreams of going to Europe, her history was very much entwined in the traditions of America. Frances' family dated back to the country's founders. Her father was a direct descendent of Elizabeth 'Betty' Washington, sister of George Washington and one of the founding mothers of the United States.

'The College of Heraldry traces George Washington's ancestry – and consequently my own – from Charlemagne and his first wife. So, I probably inherited my feeling for Europe from my remote ancestry,' Frances wrote in her memoirs. It was Frances' pride in this ancestry that partly led her to Europe when she was in her early twenties, touring the royal palaces of the dying Balkan states. Once she was living in England, she actively sought out the details of her lineage, which did indeed go back to the first emperor of Europe, and then to Charles the Bald.

If there was one element that passed down the generations to Frances, it was George Washington's love of the finer things in life, an eye for the details when it came to fashion and an appreciation of British and European style. As commander-in-chief for the Virginian forces in the French and Indian War, he ensured he looked the part by purchasing luxury clothing in London, including ruffles and silk stockings, and sketched out the uniform of his officers – blue coats with scarlet cuffs and matching waistcoats. He had never been to England, yet he tried to imitate the style of an English gentleman and furnished his Virginian plantation, Mount Vernon, with fashionable pieces shipped from London, including Wedgwood earthenware, silver-handled cutlery and a green four-horse coach, which was all the rage in London.

At the age of 17, in 1750, his sister Betty married Fielding Lewis and they had eleven children together, of which three died in infancy. Their youngest, Howell Lewis (1771–1822), travelled west with wife Ellen Pollard, building a home near Charleston, West Virginia, with enough room for their eleven children. Their oldest daughter, Betty Washington Lewis, became the second wife of English-born Joseph Lovell in 1818.

They had six children, and following Joseph Lovell's death in 1835, Betty moved to Marietta, Ohio. Her son, Joseph Junior, married a local girl, Sarah Sophia Nye, in 1852 and they had one child, Frances' grandmother, Betty Lovell, born in 1853. They lived for a time at the famous Meigs House, built in 1802 and named after its first resident, Postmaster General Return Jonathan Meigs Senior. It was arguably the most important home in town, and one of the most impressive in two-storeys of red brick with a grand porch looking out over the Muskingum River.

Despite being steeped in tradition, by the 1800s Marietta's progressive politicians championed civil rights, and there were two underground railroad stops in the town, where runaway slaves could be hidden on their journey north. Over the years since its founding, the town's historic homes on brick-paved streets were the birthplace of governors, senators and even a vice president, ensuring it made a firm mark on history. It was in this impressive little town that generations of Lewis Lovells were to live.

At the age of 23, in 1876, Betty Lovell married 28-year-old Francis Fox Oldham, a southern gentleman from Moundsville, West Virginia, who moved with his family to Marietta at the end of the Civil War. With Francis

Fox now a successful circuit judge in Ohio, the Oldhams lived prosperously in a comfortable home at 1 Fourth Street. Frances' father, Robert Pollard Oldham, was born on 19 May 1877, with his middle name chosen as a tribute to great-grandmother Ellen Pollard. Another son, Wylie Oldham, was born in 1879, but lived to only the age of 1. Despite the tragedy, his mother, Betty, gave birth to a daughter named Lovell 'Lottie' Oldham, on 29 June 1882 (the aunt Frances would stay with in Rome), later followed by another daughter, Frances Fielding Oldham, on 19 February 1889, with her middle name in tribute to Fielding Lewis, husband of Betty Washington, George's sister.

Growing up in progressive, booming Marietta at the cusp of the twentieth century, it was this open-mindedness that perhaps helped instil in his daughter a sense of independence and fun, as he sought never to restrain her from taking her own path in life.

Robert followed in his father's footsteps by studying law at the University of Cincinnati, and then enrolled at Harvard University Law School in 1898, graduating with a Bachelor of Law in 1901. After settling in Seattle, he joined the prestigious firm Bausman & Kelleher, one of the oldest in the state of Washington. By 1914, he had been promoted to partner, and earned a reputation as a major player at one of Seattle's top civil law firms. Robert was praised in 1922 by James Boswell, author of the *American Blue Book West Washington*, as belonging to 'that school of attorneys who never permit themselves to become "ruffled", but who are, at all times, calm and dignified'.[2] It was this calm, logical nature that he passed to Frances, allowing her to hold her own as a trade envoy for Britain during the Second World War, when she was the only woman in the boardroom.

Mary Bell Oldham was only 20 years old when she married and started a family, yet she settled into her life as a prominent lawyer's wife and an active and committed member of the city's burgeoning society. Frances, perhaps keeping this in mind when she was lady of Invercauld, remembered that her mother 'was loved by everyone in Seattle from the chimney sweep to the wealthiest tycoon'.

At the turn of the century, Seattle was still a small town founded on an economy in logging and fishing, but it was becoming a major transport hub on the back of the gold rush, attracting several prodigious businessmen with an eye on development. By the 1910s, Downtown Seattle was lifted by a wave of new architecture, with constructions in development and architects competing to create the tallest, sleekest buildings. Robert Oldham commuted every morning to the brand-new Beaux Arts Hoge Building on

705 Second Avenue, the city's tallest at that time, where his firm had set up offices.[3]

Many of the prominent Seattle families were recent arrivals from the Northeast or Midwest, and they wished to recreate the gentility and culture of the more established East-Coast cities, in a timber town which once had an untamed and rambunctious reputation. As a prominent lawyer's wife, Bell was an important figure in town, as the ladies' charity luncheons and tea parties were detailed in the society pages of the *Seattle Daily Times*. They dressed in the latest Edwardian fashions to arrive on the west coast: high-necked frilled blouses, corseted waists and long skirts, with their wide-brimmed hats resting on intricate up-dos. Their afternoon teas, where the ladies took turns to operate the tea urn, were always elaborately decorated affairs with vases of flowers and pretty china set out on white tablecloths.

Her status was also further cemented by being married to a descendent of George Washington, which was an impressive connection in a town steeped in American tradition, and where any daughters of hers would be entitled to join the prestigious Daughters of the American Revolution. Bell would also become a charter member and trustee of the Sunset Club, founded in 1912. It was one of the most important private clubs for women in Seattle, who gathered at its colonial-style clubhouse on First Hill.

Social events were regimented around the calendar. The Christmas season was filled with tea parties and dances and was, as the *Seattle Times* called it, 'a strenuous winter of gaiety'. From Ash Wednesday to the lead-up to Easter was a quieter period, a time for going to church, giving to charity and restocking their wardrobes with summer clothing.[4] As the summer season arrived, Seattle's comfortable residents headed off in their motorcars to their country homes in idyllic settings on a sound, lake or island.[5]

While he was very successful as a lawyer, Frances' father, known as Bob to friends and colleagues, was often focused on supporting the underdog, meaning he would sometimes give his time for free to help different causes. After arriving in Seattle, he had become actively involved in the Washington State branch of the Democratic Party. He was president of the Woodrow Wilson League, a group for independents and democrats, and later took charge of the 1924 Washington Democratic presidential nomination campaign for William Gibbs McAdoo.[6]

'We always had plenty of money, but there was no feeling in my home of the importance of making more and more in order to be richer and more influential than the neighbours,' said Frances:

My father and mother were democrats in the true sense of the word. Both had been brought up in strict Episcopalian homes in which church every day and Sunday school on Sunday was the regular routine. Father was religious, but broad-minded. He did not believe that God could only be found in the Church. He disapproved of churches in which the rich could buy the more expensive pews and the poor were kept herded in the background. He always said that he felt closer to Him in the Great Outdoors that had not been touched by man.[7]

While religion played a part in their upbringing, the Oldham children were not forced to go to church every Sunday and were not baptised, as Robert wanted them to make that decision for themselves. Instead of focusing solely on church teachings, their father taught them kindness, and to keep quiet rather than speak ill of people. It was a loving home, where they celebrated the American traditions, particularly with their heritage as a founding family. She treasured the Thanksgiving feasts, and always remembered 'the delicious scent of spices and cooking which came from pantries and kitchens'.[8]

She had an active imagination, inventing stories to tell the younger children and spending hours in the family library. Shakespeare and Dickens were her favourite authors, and she poured over atlases and history books to trace the lines of the eastern European frontier and the famous landmarks that were waiting for her to explore – Paris, with its Eiffel Tower, Rome's Colosseum and Pantheon and the Parthenon as a beacon over Athens.

Her father adored his daughter, who was curious, quick-witted, vivacious and imaginative, and he encouraged her in her desire to learn. While she was happy as a child, such was her ambition to travel that she had the intuition that her time in Seattle was only temporary. Even from a young age, she sensed that this was just the first chapter of her life, and there would be so much more for her to see and experience of the world.

Frances was nearly 11 years old when her younger sister, Mary, was born, in July 1913. Having a child ten years after her last may well have come as a surprise to Frances' mother, and having suffered a degree of ill health, it placed extra strain on her body. Mary Bell, who had once been a social butterfly, was now housebound following Mary's birth and later by a cancer diagnosis.

As the oldest daughter, Frances was expected to help with family duties, and ultimately acted like a second mother to her sister. 'I had a natural mother instinct and adored dolls until my baby sister arrived whom I considered my personal property,' she said. But this responsibility, she said, 'threw the weight of the household upon my shoulders' and it taught her lessons on the art of housekeeping and how to throw a dinner for her father and his work friends, skills that would be put to good use later in life. They may have had help from a variety of servants, including a Finnish maid who appeared on the census in 1910, but this was considered the norm in those days for a house of a certain size. As she recounted:

> The old butcher showed me all the cuts of meat – which were the best, the most economical, how not to waste and so on. In fact he became such a friend of mine that when he died he left me all his money. I learned how to buy vegetables and fruits in season, how to make a delicious dinner for unexpected guests, how to arrange menus and to cater to people's tastes. I learned this so well that my father used to say that a dinner I thought out for his business friends always led to an increase in business. Mother grew to rely on me entirely.

At first the children were educated by governesses, but as Frances recalled, 'when my mother saw signs of slight childish snobbishness in me towards the less immaculate and not-so-well-spoken children of the neighbourhood, I was immediately sent to public school'.

At first, she found it a culture shock to mix with children who were not part of Seattle's gentle class. In her memoirs, she recollected:

> I was utterly bewildered and miserable at first at having to consort with lumbermen and fishermen's children, all of whom were rough and whose vocabularies were not exactly what I was accustomed to, but I am grateful for the two years I spent there, for it was there that I first learned an understanding of and sympathy for my less fortunate brethren.

After two years there, she attended Bradford Hall Private School, with students mostly from Seattle's wealthy families. She was particularly enthusiastic about writing, constantly turning out classroom essays and short stories not just for homework but for her own enjoyment, as they fed into her highly active imagination as she dreamed of faraway places. She was fiercely independent, constantly badgering her father with questions about when she could go overseas. He only gave vague replies and no promises, and once she was in her mid-teens, she realised that to be able to travel she would need to save up her own money. And writing would be the key.

Chapter Two

By the time she was a teenager, it was clear that Frances inherited the beauty and charm of her mother and the persuasive skills of her father. At 13 she joined Seattle's Drama League and threw herself into acting in plays and performances. In April 1915, for the 351st anniversary of Shakespeare's birth, she performed as Maria from *The Twelfth Night* in an ambitious street procession devoted to the Bard's comedies.[1] She also took part in a variety of performances at Bradford Hall School, many of which raised money for charities championed by the pupils' parents, such as the founding of a new orthopaedic hospital.

On one occasion, she was a chorus member alongside her classmates for a rendition of the operetta *Princess Chrysanthemum* at the luxurious home of prominent Seattle businessman Harry Whitney Treat, high above the city at 1 West Highland Drive. His daughter Priscilla, who attended the same school as Frances, was hailed in the papers as one of Seattle's 'most charming sub-debutantes'.[2]

Harry Treat was, like Robert Oldham, a new Seattleite, having arrived from New York in 1904, buying hundreds of acres of land in the Loyal Heights and Golden Gardens areas and helping develop the trolley network. It must have been an impressive sight for the visiting schoolgirls to be inside what was considered the grandest house in town, and no doubt Frances' imagination was captured by the theatrical interiors and the horses tied up in the garden. Having travelled to Europe, the Treats filled their thirty-room Queen Anne mansion with English vintage coaches, period costumes and touches of Art Nouveau decor. On Memorial Day 1915, Buffalo Bill Cody even visited the Treat family home to perform his Wild West show for their younger daughter, Loyal, and it's likely that Frances was one of the guests.

In the summer of 1915, there were the usual weekend trips to summer houses, wilderness getaways to Mount Rainier, a snow-capped active stratovolcano, and rounds of weekly ladies' brunches at the Seattle Tennis Club. War was raging in Europe, but in cosseted Seattle it seemed a world away. However, the city swung into action when America joined the global conflict in 1917.

Robert Oldham swiftly signed up to the Washington Liberty Loan Committee, which organised parades and shows in order to raise much needed war bonds.[3] Despite her ill health, Bell also stepped up to do her part in the war, joining the National League for Women's Service in Seattle and assisting with the Sunset Club's Red Cross auxiliary, where its members rolled bandages and knitted scarves and mittens for the men fighting overseas. She also helped to establish the canteen at the Seattle Soldiers' and Sailors' Club, of which it was said 'hundreds of soldiers and sailors were hearted by her kindliness and words of encouragement'.[4]

Like other Seattle teenage girls, Frances wanted to do her wartime duty, particularly as all the activities fed her imagination and her desire to go overseas. 'We lived very close to the Boeing Airfield,' Frances recalled:

And during the First World War I used to be fascinated by the building of planes. Every time I saw a plane take off, I felt that it drew me one step nearer to my goal – Europe. This of course was long before Europe was an overnight journey from the States, but to me the link was growing stronger and stronger as each plane was completed and took to the air.

With her skills in horse riding, Frances joined the Women's Cavalry, which aimed to prepare for an attack on the States. Under the direction of a professional horsewoman, Miss Dell Von Ohl, they enthusiastically practised manoeuvres and formations on the Washington Park speedway, clad in a uniform of tailored riding jackets, shirts, ties and jodhpurs. Frances, along with several of her school friends, performed these duties beside notable Seattle women including Lois Mendenhall, wife of vaudeville impresario Alexander Pantages, who owned Seattle's Crystal Theater.[5]

Cynthia Grey, of the *Seattle Star*, described the scene in May 1917 and recollected overhearing a man dismiss them as a joke, 'Women's cavalry! I wonder what they think they could do in an honest-to-goodness war?' As Cynthia pithily replied in her article:

No, Mr Man, the women don't even dare to hope that the government will consent to accept their service in the field, but they feel that they can be invaluable in doing guard or police duty, in maintaining communications, and in the rescue of [the] wounded or injured.[6]

By 1918, when the war came to an end, Frances was enrolled at Madame Pless' School, an exclusive girl's school in Capitol Hill, founded by Myra Pless, who had been infamous in the local papers. Myra began teaching French and German to support her and her daughter Madeline when her husband, a large German count called Curt Pless, went missing in 1909. There were rumours that he had been abducted or murdered by Kaiser Wilhelm II, who was then the bogeyman of Europe. However, in 1912, she discovered that her husband was living in Virginia under an assumed name, where he was working as a realtor. He refused to care for his wife and child, and Myra returned to the Pacific Northwest, where she established her school for day and boarding pupils.

During her time there, Frances was voted class president and, in an early indication of her love of organising spectacular parties, she held dinners at the Sunset Club for students and alumni of the school and took part in charity dances and bazaars. For one event to raise money for the Lighthouse for the Blind, she was in charge of producing and selling jelly and preserved fruit and jams.[7]

Frances also proudly used her connections to help educate her fellow pupils, organising a trip in February 1919 to the Washington Supreme Court to hear a case argued by her father. The activities of Frances and her friends were regularly featured in the society columns. They held their own luncheons, always decorated with perfect table arrangements and beautiful seasonal flowers such as maple vines, marigolds and hydrangeas, or attended dances at the golf and tennis clubs, events which were usually chaperoned by one of their parents.[8] They borrowed their parents' motorcars and yachts, and made trips across the Sound or to their summer houses for weekend parties.[9] By autumn 1919, Frances was hosting a regular Thursday night dance at a venue called the Jumble Shop, which was a place for her friends to socialise with the opposite sex.[10]

As was true throughout her life, she embraced parties and dances because she loved meeting new people. Her daughter Marybelle said:

She called herself Pollyanna, because she always believed the good in people. She never believed they could do anything wrong. Always wonderful, exciting, and gay. Because that was the word that was used then. She talked about having a gay time.

These 'sub-debutante' dances were reminiscent of a passage in Henry James' *Daisy Miller*, where he described 'a flitting hither and thither of "stylish" young girls, a rustling of muslin flounces, a rattle of dance music in the morning hours, a sound of high-pitched voices at all times'.

Young women of social standing were dictated by societal codes, where girls were protected by chaperones and were expected to do as their parents instructed. While Frances' father was more liberal than others, giving her a degree of freedom, she still demonstrated a glint of teenage rebellion. She liked to recount a story of how she often left her home in the frilled organdie her mother wanted her to wear and then swiftly changed into a more daring dress once she was out of her parents' sight.

This tale was mentioned in a 1936 article in *Harper's Bazaar* in which she offered style advice for teenagers:

> I, too, was once a young girl and my one idea was never, under any circumstances, to look it! Well I remember ordering, unbeknown to my unsuspecting parents, a tightly fitting black velvet evening gown completed by a sophisticated silver lame tunic. This I kept secreted in a chest in the ball-room, to be changed into from the frilly organdie in which I bid my parents good night before departing to my party. Cautiously I slipped into the depths of darkness and exchanged the gowns, then through the garden to the waiting motor.[11]

Hers was a generation of girls coming of age at the end of the First World War, and a time of great societal changes and new freedoms for women. It was the advent of the flapper, the type of girl their contemporary, Zelda Fitzgerald, would describe as salamanders, after the Owen Johnson novel, *The Salamander*, about 'a girl of the present day in revolt – adventurous, eager, and unafraid'.

Seattle was a little behind the scenes coming out of New York and other eastern American cities, yet there was a first mention of 'flapper' in terms of fashion in the *Seattle Star*, in February 1918, describing a fashionable style of ankle-length dress available in a Seattle department store.[12] The same newspaper, in an editorial in August 1919, posed the question:

> Where do all these slim, well dressed flappers come from? In the morning, they pour out of Seattle apartments and rooming houses by the hundreds. Every car brings them into store and office and factory ... They are of a type, these flappers. They look, just now, like

the latest fashion plates from some foreign magazine … An army of flappers, dressed to the minute, and living with as little outward care as the butterflies.[13]

There was a new type of woman on the horizon, and she was rejecting the old guard in how she dressed and the way she wanted to live. The description of these girls, 'all working for a living; most of them apparently do not live at home', didn't quite fit Frances and her society belle friends, who were still living with their affluent parents and were destined to transition from a spell at college to married life. Yet Frances, forceful and determined, always had her own ideas on what to wear and how she would conduct herself. Choosing to wear her own dress to dances, rather than what her mother dictated, was a demonstration of an early propensity for carving out an individual sense of style, without constraint. She wished to forge her own life and she wasn't ready to settle for a conventional marriage in her hometown.

During this time, as well as weekend trips across the water to Bremerton or drives to Mount Rainier, Frances travelled to Portland, in neighbouring Oregon, to visit her mother's side of the family. Yet she needed to go further, to explore the places she could only dream of in atlases and books.[14]

Like Isabel Archer in *The Portrait of a Lady*, she had an aunt, Lovell Appleby Oldham, who had moved to Europe, and Frances longed to experience that life for herself. It was made even more tantalising by the letters and cards with an Italian postmark that would occasionally arrive from Lovell, who was living permanently in Rome, after having married an Italian, Guglielmo Luparini Leonetti, in 1916. Frances wrote:

The urge to go abroad was with me constantly in these early years, but my plans were constantly thwarted by my father, who hated the idea of losing his children even for a short while. Opportunities were offered by my grandfather who had travelled all over the world with his wife and daughters, and was unable to understand father's lack of interest in any but his own country. My aunts had been educated abroad and one or two had married foreigners and were living in Europe. My grandfather offered to send me to Italy to stay with an aunt and be educated there, but father would never listen to his suggestions or my pleadings.

After graduating from Madame Pless' school in December 1919, she finally experienced independent travel when she left Seattle for San Francisco by steamship in January 1920. She had enrolled for a spell at Mills College, a private liberal arts school in Oakland, California, led by peace activist and educator Aurelia Henry Reinhardt.

In June 1920, she returned to Seattle for the summer season, where she hosted a round of luncheons at the Sunset Club and invited friends to her family's summer home at Hunts Point, across Lake Washington.[15] Her studies at Mill College were short-lived, likely because her mother was increasingly bed-bound and she had to return to look after her.

Living in a sense of post-war optimism as they turned 18, Frances' friends began to announce their impending weddings. A surprise linen shower was held in honour of her friend Catherine Butler's engagement, where Frances helped serve the tea and her little sister Mary carried the baskets holding the gifts.[16]

As part of the celebrations, Catherine organised a photo shoot at the famous McBride Studio, owned by pioneering photographer and fearless mountaineer Ella McBride. She and her sixteen girlfriends, including Frances, posed for headshots, and these photos appeared in the pages of the *Seattle Daily Times* on 11 May 1919, revealing the fresh, round faces of these society girls with their waved hair cut fashionably but conservatively short.[17]

There was no mention of a particular beau for Frances during these years, either in the society section of newspapers or in her own partial memoirs, written several decades later. Sometimes, she went on dates with the officers at the nearby Coast Defense bases or the young men back from war who would be invited to debutante balls. Her younger brother Robert would bait her and tease her each time she was getting ready to leave the house. 'He was a typical younger brother, and she was driven crazy by the pranks he played. I suspect my mother was favourite, so she must have got round her father in going out on dates,' says Marybelle.

At a time when engagements were announced quickly and casual dating was frowned upon, Frances chose to remain unattached, so that she would still be able to go to Europe, despite her father's wishes. She recalled how he hoped she would be 'a good western girl' and:

> ... marry a boy from that part of the world and to make my home near him for the rest of my life. He insisted that his sisters had achieved culture but not happiness. Father always maintained that happiness lay in the earth of the West Coast. His marriage had been a very happy one, and he had a passion for the West.

One of the ways to earn her own money was by using her talents as a writer. She had decided early that writing was to be her career. 'Any kind of writing.

I was not particular,' she said. She went to the offices of the *Seattle Star*, spoke with the editor and asked for a job.

As the daughter of one of Seattle's most prominent lawyers, and with her name frequently mentioned in the society pages, it seemed an obvious fit for the paper to hire her. She was given a part-time role working under the society editor, Betty Brainerd, the daughter of Erastus Brainerd, the American journalist who was editor of the *Seattle-Press Times* (later the *Seattle Times*) and then the *Seattle Post-Intelligencer*. As founder of the Seattle Chamber of Commerce, he helped push the city's development in the 1890s as the place for miners to be outfitted before they made their way to the Yukon during the Gold Rush. Given his status, he was a member of the prestigious Rainier Club, alongside Robert Oldham, which may have helped with Frances' introduction to Betty.

With a good telephone voice and impeccable manners, Frances had a natural talent for collecting information on the latest charity events, tea parties and dances to fill the pages. These columns were incredibly detailed, reporting in minute detail on the guests, flower arrangements and refreshments served at seemingly inconsequential events. Yet, despite their laboriousness, they were a means of attracting a loyal local readership.

She learned through the society pages editorial skills in a polite form of journalism that would stand her in good stead for the glossy women's magazines. 'She taught me to respect the wishes of the people involved. If they asked for a story to be held up for a couple of days, we held it up, even if other newspapers printed it,' she said.

Alongside writing snippets in the society pages, Frances was given more assignments at the *Seattle Star*, including interviewing and news reporting. She paid close attention to the work of the editors, to 'the blue pencilling and cutting and unconsciously learned the job of editing'.

One of the first assignments she was given, due to a staff shortage, was to interview an American artist who had lived in France. As she waited with the more seasoned, and male, reporters, the artist immediately spotted Frances and allowed her to have a one-to-one interview with him. In her memoirs, she recounted that she was in her schoolgirl uniform, and with her hair in pigtails, although this is a typical flourish of exaggeration. However, what is likely to be true is that he was completely charmed by her enthusiasm and quick wit.

After years of ill health, Frances' mother died at her home in the early hours of 22 January 1922. She was only 39 years old. In those days, cancer was something that was never spoken of outside of the family, and so there are few details available about her illness. The *Seattle Daily Times* posted a warm tribute in announcement of her death. 'Because of her kindly disposition and gracious manner Mrs Oldham soon became a favourite here and her activities were devoted almost entirely to work for others,' it wrote, adding that despite her illness she 'maintained a cheerful and hopeful attitude, and the members of her family and friends were always first in her thoughts'.[18]

Devastated at the death of her mother, it had also cut one of the ties that bound Frances to Seattle, but she still felt a duty in caring for her younger sister. For the next couple of years, Frances remained at home, supporting her group of friends as they continued to get married.

In April 1923, she and her brother embarked on a road trip to California to visit cousins in Coronado. Their father arranged to meet them in Los Angeles and they then made the journey back together by motor car, taking in the national parks and attractions of the Golden State. After this trip with her family, Frances would hold a lifelong preference for exploring countries by road – something she would do frequently with her third husband, Alwyne Farquharson.[19]

Her friends may have been holding spectacular, showstopping weddings with Jean Patou dresses imported from Paris, or drifting to colleges on the East Coast, but to Frances, Europe was still the shining beacon – the green light across the water that was calling to her. She continued to enjoy parties and lunches and had fun performing on stage dressed in a maid's outfit for a cabaret at the Junior League Ball. In a photo splashed in the *Seattle Daily Times* in March 1924, Frances' up-to-the-minute sleek, bobbed haircut rested under her white maid's cap, and it's clear she carried herself more naturally than the other girls posing in fancy dress. It would reflect a love for expressive fashions with many pieces in her collection purchased on her extensive travels.

She was also being given more responsibilities at the newspaper. Betty Brainerd was forced to leave the *Seattle Star* in late 1920 when her own life made headlines. She was arrested on kidnapping charges for helping her lover take his daughter from his ex-wife, which resulted in a dramatic trial.

Working under the new society editor Lillian Keen le Ballister, Frances received her first credit as assistant in the 15 May 1923 edition. Her father was surprised at the amount of money his daughter had been saving up over several months, and he was also a little concerned that she would feel the need to work at a time when well-bred women rarely held down jobs. Did he not give her a large enough allowance, he asked? But impressed with the determination and thrift of his daughter, he agreed to match her savings, dollar for dollar.

By 1924, little sister Mary was boarding at the Annie Wright School in Tacoma, and there were fewer requirements to look after her. Frances' dreams of travel took one step closer to reality when she received a letter from a friend who was planning a trip across the Pacific to Asia. 'She offered to take me if my father would give his permission. At last the end seemed in sight,' wrote Frances:

> I was wondering what would be the most tactful way to broach the subject at home, when I received another letter from her – the whole trip had to be cancelled because of her illness. I was utterly heartbroken and had to face this bitter disappointment alone, because I had not mentioned it to anyone else.

While it was a blow to Frances' plans, as travelling unchaperoned was considered impossible for a young woman at that time, another opportunity soon turned up. A friend of her father's, who had moved from Seattle to New York, Pearl Kennedy Roberts, was only too aware of how much Frances wanted to travel. Pearl was a member of the Washington Suffragette movement and became one of the first female lawyers in the West when she passed the bar in 1910 in Montana. She established her own practice in Seattle dedicated to representing women in divorce. She went east, following her marriage in 1914, where she was known by her married name, Mrs Herbert Wilkes Roberts.

Pearl had booked onto the *Mauretania* for a Mediterranean cruise and offered to act as chaperone if the younger woman wished to accompany her. First, Frances had to get permission from her father, whose face fell when she told him the news, even though Pearl, with her esteemed background, her intelligence and drive, was an ideal companion. Having been widowed only a couple of years before, Robert was devastated at the thought of losing his daughter too. He told her it would be an impossibility for her to leave for overseas as he simply couldn't afford to fund an extended European trip.

As Frances recollected in her memoirs:

> I can still see his face when I told him I didn't expect him to pay for my trip – I only wanted his permission. And he almost fell backwards when he saw my bank balance – the balance that he had been increasing steadily by doubling every penny I had earned. 'I'll be damned!' was all that he could say.

Robert was all too aware of his daughter's determination and ambition, and he realised that he couldn't hold her back, despite his great sadness at the thought of losing her. Impressed that she had saved the money herself and knowing that headstrong Frances wouldn't take no for an answer, he finally agreed, and as she remembered, became very supportive:

> He promised to continue my allowance, and outfitted me for the trip, refusing to allow me to spend a penny of my own money. I suppose by that time he had come to the conclusion that my will was as strong as his and the outcome was inevitable. There was always a strong bond between my father and myself, and he knew instinctively when I had the whip hand.

Finally, her long-standing dream came true, and on 27 January, after a small send-off at the newly opened and incredibly grand neo-Renaissance Olympic Hotel in downtown Seattle, she left her home city for the east, where she would meet Pearl Roberts in New York. Her father typed up a list of dos and don'ts for her cross-country journey, warning her not to speak to anyone unless she had been introduced and never to go out on her own without her chaperone.

In her memoirs she described herself as being 16 when she travelled the breadth of the country by train, yet records show that she was, in fact, 22 – but still, it was a daring and rare move for an unmarried woman at that time. Young ladies didn't just take off across the United States and travel to Europe with no thoughts on when they would return.

As life went on in Seattle, and the marriages of more of her peers were announced, Frances was no longer looking out across the ocean, thinking of what could be. To those who read the society column in the *Seattle Daily Times*, they may have noticed a brief note in May 1925, among the suppers at the Tennis Club and luncheons at the Sunset Club, that 'cards from Miss Frances Oldham still bear an Italian postmark'.[20] For Frances, she was now living the dream life, and she chose not to look back at her old existence, only forward.

Chapter Three

With her note from her father in her purse and her suitcases packed with what she hoped would be the right clothes for a trip to Europe without a return ticket, Frances Oldham arrived at Seattle's King Street Station to head east on 27 January 1925. It was a cold winter day and, as typical for Washington, the rain was drizzling as she boarded the racing green and cream–painted carriages of the North Coast Limited.

The eastbound train carried passengers on the 2,331-mile journey from Seattle to Chicago's Union Station; a trip which took almost seventy hours and involved three nights on board, becoming an event in itself. The track traversed the wild, rugged landscapes of the upper states, and travellers were promised spectacular views of the Montana Rockies as the train carved through snowy pine-clad mountainsides and sliced across the great plains of North Dakota.

To ensure the comfort of its often-wealthy guests, the train featured Pullman sleepers, a dining room and an observation car for passengers to enjoy the wide vistas opening out in front of them. The leisurely pace of the journey allowed Frances to mix with her fellow travellers, of which she must have been the youngest lone female, and on the second evening, while she was relaxing in the observation car, a 'nice-looking gentleman' approached her to strike up conversation. 'I was very embarrassed,' she recalled, somewhat more coyly than was likely the reality, in her memoirs:

It seemed to me that it would be extremely rude not to answer him, but at the same time I did not wish to disobey my father's instructions so soon. So I handed him the sheet of paper, putting my finger to my lips as a sign of enforced silence as I did so. He read it over and laughed very heartily and invited me to dine with him and we became good friends for the rest of the trip.[1]

After arriving in Chicago, taking in the Art Deco splendour of Union Station, she transferred to the Baltimore and Ohio Railroad to Marietta, Ohio, to visit her grandmother, Bessie, now widowed after Francis Fox Oldham's death in 1912. Finally, she arrived in New York City, where she stayed with the woman who would be the chaperone for her journey to Europe, Pearl Kennedy Roberts.[2]

The city was the pulsating heart of modernism in the twenties, and the fastest-developing and most vertical in the world, with new sky-high constructions and bridges being built, theatres and dance halls glowing with huge neon signs, and everywhere people talking of money – how to make it and how to spend it. The energy and pace were frenetic and seemed a world away from her life in relatively sleepy Seattle:

> New York surprised me. I couldn't help noticing how important money was considered, and how social position seemed to depend on the size of the pocket book rather than on birth, breeding and manners. I was bewildered by the display of wealth, the extravagance and ostentation. We had always lived so simply at home that this new life seemed to be almost shocking. Years later, when I reached London and dined with Royalty, I discovered that their standards were the same simple ones of my family.[3]

Frances spent two weeks in New York, where she had a thrilling time experiencing the city's society events and the hottest nightclubs, which blasted with jazz as revellers took to the dancefloor to try out the latest dance crazes, including the addictive Charleston. At one event, she met an attractive Italian man from one of the ancient Roman families, who was studying architecture in the United States:

> He was most attentive to me, and tried to arrange to see me again. But I told him that was impossible – I was sailing in a day or two. When he heard that I would be spending some time in Rome, he was delighted, and told me he would be there to meet me and we would continue our friendship in his own country.[4]

On 17 February, she and Mrs Roberts boarded the Cunard's most celebrated ocean liner, *Mauretania*, for Rome, which would make a number of stops at Mediterranean ports on the way.[5] After being shown to her cabin, she opened the portal door to find it filled with flowers – a beautiful bouquet from her father to wish her luck on her journey and another from the unnamed Italian gentleman, with a promise to see her again.

'The trip was exciting to me – after all, wasn't I on my way to Mecca?' she said. The ocean liner, known as 'the grand old lady of the Atlantic', was the largest and fastest in the world at that time. Its first-class passengers were treated to luxury in the Italian palazzo style, with magnificent marble staircases, comfortable verandas to while away the hours watching the ocean and horizon, a library flanked with Grecian pillars, a dining room over two floors which was sunlit by a huge dome and French-furnished lounges with potted palms.

Relaxing in these majestic surroundings, she began chatting to a young Englishman, Ernest Charles de Rougemont, who was travelling with his 51-year-old uncle, Ernest Frederick de Rougemont. Ernest Junior was the same age as Frances, had been educated at Harrow and Trinity College and was the son of the chairman of Lloyd's of London insurance brokers. He was planning to follow in his father's footsteps, starting with a position as an underwriter. Before he settled down in his career, he and his uncle, also working at Lloyd's, had travelled the east coast of the States, from Miami and Key West to New York. On this trip, the elder Ernest met a New York artist, originally from Pennsylvania, Rebekah Davis Miller, who was in her mid-forties. They fell in love and would be married later in the year.

Frances got on so well with the two de Rougemonts that they joined up with her and Mrs Roberts when embarking at the Mediterranean ports, en route to Rome. The *Mauretania* made stops at Madeira, Gibraltar, Athens, Haifa, in British Palestine, and Alexandria in Egypt, allowing her to experience for herself the places she had only visited in her imagination.

As they went ashore together and explored the dusty ports and crumbling old towns, she and the younger Ernest began to feel more than friendship growing. The young Englishman had never met a woman like her before – so enthusiastic about everything that she saw, and with an infectious energy that made her a joy to be in the company of. She was having such a good time that it was at this point that she wrote to her father, to tell him that 'I had torn up his paper of tabus'.[6]

On arrival in Rome, Aunt Lovell, now Signora Leonetti, greeted them at the port and took them to her home in the city. Lovell had married into a wealthy Roman family, and with three young children, Francesco, Luigi and Lorenzo, she was fully ensconced in Italian life. Although, after spending time with her aunt, Frances would begin to suspect that she wasn't very happy in this marriage.

A few days after she had arrived, the Italian nobleman from New York turned up at the Leonetti home with a bunch of flowers and offered to take Frances to see the sights of the city in his motor car. They explored the Roman Forum and the Colosseum, which in those days could be driven around, and visited the olive groves and hillsides of Lazio, via the cobbled Appian Way.

Each day he became more attentive to her, but her aunt Lovell, who was of a different generation where single women didn't get into motor cars alone with men, disapproved of these unchaperoned dates. For a woman like Frances, it was all part of the newfound liberation of coming of age in the twenties, a time of unprecedented independence for women.

Following a whirlwind romance, he proposed, but her aunt was still worried that Frances was throwing herself into a situation that she didn't fully understand. Lovell knew from personal experience what it was like to be an American woman marrying into a traditional Italian family and she warned that her life would be a lonely one as she would be expected to accept his infidelities but would also be a victim of his terrible jealousies.[7]

After listening to her aunt's warning, she observed his behaviour, and began to notice how possessive he was. It offered a glimpse into the future of what her life would be like as his wife. She was quick to realise that this was not the destiny she had planned out. She'd only just arrived in Europe, and she wasn't ready to sacrifice her freedom or her travel plans.[8]

It was on the drive to his family's old *castello*, where she was to be introduced to his mother, that she broke the news to him that she couldn't accept his proposal. She recalled:

> Angrily he accused me of leading him on, of encouraging him to fall in love with me for the pleasure of turning him down. I was quite baffled, being too inexperienced at the time to handle the situation. I tried to explain to him that I had enjoyed his company and thought that we had had fun together and that I had never had any intentions of playing fast and loose with his heart, but it was no use.[9]

In a rage, he turned the car around and dropped her back at her aunt's house. Once he'd driven away, she realised she'd had a lucky escape and hoped it would be the last time she would have to see him. But like many women who say no to a man, he wouldn't accept her answer, and continued to pursue her, despite her clear rejection. 'He followed me everywhere I went in Italy with the idea of persuading me to be his mistress,' she wrote. 'I was quite petrified, but I was learning a great deal about men.'[10]

When Frances received a letter from Ernest de Rougemont, who was now in Paris and asking to see her, it seemed like the right time to move on, and she persuaded Pearl Kennedy Roberts that they should continue with their travels. They piled their suitcases into a motor car, and were driven along the winding roads of Tuscany, with its luscious grape fields and hillsides dotted with ancient terracotta-roofed villages and poplar trees. Frances relished the breeze in her hair and the joy of imagining the next adventures that awaited her in Florence, Venice and Paris.

She and Mrs Roberts registered with the American Embassy in Florence on 8 April 1925, alongside Rebekah Miller, the American artist who she had met on the *Mauretania*, alongside the de Rougemonts.[11] Whether or not she had been in Rome alongside Frances is unclear, but as Americans abroad, they followed in each other's footsteps.

In anticipation of Paris, Frances was anxious to swap her Seattle garments, now looking a little frayed from her travels, for clothing that would make an impression in the fashion capital of the world. She heard that the place to buy the latest Paris designs in Florence was from a little boutique in the burgeoning fashion district run by a Russian countess.

As she climbed up the dark, steep staircase inside one of the imposing Renaissance buildings on the elegant Via de Tornabuoni (known as 'the drawing room of Europe') and pushed open the door of the top-floor converted attic, she entered a magical space, which she later credited with changing the course of her life. It was here that she would meet a woman who introduced her to new possibilities and connections that a girl from Seattle never thought possible.

The Cassini Model House, close to the Gucci salon, which had opened in 1921, was owned by Marguerite Cassini, an Italian countess who had previously lived in America. She was the daughter of a Dutch singer, Stephanie van Betz, and a Russian diplomat and count, Arthur Pavlovich Nicolas Cassini, and they had arrived in Washington DC at the turn of the century. Marguerite carried the pretence that she was his adopted daughter and her mother his servant, due to the scandal of the count having a child with a woman of low social standing.

As the oldest daughter, Marguerite acted as host at the Russian Embassy, and the beautiful, flamboyant young woman became an important figure in the capital's social scene, alongside her best friend, Alice Roosevelt. They were notorious for running out on expensive parties that had been thrown in their honour, smoking in public and, in Marguerite's case, her extraordinary, and expensive wardrobe of skin-tight gowns and elaborate hats. Her son Oleg Cassini, later an internationally renowned designer who worked closely with

Jacqueline Kennedy, described his mother as audacious and a 'glorious flirt', who possessed a velvety voice and 'the devil's beauty, as much a consequence of personality'.[12]

Marguerite skipped to Europe, where she married a Russian count, Alexander Loiewski, but following the 1918 Revolution, was forced to flee to Montreux, Switzerland, with her two sons, Oleg and Igor. She struggled to provide for her family on limited funds and with only a few possessions of value, except for a Fabergé cross, which she was reluctant to sell.

Visiting Montreux were old friends from Washington, who persuaded her that with her innate sense of style and knowledge of how to be daring in her dress without crossing the lines of propriety, she should start her own fashion business. With money borrowed from her friend, Queen Sophie of Greece, she opened a small boutique in the Grand Hotel, selling hats and handbags, and then made the decision to move to Florence, where she could set up a business to cater to the growing number of American tourists.

At first, she sold hats from the salon owned by the Countess Fabricotti on the Via de Tornabuoni. Once she had the confidence, she opened her own boutique based on a simple idea. She would go to Paris twice a year to study the collections and then create her own cheaper, but equally elegant, variations. It quickly became one of the places where the most fashionable women in Italy would buy their couture.[13]

Frances was struck by the 'delightful lazy atmosphere' of the tiny showroom, as salesgirls flitted around, helping customers try on narrow calf-length jersey day dresses with cloche hats, and shimmering fringed evening gowns with their waistlines low at the hip. She had timed her arrival with that of a group of Americans who spoke no Italian and, amid the chaos of different languages struggling to be understood, the countess had sought refuge in the back room. When she finally emerged, she offered a hurried greeting to Frances as she went back to struggling with her patrons.[14]

To try and help with the obvious stress, Frances offered to act as translator for the other American tourists, using her basic Italian and French. For the next couple of days, in between her fittings for her new wardrobe, she helped out as a volunteer salesgirl, offering honest fashion advice peppered with a flow of platitudes as to what styles might work better on a customer.

By the time her new wardrobe was ready, the countess was so impressed with her aptitude for sales that she offered Frances a partnership in her couture enterprise. Perhaps Frances reminded Marguerite of herself when she was younger – the daring sense of style, the magnetic personality that could win over strangers – and so the countess considered this young American to be a real asset for the business. As sales manager, Frances would be tasked with going on buying trips to Paris with the countess, where they would view the seasonal collections and quickly snap up the most interesting pieces, which would then be copied in the Florence workrooms. It sounded like an ideal job, and Frances was tempted to accept, as she was beginning to realise that her fascination lay in fashion.

'Clothes, design and color had always interested me, and I had enjoyed picking out the dresses and colors that would make the customers look their best,' she said. But she was also filled with excitement at the thought of visiting romantic Venice and Paris, the cities she had dreamed of when studying her childhood atlases, and so she reluctantly turned down the offer from the countess. Besides, she had promised Ernest that she would meet him there:

> I had not made this long trip from Seattle to see nothing but Italy and terminate my travels in a dress shop. I told the Countess that I had a beau waiting for me in Paris whom I would not disappoint. Being a Latin, she naturally understood perfectly, so she gave me her blessing.

As a parting gift, the countess insisted on giving Frances a note of introduction to her Russian friend, Lady Olga Egerton, who was the head of the Paul Caret salon on Paris's Rue de Rivoli and would be able to offer her assistance to a novice American girl in the French capital.[15]

Chapter Four

By 11 May 1925, Frances was in Venice, where she explored the piazzas and palazzos along the Grand Canal during the day and enjoyed a gondola ride on moonlit waters at night. While Pearl Roberts was due to return to New York, Frances was able to meet a familiar face from Seattle, a woman who went by the name James A. Sheahan, who was travelling with her family in Europe and took over as temporary chaperone.[1]

Two days later, on 13 May, she and Mrs Sheahan arrived in Paris's Gare de Lyon, having taken the Simplon *Orient Express* from Venice, alongside a group of esteemed Seattleites, which included the writer Bertrand Collins, Judge Thomas Burke, the railroad builder responsible for developing transport in Seattle and Washington, and Clarence Blethen, the owner of the *Seattle Daily Times*. During the journey, Blethen and his wife so enjoyed their conversations with Frances, as she regaled them with the tales of her travels, that he encouraged her to write down the stories that she told so eloquently, with a plan to publish them as a regular column for his paper.[2]

Blethen had inherited the *Seattle Daily Times* from his father, Colonel Alden J. Blethen, who had transformed the small-print-run paper into the leading daily in Washington State. He wished to build on the success of his father by making the paper more family friendly, reducing scandal crime reportage and aiming for the middle classes by highlighting local success stories. Frances, as the sparkling daughter of a celebrated Seattle lawyer, was an appealing contributor, particularly given that she was now living a dynamic life abroad.

As she stepped out of the bustling station and on to the bright Paris boulevard, thronging with motor cars, she felt the warm air on her cheeks from the spring sunshine. She'd first arrived in Europe in winter and it was now almost summer. She took a taxi to her hotel, and from its window admired the rows of chestnut trees and bursts of colour from the flowers now in full bloom.[3]

Paris in 1925 was the centre of art and fashion, a thriving hub of creativity, where it was, for Americans, cheap enough to dine in gourmet restaurants every night and enjoy cocktails at the Ritz. It was the home of Coco Chanel; avant-garde artists like Picasso, Man Ray and Jean Cocteau; the lost generation of American exiles, Ernest Hemingway, Henry Miller, Gertrude Stein and F. Scott Fitzgerald; African American jazz musicians playing in the clubs of Montmartre; and the White Russians, who had fled the Revolution and brought with them their folk traditions which infused the city with Slavic art.

It was a city where Frances could just take her time walking the streets, breathing in the sweet scents and soaking up the sights and sounds, with its pavement cafes, the accordion players in their berets on street corners, bright flower kiosks and the ateliers selling chic clothing in luxurious fabrics. One could stroll by the River Seine watching the sun's rise and fall reflected on its grand buildings, with the Eiffel Tower, Notre-Dame and Sacré-Coeur as steady landmarks that revealed its immense history. Paris was, as Goethe wrote, 'a universal city, where every step taken on a bridge or square brings to mind a great past, and where history has been played out on every street corner'.

Frances was window shopping on the city's grandest street, Rue Royale, known as the fashion centre, when she noticed a sign for Paul Caret at No. 26, the salon Marguerite Cassini had raved about. She went back to her hotel to collect her letter of introduction and called into the salon to ask for Lady Egerton.

Lady Olga Egerton was, in fact, a Russian princess, born Princess Olga Labanov-Rostovsky to a noble family who owned vast tracts of land across Russia and eastern Europe. She was married first to a Russian diplomat and after his death, she wed Sir Edwin Egerton in 1895, who served as British Ambassador in Rome and Madrid, and then as Minister to Greece, when they moved to Athens.

Following the Greek-Turkish War of 1897, Lady Egerton was supported by her friend, the Queen Consort of Greece, Olga Constantinova of Russia, in establishing the Royal Hellenic School of Needlework and Lace in Athens, which provided employment for female refugees who had arrived in the city. Lady Egerton, already accomplished at embroidery, studied Byzantine needlework and antique lace techniques, and the school soon became renowned among fashionable circles for the textiles they produced.

Sir Egerton passed away in 1916, and their only son was tragically killed in the First World War. In her grief, Lady Olga settled in Paris, where she founded her own salon, Paul Caret, while her sister, Princess Alexandra Labanov-Rostovsky, managed a branch in London. In the same way that her Hellenic school was designed to give displaced women employment, the Paris salon employed exiled Russian women who arrived in Paris penniless following the Revolution of 1917.

The saleswomen, cutters, fitters, embroiderers and models were all Russians of 'high breeding', once important figures in the Tsar's court, who had lost everything, including their homeland. Coco Chanel was similarly inspired by the Russian émigrés and their Slavic folk art when she released her 1923 Russian collection, featuring embroidered *rubachka* tunics, dramatic coats lined with fur, and ropes of faux pearls and crosses.

While it's Chanel's name and designs that live on, in the twenties Paul Caret also inspired headlines for their luxury couture. They incorporated Lady Egerton's skills in Hellenic and Russian folk stitchwork for the embroidered georgette silk dresses, gold and brocade sheath dresses, as well as plaid coats for wearing at Palm Beach and reams of shimmering lamé. In 1921, the London society magazine, *The Sketch*, wrote, 'Pleasant experience has taught a great many women that Paul Caret frocks are things that no one who wants to establish a reputation for good dressing can afford to be without.'[4]

When Frances handed over her letter and hailed her time in Florence with Marguerite Cassini, Olga was immediately taken by this American girl, so warm and charming, and whose words tumbled out of her enthusiastically. Rather than continuing to stay in a hotel, Frances was invited to sleep on the sofa in what Frances described as Lady Egerton's 'delightful little apartment'.

To Frances, Lady Egerton was an 'unusually brilliant woman with sharp blue eyes softened by a comprehensive smile. I liked her instantly, and her cordiality to an American stranger was beyond mere words of gratitude.'[5]

Frances contacted Ernest de Rougemont to inform him that she was now in Paris and staying at Lady Olga's apartment, and they arranged to see the city together. She found Paris incredibly exciting, and as she and Ernest wandered the streets, it was as romantic as she had imagined. He was quiet, kind and considerate, always behaving like a gentleman, and while she later confessed that he offered less excitement than the fireworks and drama of her Italian pursuer, her time was a whir of excursions to see the sights, dinners in the Bois de Boulogne and dancing at Montmartre's top night spots.

After ten days together, he had to return to England for work, but he invited Frances to come to visit him so she could meet his mother and the rest of his family at their home in Kent – Dennett Lodge, in Crockham Hill. She purchased a couple of outfits from Paul Caret that would be suitable for the London season and booked her travel from Paris to England, which in those days involved taking a train from Paris to Havre, travelling by ship to Southampton, and then taking a connecting train to London.

As a parting gift, Lady Egerton gave Frances a letter of introduction to her sister, Princess Alexandra Lobanov-Rostovsky, who oversaw the London Paul Caret salon on Orchard Street. Like their salon in Paris, the London atelier had an international reputation. The Maharani of Jodhpur had visited in May 1925 and enjoyed tea, served with bread and butter, with Princess Alexandra before being fitted for couture.

As the princess told a newspaper in March 1927, Paul Caret made the gowns for Europe's most fashionable queens – the Queen of Romania and the Queen of Spain. 'We make for members of British royalty too – Princess Mary and Princess Louise,' she added:

> My sister revived the ancient embroidery industry of Rhodes, which was becoming a lost art, and the beauty of the work appeals to women of highly cultivated tastes. We decided to go into trade because we were so successful during the war selling bonds and working for the Hoover fund. Neither my sister nor myself is an expert designer, but we know where to find them.[6]

After arriving in London, Frances booked into Selfridge's Hotel on Orchard Street and it reminded her of the modern Olympic Hotel in Seattle – the place where her friends had bid her farewell. When she awoke the next day, she realised that Paul Caret was almost opposite her hotel, at 16 Orchard Street, and with her letter from Lady Egerton, she prepared to introduce herself to Princess Alexandra.

As she opened the door to the salon, she was struck by its 'quiet taste', with old Venetian lace curtains in the window, reflecting the regal style of its owner, a woman who had been maid of honour for Grand Duchess Elizabeth Feodorovna. There were two showrooms, one downstairs and the other upstairs, and she was led up the steps by an assistant, who she later found out was Lady Cynthia Bernard, just one of the many women of high society she would be introduced to in the salon.[7]

Princess Alexandra, known to friends as 'Fafka', as it sounded like the diminutive, 'Sasha', appeared as an intimidating figure, seated at an old Victorian desk with a ram-rod straight posture and dignified air. Like her sister in Paris, she was immediately charmed by Frances, and with her inherent kindness, offered the young American employment in the salon and a place to stay. 'I was in England without friends or a mother – that was quite enough for the princess,' wrote Frances. 'She literally put her delicate arms around me as protection, and has gone far out of her way to give me a most unusual acquaintance in London!'

Before beginning as a sales assistant and model, Frances first visited Ernest's ancestral home, Dennett Lodge in the Kent countryside. The invitation to meet his parents was a sign that their relationship was serious and that he may propose. With its beautiful, landscaped gardens and surrounding elm woods, it was exactly how she had imagined the grandeur of a stately country home. The de Rougemonts were the epitome of English courtesy and charm, but there was a strict set of rules when staying in their home, which was notably different to the lazy existence at her aunt's house in Rome. As she wrote in her memoirs:

> I was shocked and surprised when I was awakened on the first morning by a maid snapping up the window shades, letting the morning sunlight pour in on my face. She placed a tray containing a cup of tea and a plate of thin bread and butter on my bed table, and with a cheerful good morning she left the room. I looked at my watch. It was eight o'clock. I turned over and went back to sleep. When I arose a couple of hours later and went downstairs, I found that breakfast was over and the business of the day was in full swing. I received disapproving looks and no breakfast that morning. From that day on I conformed to the house rules, drank my tea at eight and arrived down in time for the gargantuan family breakfast at nine o'clock.[8]

Staying in their home, Frances realised that this life was not for her. She still wanted to explore new places, and being married into an insurance broker family, no matter how warm and welcoming they were, wouldn't satisfy her. Ernest was perhaps too polite, too proper, when she was looking for someone who could excite her and who was on the same level when it came to embracing what the world had to offer:

> The family took me wholeheartedly to its bosom, and I fitted in very well with their life, but my decision was made that first morning. It was not the way of life I would choose for myself, but although I refused to join my life with that of my English beau, he and his family have always remained my very good friends.[9]

In September, she was invited to the wedding of Ernest's uncle and Rebekah Miller, with whom she had spent time in Florence. Both bride and groom were past those first flushes of youth, and the quiet ceremony took place at the church in Crockham Hill, with Ernest Junior as best man. Such was the impression that Frances had made on the family, from that first meeting on the *Mauretania*, that she was elevated to bridesmaid alongside Rebekah's sister, Mary.

There were a number of marriage proposals that she turned down, said Frances' daughter, Marybelle. 'She was very attractive. Men fell like flies for her, not only for her looks but for her personality, which was larger than life. They would never have met someone like her before.'

Despite the proposals, she was steadfast in her decision to enjoy all that London's social scene had to offer and was welcomed into the princess's home near Buckingham Palace.[10] Princess Alexandra had never married and having been forced to flee to England after the revolution, she was still firmly attached to the traditions of her homeland, where she had been an important figure at court. Frances said:[11]

> She ran her London house in the same grand manner as her home had been conducted during the pre-revolutionary days when she was a member of the Tsar's Court. She insisted on punctuality, and would bang on the floor with her cane if I were a split second late. 'A lady never keeps anyone waiting,' she would say. I had never known this kind of discipline at home, but I loved the Princess so much that I did not resent her martinet treatment of me.[12]

Frances assisted in welcoming society ladies as they arrived for fittings at the Paul Caret salon, and she wrote home to rave about the 'most superb gowns' they sold. Despite the, at times, brisk behaviour, she developed a close friendship with the princess, who referred to her as her niece to help with the introductions to society. Frances would in turn call her 'Aunt Fafka', and her 'fairy godmother'.

Being cared for by the princess led to her being introduced to members of the English aristocracy, including the Duchess of Buckingham and Chandos, who she described as 'a wonderful old lady of over eighty with a fabulous memory and salty humor', and Prince Arthur, Duke of Connaught and Strathearn, the seventh child of Queen Victoria, who would become a long-standing friend of Frances until his death in 1942.

She was conscious of her status as a young American woman with no money among these established figures of the Old World who followed the archaic customs and dictates of the day. Yet it was testament to her ease and warmth that she was adopted by all those she met. As Frances said:

> There is an old saying that in England, before a stranger can expect to receive hospitality, he must be prepared to give 'cutlet for cutlet'. That, as far as I was concerned, is a complete fallacy. I had nothing to offer and was unable to offer any hospitality in return, but I was received everywhere for myself alone.

These acquaintances would serve as material for her new column in the *Seattle Daily Times*, which, as had been discussed with its owner, Clarence Blethen, would be a series of travel pieces detailing her experiences as an American in Europe. To introduce its readers to her first column on 5 July 1925, once she'd arrived in England, the newspaper described her as 'one of the most prominent members of the younger set here', and said she had met:

> [a] number of the world's most noted personages, has been entertained by them in a delightful, informal way, and in general has found an infinite variety of interesting things to write home, which she does in her own charming and refreshing manner.[13]

Her dispatches would be addressed as a letter to a fictional friend called 'Billie', where she enthusiastically recounted her 'jaunt through Europe' so far. It opened with the line, 'Lunching with a Princess of royal blood does sound rather like a fairytale, now doesn't it, Billie?'[14]

Sailing into the salon one day was Princess Maria of Greece and Denmark, the daughter of King George I of Greece and his wife, the Grand Duchess Olga Constantinovna of Russia. She was a good friend and client of the Labanov-Rostovsky sisters, and after being introduced, Frances received a prestigious invite for luncheon at Marlborough House.

The Queen Anne-era villa, with its famous landscaped gardens facing on Pall Mall, was the London home of Princess Maria's aunt, the widowed Queen Alexandra, and prior to this had been the abode of her husband, Edward, Prince of Wales, and the gathering place of his notorious Marlborough set of friends. When he was crowned Edward VII in 1902 and Alexandra as queen, their son George moved into Marlborough House with his family until his coronation as King George V in 1910.

After choosing an outfit suitable for dining with a princess and completing the look with a fur coat, despite the warm weather, Frances was collected in a motor car by Princess Maria and her daughter, Xenia, who was now living in New York City after marrying William Leeds, the son of an American businessman known as the 'Tin Plate King'.

'Meeting a Princess, and then having her personally conduct you to luncheon at a famous old palace isn't an everyday experience! I was duly thrilled as we emerged from the car with the footmen in royal livery to assist us,' she wrote in her column. They were led along the dark hallways of the palace and into a bright drawing room covered with chintz drapes and wide windows looking out onto the landscaped gardens.[15]

Frances, wishing to ensure she was dressed correctly for the occasion, kept on her fur coat as she was seated for lunch. Princess Maria interrupted the chattering and turned to Frances, 'Do take off your fur coat! We all know now that you have one!' The moment broke the ice, and as she recounted, after some laughter, she removed 'the objectionable fur garment'.[16]

As the liveried footmen brought out each course, she couldn't help but think back to how far she'd come from Seattle and all those parties she would organise with her friends, with the carefully crafted seating arrangements and coordinated flower displays for the tables. The only difference now was that she was seated in a palace with two princesses.[17] She signed off her first column, 'I must scoot and array myself for my new habit – the English 5 o'clock tea!'[18]

She had made such an impression that she was invited to another lunch with Princess Maria at Marlborough House, where they had a picnic lunch on the balcony. They ate sandwiches while chatting 'in the most cosy, unpretentious fashion. I could not help wondering what a few of the professional New York hostesses would have thought, had they seen us that afternoon.'[19]

★ ★ ★

Women in the 1920s were learning to value their individuality. It was only seven years since they had won the right to vote (and five in the United States), and this permissive time meant women could go on dates unchaperoned, riding in motor cars or to the new entertainment venues that were springing up. As a young, unattached woman living abroad, Frances embraced this liberty in how she lived her life, while also ensuring her behaviour was appropriate to her class. It would still have been unusual for a young woman like Frances to be living so independently, without the protection of her family. She enjoyed being single, and with her looks and personality, was in high demand for dates with young men.

'I had the typical American girl's idea of stringing along dozens of Beaux at the same time,' she said and, given her proximity to Buckingham Palace, she was wooed by several officers from the Household Cavalry. With pride in their status as protectors of the sovereign, these men were very serious in their duties, and sometimes her irreverent humour could be taken the wrong way, as to 'laugh at them in any way is a venial sin'.[20]

One of her dates, a member of the Irish Guards, called Frances to ask if she would watch him on parade because he wanted her to be able to admire him in his bearskin hat. Without thinking, she saucily replied, 'Why, good lord, Peter! You're bad enough in your clothes!' He didn't find the remark very amusing and, she wrote, 'this levity severed my romantic and diplomatic relations with him and his brother officers for some time'.[21]

While Princess Alexandra was 'delighted and amused' at the dates Frances was going on, she was also absolutely attuned to whether someone was from the 'right' family. She followed the lineages as detailed in the *Debrett's* and *Almanach de Gotha* manuals as if they were gospel. She could tell immediately what standing in society someone had on hearing their family name, and whether they had strong connections to royalty.

Frances may have received marriage proposals from several wealthy, titled men, yet she didn't feel ready to settle down, despite the princess pushing on her the importance of blood lines. She was particularly keen for her ward to accept a proposal from a French aristocrat whose mother was a close friend, but Frances was enjoying her time in Europe too much to give it all up for one man. In fact, after six months in London, she was keen to travel further and to explore more of eastern Europe, where she believed her distant ancestors came from.

An opportunity arrived when she met an American diplomat's wife in London, Eno Ham Johnson, whose husband, Ely Elliot Palmer, was the American Consul General in Bucharest. Eno had written a 1918 book entitled *From Mexico to India*, which detailed her experiences travelling with her husband's diplomatic postings. Before Bucharest, they were in Madrid, and their home had been a popular gathering place for Americans in Spain.[22]

Frances and Eno no doubt bonded over their love of travel and their experiences of being North Americans in England, and when she expressed a desire to visit the Balkan states, Eno offered up an irresistible invitation to come and visit them in Romania. Frances lit up at the thought of experiencing new cultures. 'Fresh fields and pastures new was my theme song at that time, and this was a heaven sent chance,' she said.

Chapter Five

Princess Alexandra had reservations about her young ward going to Romania, with prejudices around the people there and the idea of, in her words, 'fresh innocence being let loose in such a sink-hole'. As she had been with her decision to leave Seattle, Frances was single-minded in her plans to visit eastern Europe, and to ensure her safety, the princess gave her a letter of introduction to the Queen of Romania, who was one of her most important clients.[1]

In December 1925 Frances left London to embark on her new adventure, which took several days on the train, cutting from western to eastern Europe. After travelling from London to Paris, she transferred to the *Orient Express*. It was a dramatic journey through Germany's Black Forest, over the Austrian Alps to Vienna, then into Hungary and Budapest and across Romania to its capital, Bucharest. The city was considered 'the Paris of the Balkans', with its impressive boulevards and grand buildings. Wealthy women displayed their imported French fashions in the elegant cafes, which served French patisserie and the finest cuisine by Parisian chefs. There was also a heavy Turkish influence and a sense of decadence in the air, with its coffeehouses, bathhouses and illicit drinking dens.

Eno Palmer had a reputation as 'one of the most noted hostesses in Central Europe',[2] and having lived in Bucharest since 1921, she gave Frances an overview of the tempestuous political situation in the country. Queen Marie of Romania was English born, a granddaughter of Queen Victoria, but with strong Russian heritage, as she was the granddaughter of Tsar Alexander II of Russia. On her marriage to King Frederick I, she carved out a cultured role in Romania, becoming much loved for her championing of the country's rich heritage, her intellect, diplomacy and support of the arts.

Her eldest son, Carol, sparked a constitutional crisis when he renounced the crown, and it would automatically pass to his brother, Michael, who was only 5 years old. Carol was considered the first true Romanian heir to the throne following the country's freedom from Turkish rule and so the decision threw the crown into turmoil. The queen's daughter, Elisabeth had become Queen of Greece on her marriage to King George of Greece, but following the 1923 coup, they were forced into exile and returned to live in Bucharest.

For Frances, the atmosphere in Bucharest at that time was 'electric. One felt as if black clouds were gathering darker and darker, lightning and then thunder. It was like living in a Graustark or [Princess of] Zenda novel.'[3]

While Frances' newspaper columns were at times humorous and light, she also wished to capture the mood of the places she was visiting and to elevate her reportage to something more insightful. She loved to experience the real energy of a place, to embrace its people and get a sense of what was happening on a deeper level, rather than merely being a tourist passing through. As she recounted her time in Romania for her column, she offered an insider's look at the political situation, which at the time of her visit was fraught with questions as to the future of the Romanian crown. She was experiencing the dying embers of the eastern European royalty, where Queen Marie would be the last queen before Romania's monarchy was excoriated by Communism.

'Europe is still full of shadow Queens – they themselves remain quietly and discreetly in the background,' she wrote, in one of her dispatches to celebrate female rulers. 'In Queen Marie of Rumania Americans see a Queen who never effaces herself. She is in the limelight. It is her husband, King Ferdinand, who is in the shadow.'

Through her connection to both Eno Palmer and the Labanov-Rostovsky sisters, Frances was welcomed into the royal residence in Bucharest, Cotroceni Palace. The French neoclassical architecture was balanced by Queen Marie's embracing of Romanian culture in the interiors, with the heavy Turkish tapestries, wood-panelled walls and ornately carved furniture.

Frances' bedroom, with its luxurious bed, reminded her of the *Arabian Nights*, and she was taken by surprise after her first night's stay, when she was woken in the morning by a young girl carrying a sitz bath on her head. Frances watched curiously as she placed the bath in front of the big porcelain stove and then lit the firewood. A dozen or more girls entered the room in single file, each carrying a large pitcher of steaming water on her head, and then each emptied the hot water into the large vessel. 'I began to get nervous and asked them to go away, but of course they did not understand what I was saying,' she wrote:

I was lifted, protesting from the bed, my nightgown was removed, and I was carried over to the receptacle, lowered into it, and was given a bath by the little peasant maids. I didn't know whether to be insulted, humiliated or amused, but I remembered that when in Rumania one does as the Rumanians do, and submitted to the indignity goodnaturedly.[4]

She relished the chance to try lavish menus of rich new foods, with meat smorgasbords and a plum vodka, Ţuică, to begin, followed by mămăligă, a cornmeal gruel topped with poached egg and lashings of sour cream and served with goats' cheese and 'well-baked peasants' black bread', which would be a favourite dish she would refer back to time and again.

'After my first meal in Bucharest I ceased to be surprised at the voluptuous figures of all the females over sixteen years of age,' she said.[5] Eno had shared similar concerns about the rich food being served in Bucharest. She told a reporter in 1928, 'It is most difficult to retain one's figure in Rumania. So much cream is used in all the dishes, and they are so delicious.'[6]

Having made an impression at the palace in Bucharest, Frances was invited to visit the royal hideaway of the queen, Peleş Castle, positioned in the Carpathian Mountains, near the village of Sinaia. With its sky-piercing spires and timber-clad turret, its mix of neo-Renaissance, Swiss and German architecture and its backdrop of dark pine forests and snow-covered peaks, it was a place that filled her with wonder. The interiors of the palace seemed to bridge the gap between the west and east, with their intricate carvings that still bore a Turkish influence, ornate rugs and tapestries and huge banquet rooms with low seats covered in cushions.

When Frances was invited to meet with Queen Marie in person for tea in the palace, she was led into the large reception hall, which featured Turkish divans and a large white marble table with two black cocker spaniels resting on it. 'Though middle-aged and the mother of five children, she is truly a radiant beauty,' was Frances' first impression of the queen, who was dressed in mauve chiffon and ropes of pearls. 'After I made my curtsey, she came forward and greeted me cordially, putting me completely at my ease.'[7]

Frances reported on her conversations with the queen with her typical embellishment in the dialogue to appeal to her readership back home, who would be thrilled that one of their own was embraced by European royalty. 'You are the little American girl I've been hearing so much about. You have writing aspirations, have you not?' the queen asked her. She admired the Paul Caret suit Frances was wearing, with its high collar decorated with a gold leather band. 'I know the owners, Lady Egerton and Princess Labanov, very well. They are such dears. I am sure it must be very nice for you to be under their protective wings.'[8] The queen led the way to the dining room where tea was served as a buffet, with caviar on toast, cheese, muffins and pastries, and they then moved through to the music room where they sat on the divans and listened to the golden harp being played.

As Frances prepared to say goodbye, the queen spoke of her hopes to visit the United States. A few months later, she embarked on a successful diplomatic tour of the country, where she was greeted warmly by the people who had read of her almost mythical status in the newspapers.

Her husband died a short time later, and she became queen dowager, while Carol's son Michael was named king. However, Carol returned to claim the crown and sought to crush his mother's popularity. She retreated to her palace on the Black Sea and died at Sinaia in 1938, where Frances had been entertained more than a decade before.

Staying at Cotroceni Palace in Bucharest over Christmas 1925, Frances was pursued by several eastern European suitors, who took her horseback riding, for moonlight sleigh rides or for cruises in their carriages along the main boulevards. 'You ride, don't you?' the queen had asked Frances over lunch. 'Oh, don't say "not well", because I've seen you, and besides every young diplomat or army officer is pleading to accompany you.'

There was one who she referred to in her memoirs as 'Prince Giecka', who would take her on sleigh rides across his land and fox hunting on the frozen River Danube, where they would lie on the ice, hidden by snow drift, waiting for the red foxes to appear. 'Giecka used to give me the fox skins after the animal had been skinned,' she said. 'The hides were scraped, but not cured, and after a few days they got very smelly and I had to get rid of them without letting him know, or he would have been deeply insulted.'[9]

Another of her suitors, who was known as something of a Casanova in Bucharest, 'an unbearably handsome Pole', would invite her riding in the mornings along the Șoseaua Kiseleff, one of the city's principal boulevards, known to visitors as the *Chaussée*. While she was warned repeatedly about him, she found him 'gay, charming, courteous and witty and loads of fun'. When he invited her to his sister's house for tea, she arrived to find there was no sister and the invitation was a ruse to be on his own with her. She managed to make her excuses to leave, despite him falling to his knees with a marriage proposal. She wrote in her memoirs:

To my embarrassment and surprise, as soon as the coachman started the horses on the homeward journey, he fell on his knees at my feet, put his head on my lap and begged me to marry him. The big bad wolf had found an honest woman at last! I told him very gently that I was not in love with him, and therefore could not marry him. Unlike my Italian beau, this did not enrage him. He remained my friend and to this day has never married.[10]

There was also a Hungarian baron, known as 'Upos', who had worked as a diplomat in London. His Transylvanian estate had been ceded to Romania as part of the Allies' Treaty of Trianon, following Austria–Hungary's defeat in the First World War. She met him in a restaurant in Bucharest, where he was drinking too much due to his misery at his ancestral land no longer being part of Hungary. They became friends, having long, melancholic conversations about the future of the world. He was convinced there would be another world war, born from the sufferings of the last one, and which would be even more devastating.

He invited Frances to his family's estate in Transylvania, where she was instantly captivated by the magic of the place. His palace, she said:

… was like something from a Hans Anderson fairy tale standing over the frozen lake, hemmed in by the Carpathians, the snow sparkling in the moonlight like Christmas cake frosting. My entire visit was like a dream. The local people sang at night outside the palace, weird, sad songs handed down through countless generations. He took me for romantic sleigh rides under heavy sable rugs in the moonlight all over the estate. There is no doubt that for a while I was completely under his spell, and why I did not remain there forever is still a mystery to me.

Her weekly article for the *Seattle Daily Times* had not only provided her with some extra income but had fuelled her desire to be a roving journalist, so she could write dispatches from wherever she travelled. She had also come to realise, as she experienced so many different cultures and met so many fascinating people in the Balkans, that she would never go back to the United States to live – her home would always be in Europe.[11]

The trip to the Balkans would also influence her sense of style for decades to come. The eastern European mood was evident in her collection of embroidered blouses and jackets, her sartorial preference for bright colours and a love of Turkish harem pants and turbans. All these touches can be seen in her fashion choices throughout the thirties, and in the dramatic tartan outfits she later designed when living in the Highlands.

Chapter Six

Frances returned to London in spring 1926, where she continued to live with Princess Alexandra while assisting her at the Paul Caret salon. She was both a salesgirl and model – bringing a natural flair to their luxurious beaded and sequin dresses, peacock-hued suits and silk blouses. She now sported a fashionable shingle haircut, which was captured in a portrait by the Russian artist Leo Klin and published in the *New York Herald Tribune* in October 1926. Guests to the salon that year, where Paul Caret was described by one reporter as a design house who 'weaves dreams and turns them by magic into frocks',[1] included Crown Princess Louise of Sweden, who ordered a georgette rose evening dress.[2]

Building up her experience in writing for more publications, Frances was hired by the Newspaper Enterprise Association (NEA) as a correspondent, and her syndicated articles appeared in local newspapers across the United States, providing an insider's insight to Europe's politics, written in a travelogue style. As an overseas reporter, she was more than merely an American traveller abroad – she used her charisma to ask pertinent questions to the highest dignitaries.

In one article from Berne, Switzerland, in December 1926, she interviewed President Heinrich Häberlin on the subject of immigration and his appeal to the United States to accept more Swiss citizens. When the Queen of Spain visited the Paul Caret boutique in November, Frances took the opportunity to ask her whether she was planning a trip to visit the Spanish-speaking countries of South America, which she duly reported in one of her articles.

In her dispatches to the *Seattle Daily Times*, she praised Princess Alexandra as her 'fairy godmother', as it was the princess who, in August 1926, arranged for her to be presented to Mary, Princess Royal, the only daughter of King George V, at a charity garment sale to raise money for the Officer's Families Fund.[3] She arrived at the address on Grosvenor Square dressed in her smartest black 'smoking' coat and skirt and was led by a footman into a drawing room where

Princess Alexandra was waiting for her. Given her striking looks, Frances was asked if she would model some of the knitwear and outfits created for the charity event. She agreed to try on a pale blue two-piece suit, which it was hoped Princess Mary would purchase, as it was reportedly her favourite colour.

As Frances recounted in her *Seattle Daily Times* article, Princess Alexandra introduced Frances to Princess Mary as her 'little American godchild', and Frances offered a low curtsy. She then gave a florid description of the conversation:

'Oh, do let me see your frock,' the Princess exclaimed. 'And how long have you been over here?'

'I came here for three months, Your Royal Highness, and I've been here a year and a half.'

'How flattering to us! I like that color. Should I have it? There are so many things that are lovely that I want them all. And when do you go back to your splendid country, Miss Oldham?

'Oh, don't ask her that,' said Princess Alexandra. 'She doesn't know herself. Besides, we don't want to lose her.'

'So that's how it is! Well, stay as long as you can. We like Americans to be happy in our country.'

After the charity event, Frances darted off for a lunch appointment with Geoffrey Hope-Morley, High Sheriff of the County of London, at the Embassy Club. They were then due to watch the famous match between Eton and Harrow cricket clubs at Lord's Cricket Ground.

The annual game between the two public schools was one of the highlights of the London season, with the sought-after seats at the grandstand filled with ladies in their finest chiffon and with matching parasols and gentlemen in morning suits and top hats, with a blue cornflower in their buttonhole to represent Harrow or a carnation for Eton.[4]

After two years in London, Frances had established herself as one of the most popular young women on the social circuit, with invites to charity events such as the 184th anniversary of the opening of the Queen Charlotte Hospital in May 1928, where she was one of fifteen 'pretty maids of honour'.[5]

In the summer of 1928, she returned to the Continent, where she once again visited Bucharest. She was invited for afternoon tea with Elisabeth, exiled Queen Consort of Greece, and her husband George II of Greece in Cotroceni Palace. 'All afternoon an unspoken question had hovered on the tip of my tongue. I so wanted to ask this young pair why they had resolutely refused to abdicate the throne, preferring exile and poverty instead.' While living in a palace may not seem like poverty, she insisted they led a very simple life. Frances was invited to dinner one evening and afterwards they settled down for card games. She wrote:

> I learned that the Queen is keenly interested in the game which swept all over America like a prairie fire – mah-jong. Almost any evening in the royal palace you can see a party in which are included the young Queen and several young diplomats all of whom are adepts at the game.[6]

After time spent at the palaces of Bucharest, Frances travelled by train to Paris, returning to stay with Lady Olga Egerton in her chic apartment. She wrote of enjoying 'the gay life which Paris so well affords – seeking novelties, dining, dancing or racing, I answer no questions, therefore tell no lies and am able to sleep the light sleep of the just'.

On top of the *Seattle Daily Times* and the *Amalgamated Press*, she was also earning money by writing pieces for *Vogue*, *The Spur* and *London Sphere* and, in her delight at being a working woman in Paris, 'life rolls on at an amusing pace'.[7] Evenings were spent at exclusive nightclubs, including the Blue Room, one of Paris's chicest nightspots which took its name from the blue satin brocade that covered its wall. It stirred to life after 11 p.m., when the tables gave way to the dancefloor, which simmered with an exclusive crowd of politicians, American millionaires and actors.

One evening, Frances was seated at a large table covered with buckets of ice, bottles of vintage champagne and brightly coloured cardboard aeroplanes. She had been invited by a dashing war hero, James Rodney, to celebrate an acquaintance purchasing a new three-engine Fokker. James was from a family of keen aviators. His uncle, the Honourable Freddie Guest, was the founder of Britain's auxiliary air force, and Freddie's wife, Amy Phipps Guest was equally daring. She was the owner of the aeroplane *Friendship*, which carried Amelia Earhart across the Atlantic in June 1928. Amy had been fully prepared to be the first woman passenger to cross the ocean by air, if not for her family persuading her not to go.

The new aviation age was upon them, and this sense of excitement and adventure was in the air in the Blue Room that night. As she recounted in her *Seattle Daily Times* column, the owner of the plane had even offered to take Frances on a hunting expedition to Africa, via Spain and Egypt in October, with James as a pilot. When Frances spotted an old friend from Seattle, Tove Janson, and her husband, the Hollywood actor Monte Blue, through the throngs of people on the dancefloor, she caught Tove's eye, and they both came over to say hello.[8] 'We knew you were somewhere over here and it is so good to find you, honey,' said Tove as Frances embraced her.

Frances was thrilled to see a familiar face from home, and they arranged to meet for a catch-up over lunch the next day at Chez Capulin, which she described as 'one of those delicious restaurants in the Bois, in warm sunshine under the trees'. Seated together at an outdoor table, Frances noticed how Monte was as romantic to his wife as he was on screen, doting and affectionate, and presenting her with a bunch of violets, even after being together for four years. Seeing them together was reassuring to Frances that perhaps marriage wouldn't stymie the freedoms she enjoyed; one of the reasons why she had turned down so many proposals on her travels.[9]

She and James had become closer as they spent time together in Paris; he was dynamic and handsome, and they both shared a passion for discovering new places and new experiences. Lady Egerton would often take them for dinner at the latest Russian hotspots with, as Frances described, 'softly shaded lamps and such tzigane music stirs even the cold blood of the Englishman', and where they tried delicacies, from caviar to the meat of 'a delicious Russian bird which feeds on nuts'. They wandered the streets of Montmartre, hopping between different haunts to drink champagne and dance to jazz and then to revive themselves with bacon and eggs at one of the tiny little bars down a cobbled street. She wanted to be sure she had made the right decision in accepting James' proposal, and after having given it much thought, their engagement was announced on 30 July 1928.

Captain James Henry Bertie Rodney, like Ernest de Rougemont, had been educated at Harrow and Trinity College, Cambridge, but ten years prior. He was born on 29 March 1893 in Felthorpe, Norfolk, to George, 7th Baron Rodney and Corisande Evelyn Vere Guest, whose grandfather was John Spencer-Churchill, 7th Duke of Marlborough. The 1st Baron Rodney was a British Naval officer who saw victory over the French in the American War of Independence and was awarded a peerage in 1782.

Almost immediately after marrying Corisande, George Rodney showed his abusive side, and she moved out of their home in 1899 after he struck her in her eye. Rodney, in turn, moved in with Corisande's former lady-in-waiting, Annie Turner, and she filed for divorce on the grounds of cruelty and adultery. When divorce was granted in 1902, Corisande took James and his three brothers to live at the Guest family seat at the gothic Canford Magna Manor in Dorset. James' father died in 1909, and the title of Baron Rodney passed to James' older brother, George.

James' studies at Cambridge were cut short following the outbreak of the First World War. He enlisted as a lieutenant of the 5th Battalion Rifle Brigade and then transferred to the Royal Flying Corps as flight lieutenant in 30 Squadron in November 1915.[10] He served across the Middle East and Egypt and was awarded the Military Cross for his service in Mesopotamia, where he was shot down and severely wounded. He was also bestowed with the Distinguished Service Order for his bravery.[11] Following his demobilisation in March 1919, he worked for shipping firm Harris & Dixon, of which his cousin, Ivor Guest was vice chairman.

From his time in the Royal Flying Corps, and later the Royal Air Force, James Rodney was passionate about flying. Having been stationed in Egypt and Mesopotamia (now Iraq), he felt a strong connection to the region, naming his yacht *Afrika*. He shared this passion with his uncle, Freddie Guest.

Freddie had fought in the Boer War, acted as private secretary to his cousin, Winston Churchill in 1906 then, following the outbreak of the First World War, served as aide-de-camp to Field Marshal Sir John French on the Western Front. He also fought in East Africa, where he was awarded the Distinguished Service Order. After being invalided out of the war, he joined the Liberal–Conservative coalition government, serving as chief whip from 1917 to 1919 and Secretary of State for Air from 1921 to 1922. As well as his political career, he was a talented sportsman, winning bronze for polo in the 1924 Olympic Games.

What bonded James and Freddie together was the Auxiliary Air Force, set up to ensure there was a supply of trained men to fight for their country if needed. When Freddie founded the 600 (City of London) Squadron in 1926, his nephew James became adjutant and chief flying instructor.

The members of the squadron were expected to supply their own aeroplanes, and then learn how to fly them. Because of this, recruitment came from the city's financial and legal establishments, such as Lloyd's or the Stock Exchange. It was considered an elite corps, appealing to the type of rich young men who would have gone to battle on horses, but now could fly machines, with the skies as their new playground.

With his flight experience and military honours, James was considered the obvious choice to lead. On top of this, he had a sense of daring, as demonstrated when he performed a parachute jump from the wing of a Vickers Vimy bomber at the August 1926 Bank Holiday Camp at Northolt. This opportunity allowed him to travel across the country and to the Continent, as he would often transport new planes between the bases.

James had been married previously. In 1923, he had wed Phyllis Finch-Noyes, a Gaiety chorus girl known by her stage name Phyllis Desmond. Their marriage was short-lived and dissolved by 1927. It was probably then that he crossed paths with Frances, perhaps at one of the social events she attended for Old Harrovians. His energy and adventurous spirit, along with his tall, chiselled good looks, enhanced by a debonair moustache, would have been incredibly attractive to Frances. Rather than the thought of having to give up her love of travel to settle down in the Home Counties, he could pilot his plane and take her on trips overseas.

Frances spent August 1928 in Corsica with the Honourable Theodosia Meade, enjoying a last holiday as a single woman, and while she was away news of her engagement reached the United States. The *Seattle Daily Times* reported in August 1928:

> Recent letters from Miss Frances Oldham speak interestingly of the round of entertaining in London which is following close upon the announcement of her betrothal to Captain the Honourable James Henry Barty [*sic*] Rodney, DSO. They have been guests in the last few weeks of the Duchess of Buckingham, the Countess of Albemarle, the Duchess of Somerset and HH Princess Alexandra, and last week Miss Oldham was entertained at a tea by Princess Olga, Lady Egerton, at which HRH Princess Victoria, sister of King George, was among the guests.[12]

She and James were married on 23 August 1928 in an intimate ceremony at a registry office in London, where it was witnessed only by James' immediate family and a couple from Seattle who were visiting their children.[13] Frances made a startling entrance; rather than wearing traditional bridal white, she chose a blue tailored suit, worn with a blue leather coat with grey fur collar, a Reboux cloche hat and a corsage of white orchids.[14]

She was never going to be a conventional bride, and this choice of costume revealed her tastes. Her blue suit and leather coat may also have come from Paul Caret. An article in the *Daily Mirror* in October 1926 mentioned the salon's beautifully tailored leather coats with fur collar.[15]

The lunch reception was held at the Ritz and was hosted by James' mother, Lady Corisande Rodney, and her brother, the Honourable Henry Guest. After dinner and speeches, the newlyweds were taken by car to Croydon air-field, where a private plane was waiting to whisk them off on a three-week honeymoon tour of Europe, which included a visit to Romania, where they had dinner at the palace with Queen Marie.[16] She was excited to share her love of the country, and the happy times she spent there, with her new husband. A photo captures them boarding the plane, with Frances in her wedding outfit and James with his pilot cap and goggles and a scarf knotted around his neck – the very essence of modernity, as they anticipated their next adventures.

Part Two

The Hon. Mrs James Rodney

Chapter Seven

Landing back in England from their three-week honeymoon in mid-September 1928, the Rodneys moved into their first homes together: first at 52 Warwick Square, in Pimlico, and then to a flat belonging to James' uncle, Ivor Guest, in the famous Albany apartment complex in Piccadilly. The social life didn't stop with marriage. With James' aeroplane, they could visit friends by air, reflecting the burgeoning interest in aviation and all its possibilities. For the upper classes, owning a plane was like investing in a high-end motor car.

'Flying high has always been the ambition of men and women of fashion throughout the ages – but what generation has had such ways and means as our own?' Frances wrote, in one of her syndicated columns. 'A few hours will see them arrive, and if after the cure they look in at the Lido or South of France for the odd spot of fun, it is only a few hours off the homeward track: so why not?'[1]

At the end of September, the Rodneys flew in for a weekend party in Selsey, West Sussex, at Norton Priory, a rambling, ivy-covered country house owned by Mr and Mrs Norman Holden. To accommodate the number of flyers in their group of friends, the Holdens had cut away hedges and trees to make a landing ground on the lawn. A newspaper article noted, 'Things seem to be moving so quickly in the world of aviation' that Commander and Mrs Redmond McGrath were the 'the only people who arrived by car'.[2]

Women were very much encouraged to take up flying and one of the first young women to get her 'A' licence from Hanworth was Diana Guest, Freddie's daughter. She took after her mother Amy, who had wanted to be the first woman to cross the Atlantic as a passenger but settled for Amelia Earhart going in her place. Diana was so crazy about flying that, according to Frances, she decorated her bedroom to fit with her passion. The walls and ceilings were sky blue and on one side was a map of her father's last air route to Africa and another wall had an aviation map of the world.[3]

In November 1928, Freddie worked with the government to form National Flying Services Ltd (NFS), a central organisation to coordinate the nation's flying clubs and aerodromes. Its headquarters was established at Hanworth Park, now within the London Borough of Hounslow, which reopened as London Air Park aerodrome in August 1929. James kept a cottage on the grounds of Hanworth before his marriage, and as senior pilot and manager, he spent much of his free time there. Hanworth Park House was the office space and country club, which held aerial tea parties from the garden, attracting high-flying celebrities like Amy Johnson and Amelia Earhart, and where the Graf Zeppelin airship was displayed in August 1931.

Surrounded by a husband and friends who were obsessed with flying, Frances also embraced its opportunities. A September 1930 issue of the *Bystander* listed her as one of several society women who had been awarded a flying licence at Hanworth Park.[4] In an article in the *Sunday Dispatch*, she encouraged the 'high-spirited, modern woman' to get their 'B' licences, so they too could have freedom of flying and be able to take over the controls from their husbands. 'My advice to young women of 1930 is to take up aviation,' she wrote:

> Flying is one of the few sports really fit for the strength of the womanly woman. It gives her quicker mind a chance, her imagination the opportunity for which it longs, and employs the dull hours of a long day in healthy fresh air.[5]

For Frances, part of the attraction of James was his intrepid spirit, and they could hop in his plane and be over the Channel, or 'zip' over to Romania or the Czech Republic, for golf tournaments in Marienbad, in a matter of hours.[6]

Travelling was still incredibly important to her, and she hadn't wished to lose that thrill when settling down to marriage. She recollected fondly the dinners with the Queen of Romania and referred back frequently in her columns to glugging glasses of *ţuică*, the national spirit, distilled with plums, and one of the best meals she had tasted, *mămăligă*, topped with poached eggs and sour cream.

In a November 1930 *Daily Mirror* article, she chastised the type of English-speaking traveller who 'carries all their national prejudices abroad and tries to live as the perfect Englishman, or the perfect American, no matter where he may be'. In Frances' curious mindset, travel was all about experiencing other cultures and embracing them as if you were a local:

One doesn't travel for comfort, one travels for knowledge, understanding, and interest in people. At least, that is how I have felt about
travel and often have I sat up all night in a third-class carriage on the
Continent, not for comfort – nor even to save the money, perhaps – but
just to watch the people of the country as they really are.

The experiences one has in a tiny Italian hotel or during a boar hunt
from a crumbling Hungarian castle are far greater and more amusing
than the comfortable life one leads in the Ritz of the world. 'When in
Rome do as Rome does' is the only way to enjoy its charms to the fullest.
If she eats spaghetti done in a curious way, eat it with her, and often one
finds it excels our own preparation. If Spain dines at ten, dine at ten with
her. And if sweet jams are eaten by the spoonful between sips of cold
spring water in Rumanian palaces, one must not ask for bread. Only in
this way can one see the foreigner as he really is. A charming host, sporting in most cases, and hospitable according to traditional ideas.[7]

In December 1928, Frances returned to America for the first time in four years,
bringing her new husband to meet her father. The Rodneys boarded SS *Olympic*
at Southampton on 12 December 1928, and after a week crossing the Atlantic,
they arrived in New York. They spent a couple of days experiencing the thrills
of city life, where the feverish energy of the prohibition era was gathering pace,
with its parties and speakeasies driven by a seemingly booming economy that
would crash spectacularly ten months later.

They took the train across the country, switching to the North Coast Limited
at Chicago's Union Station, as they traced the same transcontinental route Frances
had travelled as a single woman. Christmas Day was spent on board the train,
where they were served their Christmas meal in the dining cart, complete with
flaming Christmas pudding. She was so thrilled by the sight and taste of it, laced
with citrus, spices and maraschino, that she begged the cook for the recipe.[8]

They arrived in Seattle on 28 December 1928, with an announcement in
the local papers of the return of a local society darling. Back in Washington,
she was struck by the differences in dinner times, having become accustomed
to the English rules of dinner at 8 p.m.:

On arrival in New York we were not surprised to find their times about
the same as our own. But as soon as we left that cosmopolitan city, how
extraordinary to find our dinner hour six to six thirty. At first we had
no appetites! But slowly we became more accustomed to no tea, and
early dinner![9]

They spent a couple of weeks in the city, staying with her father and his new wife, Alice Pickering, who he had married in 1926, and catching up with friends from her school days.[10]

The Rodneys then travelled to Canada to visit James' brother, George, Lord Rodney, who had rejected a life in England in favour of carving out his own destiny as a pioneer in the New World. He had bought a plot of land in Fort Saskatchewan, Alberta, where he and his wife, Lady Marjorie Lowther, daughter of the 6th Earl of Lownsdale, roughed it as hired hands for two years before building their own log cabin and establishing a successful cattle ranch, while they raised their four children.[11] The décor of their cabin would stay in the mind of Frances as she thought about decorating her own first home as a married woman. In her writings, she highlighted the cabin's pine and stone contrasting with the white plaster, scarlet fittings and bear-skin rugs, and their novel technique of using the wrappers around tins of vegetables and fruits to fashion patchwork wallpaper.[12]

At the beginning of May, Frances and James returned to England, sailing on RMS *Berengaria* from New York. Now going by the name of the Hon. Mrs James Rodney, privately and professionally, and with her desirable position as a stylish society figure, by 1930 she was being commissioned to write opinion pieces for the *Daily Mail* and the *Daily Mirror*.

The beginning of the thirties was marked by the rise of society gossip columnists who offered first-hand accounts of their aspirational lifestyles. The stock market crash of October 1929 not only wiped out savings and destroyed businesses, but resulted in less tolerance for the frivolities of the previous years. The columnists would also act as moral arbiters, offering sage advice and guidance to their readers at a time when the Bright Young Things were criticised for their debauched behaviour, depicted so shockingly in Evelyn Waugh's *Vile Bodies*.

In a forthright article in *John Bull* in December 1931, Frances echoed the thoughts of the time, that the careless, reckless behaviours of previous years were not as amusing as they once had been:

> Good riddance to those publicity-loving, notorious 'Bright Young People', of whom we heard so much not long ago! Whether they have really sobered down and become ashamed of their outlandish pranks, or whether the present parade of long skirts and gallantry has replaced the 'cocktails and laughter' period would be impossible to say.[13]

She had left behind the single and care-free Miss Oldham, who had been hesitant to settle down, and instead embraced her new position as a married English woman.

As the wife of a baron's son, Frances was now established as one of London's popular hostesses with an eye-catching wardrobe, and so she was a natural fit as a society columnist. Her articles offered an insight into her world, and they reflected her love of travel, where she covered topics such as the mealtimes in different countries and how they revealed the national characteristics. She also used her columns to deliver messages to women which, at times, sound conservative to modern ears, such as her advice on how to hold on to a husband in the face of rising divorce rates. She suggested women consider it a privilege, as a wife, to see that his favourite dish was well prepared, a fire was lit for his return on a cold winter evening and to learn backgammon or bezique to entertain him.

Most women, once they married, were expected to give up their careers, if they'd had one, but for Frances, there was no question that she would stop writing. By the 1930s, around a third of women in Britain worked outside of the home, but for married women that was one in ten. The endless task of taking care of the home was considered solely women's work, and Frances strived to do both, although she was in a position to have a cook and maid to help her with these duties.

The newspapers she wrote for were focused on promoting family values during a period where there were concerns about falling marriage rates and an increase in divorce, and so her columns were expected to reflect the same. She did, however, celebrate the rise in the numbers of working women as a result of the societal changes following the Great War, in her column in the *Daily Mirror* in February 1931:

> Today nearly every girl of good family has the chance of earning a decent living. Times have changed, and even conservative men realise that if the necessity arises their daughters be capable of supporting themselves.[14]

While life moved faster for modern women than a decade before, with cinemas, telephones and more opportunities with work (or sport, as she noted) leading to women delaying settling down, she considered marriage 'the greatest of all the careers open to women, and the holding of a husband requires far more clever handling than any other job in life'.[15]

It was evident that she was speaking from her own experience of being ecstatically happy and in love with James, and this was revealed in a July 1931 article for the *Daily Mail*, entitled 'Marriage is such fun!':

> Real happiness comes only with permanent companionship. I often wonder how I managed at all before I married, remembered the desperate loneliness of coming home after the party with no one to share my exhilarated high spirits, the meal eaten in solitude because I lacked the energy to arrange for guests, the desperate weariness when disappointments could not be discussed with a kind, understanding partner. It wasn't living – one simply exists until marriage.[16]

When she and James moved into their home, they took on domestic jobs together – building bookshelves, painting rooms and converting apple boxes into storage space. She enjoyed whipping up dinners, mending his garments, sharing his worries and pleasures and making those little gestures of a devoted wife, such as ensuring his chair was placed by the best reading lamp. In prescient words because she would live in both a mews and a castle, she wrote that 'Marriage in the true sense of that word cannot exist unless the home, whether it be a castle or a mews, belongs to both – a haven of rest for two souls who respect each other with a grave':

> Tender fondness. How often this has been proved to me during my few years of marriage! For during our travels I have felt at home in trains, hotels, other people's houses, and ships, so long as my man has been with me. Yet even under our own roof I feel sadly abroad when he is unable to be there.[17]

In these articles, she also revealed her friends' struggles with the recession, and how they were forced to cut down on their luxuries. Perhaps in a reference to her husband's uncle, Freddie Guest, she noted one man who was contemplating selling his flat in order to keep his fleet of planes.[18]

She also wrote pieces for *Vogue*, although these were uncredited. In those days, most of its articles were not by-lined, so it's not possible to know for sure what exactly Frances contributed, or how frequently. It is clear that she was attending and reporting on the fashion collections, where shows took place in the designer's atelier or 'house'. She was in Paris for the spring collections in May 1930, which reflected the new femininity of a new decade. 'I watched mannequins parade in all this season's ravishing garments and tried to glean the most intriguing of novelties,' she said.

Editors and buyers would gather in the showroom to watch mannequins hold a cardboard sign with the number of the garment they were modelling. The models moved quickly, to try to discourage copycats, which was becoming a problem for design houses, particularly given the economic climate. It was the business model that Marguerite Cassini had made a living from, and in March 1933, Frances spoke with authority about it to a columnist under the title 'Diary of a Modern Young Man', at one of the exclusive shows:

> Shows are guarded with the greatest care, the Hon Mrs James Rodney tells me, yet somehow the 'bandits' manage to scrape through. Tiny cameras hidden in the lapel of a fur coat have even been employed in snapping the mannequins, although some artists trust their memory to duplicate the designs.[19]

In one of her columns from 1930, she wrote of her preference for having her clothes made in London and advised her readers to glean ideas from French couture while still going to their trusted tailors:

> I prefer to have my own clothes made, and properly fitted, in London town. People often ask me why – well, here's my reason. My people take more trouble and certainly do turn me out in models which fit me, not their mannequins, you see.
>
> Perhaps it's because I live in London and not in Paris, but in the big couturiers in Paris, unless one is fitted at least four times, the gown is totally unlike their own model, and unless one is spending a small fortune they take no trouble at all. My own experience is to do your looking in the French capital and your choosing and buying in the English if real chic is your goal.[20]

The Depression particularly hit the fashion industry, as the customers who had bought on credit now couldn't pay their bills, and with disposable incomes drying up, there was less of an appetite for luxury goods. Frances told her *Daily Mail* readers that the chicest women she knew were dressing on a budget, as the secret of real style was 'knowing what to wear and how to wear it'. Just as the Wall Street Crash of October 1929 had changed the fortunes of so many, it also marked a dramatic shift in fashion, from knee-revealing flapper dresses to floor-skimming elegance. In an article in May 1930, she spoke of her relief at not having to disclose 'every secret as the "flapper" dress of past seasons allowed … Surely we all realise that the subtle lure of hidden charms intrigue men's curiosity.'[21]

She said:

> It is my belief that the long dress has come to stay … Here at last is the chance we have longed for – soft, clinging gowns to the floor, tight-fitting bodices – and for the first time since many of us grew up we can show off our small waists and straight, smooth backs.[22]

In advice that she would reinforce during the Second World War, she believed that every young woman should be taught how to cook with fresh ingredients, how to use up leftovers and 'how to keep the ice-chest free from scraps or waste'.[23] She was a champion of frugality, rather than wastefulness, and these lessons would be very much part of her ethos for the rest of her life.

Frances was a woman with unending drive and ambition, and she spoke admiringly of the woman who was capable, who could adapt to having to work for a living to supplement their incomes, given the hard times everyone was facing. She wrote in one article:

> What does it matter whether we drive delivery vans or select succulent vegetables in the 'A.M' so long as each is earning his or her daily bread? Modern chic has proved that we are definitely off the 'Simply don't know how – couldn't boil an egg' snob standard.

It was during this time, as a devoted wife and renowned hostess, that she developed her unique interior decor style. She and James moved into a charming mews house in Gloucester Place Mews and the way she decorated it would become her signature, and further expressed later in life, when living in Braemar and Invercauld castles. Marcia Brocklebank, a close friend of Frances, who first met her in the sixties at Invercauld, described her definitively as 'colourful', and this affection for the emotional power of colour was evident when she was establishing her first home.

She mentioned in a January 1931 article in the *Daily Mail* an 'amusing' bathroom in a Paris bachelor apartment she'd visited, where it was painted bright primrose yellow, with a shiny yellow tile floor, black enamel fittings and a black chenille bath mat and rug. This strong yellow theme would recall the way she chose to decorate her own bathrooms at Braemar.[24]

In an article in December 1930, she enthused about how colour 'mixes' had 'reached their height in modern home decoration'. There 'seems to be no arrays of shades which are not used together ... like flowers in a herbaceous border', and her own 'minute abode' was praised for its 'cosy atmosphere', which she achieved through bright paints and shaded lighting. In the living room, the walls were a soft moss green, the carpets deep smoke blue and the curtains a vivid cherry red. She featured yellow and pink-orange pleated lampshades, a bookshelf with colourful spines, bowls of bright flowers resting on tables and the cover of her divan was a patchwork of pieces she had collected on her travels – a blue and black Spanish shawl, red, gold and blue Mandarin coats and a Romanian peasant's skirt. She also confessed that 'Yellow and green cushions complete this ridiculous makeshift'.[25]

As well as her interiors, she spoke of using colour to plan out interesting meals for her guests, where she sought to achieve a particular harmony. She described one dinner she attended, where all the food that was served was black – from the caviar to the black cream mushroom soup, a blackcurrant fool and coal black coffee. 'An all-white meal would have been just as bad. And I myself have been to all-pink luncheons which are even more upsetting!'[26]

She recommended to her readers serving a soufflé delicately flavoured with passion fruit juice, 'so light it tastes like sweetened air', a cheese board after the main meal, and coffee made by the hostess herself, 'since only she can be sure of the delicious result'.[27] She also suggested a few simple American snacks which, in the early thirties, were considered quite a novelty:

> I have brought back many tea-table recipes from Canada and America. One was nothing more than a biscuit covered with the beaten, sugared white of an egg and toasted in a quick oven. Another was ordinary peanut butter placed between two slices of bread and toasted.[28]

Now she was married into a titled family, her life was even more entrenched in committee events and society weddings. Her mother-in-law, Lady Corisande Rodney, presented her at court to King George V and Queen Mary in May 1930, with Frances dressed in a pristine white gown decorated in ostrich feathers. In June 1932, she and James attended an engagement reception at Grosvenor Square for Captain Henry Rogers Broughton and Diana Fellowes,[29] and in May 1933, she was invited to a 'midnight party' at 22 Bruton Street, with a guest list of Bright Young Things including Randolph Churchill, Diana Mitford, Joan Guinness, Lady Pamela Smith and the noted interior decorator, Sibyl Colefax.[30]

Frances also took part in charity work, including supporting the National Birthday Trust Fund, which provided anaesthetics for women in maternity hospitals. She worked with Lucy Baldwin, maternity care activist and wife of the former British Prime Minister Sir Stanley Baldwin, to organise an aerial pageant at Hanworth Park, which was attended by Sir Philip Sassoon, the Marchioness of Cholmondeley, and Air Vice Marshal Sir Sefton Branker, among other notable guests.[31]

Her photograph frequently appeared in the pages of society magazines like *Tatler* and the *Bystander*, with captions that highlighted her on-point wardrobe. The 26 December 1928 *Tatler* featured a full-page portrait by the pioneering society photographer Yevonde, with Frances sporting a chic bob, pearls and a sequined sheath dress. She was featured in the *Sketch* in February 1933, wearing a white feather skull cap, which the caption said had created a stir at the Ritz and she was pictured wearing it again when with James at an exhibition of miniatures by Rudolf Sternard. The hat was a particular favourite of Frances', and she would continue to wear it forty years later.

In another portrait in the *Sphere*, she was wearing the same hat with a 'slimming and original suit' from Paul Caret. As the caption read (or warned):

> The achievement of absolute smartness demands intelligence – smartness is not super-imposed but evolves naturally from the very fiber of the wearer. No effort on the part of the dressmaker can make you smart if you have a dowdy mind.[32]

A few months later, she was gracing the front cover of the *Sketch*, modelling a veiled hat, tilted at an angle, with her shoulders circled by a white fox stole. As these photos indicate, Frances was a woman who knew how to dress for every occasion, choosing an outfit that not only hit all the right notes, but also added a new twist, a different flavour to what had been thought of before.

She was pictured in the *Bystander* wearing de rigueur beach pyjamas in the South of France in August 1930, and at a cocktail party at the Paul Caret salon in November 1932 she was topped with Elsa Schiaparelli's famous 'mad cap' hat. The surrealist Italian designer would become a good friend of Frances' during the thirties.

In 1934, Schiaparelli was encouraged by her Scottish lover, Henry Spence Horne, to expand her Paris business by opening a salon in London, and his brother, Sir Allan Horne, provided his Mayfair property at 36 Upper Grosvenor Street as a showroom and workroom. She lived on the top floor and imported some of her Parisian staff to work out of the building. She called it an 'enchanting life' in London, as she became a fixture at all the places Frances enjoyed: the Ritz, Quaglino's, the Embassy Club and the Café de Paris.

Schiaparelli created clothes that suited new freedoms, so it was natural that a woman like Frances would embrace the practical silhouettes and washable fabrics, alongside the creative flourishes that transformed couture into an art form. Schiaparelli's headwear particularly appealed to Frances, who enjoyed her snoods and mad caps, and who, like the designer, chose to wrap a turban around her head.

Rather than selecting the simple elegance of her rival Coco Chanel, Frances preferred Schiaparelli's more provocative creations. Both Frances and the Italian designer had a commonality in embracing bright colours for both their interiors and clothing, with Schiaparelli introducing brilliant violets, blazing oranges and, of course, her famous shocking pink, which she made her signature in 1937.

'Really good clothes never go out of fashion,' said Schiaparelli, believing that clothing was architectural and the body used as a frame. While she embellished fashion with fun, she also understood her greatest customers were 'the ultra-smart and conservative women, wives of diplomats and bankers, millionaires and artists, who liked severe suits and plain black dresses'.

Several of Schiaparelli's garments and hats are included in Frances' collection of clothing held at the National Museum of Scotland. There are soft black felt hats, one with a kick like a scorpion tail, with the label 'Schiaparelli London'. There's a black tailored dress with a ruched waist and large buttons down the front, and a body-hugging black skirt and a top with a slashed neckline. They were business efficient, for a working woman about town, yet worn with individual flair.

Frances may have lauded the benefits of being a devoted wife and taking pride in keeping her home, but she was also fiercely ambitious in her own career. As well as writing for the dailies, by 1932 she was commissioned to pen travel articles and highlight the latest society hotspots for the British edition of *Harper's Bazaar*.

The fashion magazine was founded in America in 1867 by a trio of brothers, known as Harper & Brothers. It grew from a sixteen-page weekly, showcasing Paris fashions, to being expanded in 1901 to a weightier monthly edition.[33] In 1912, it was purchased by the country's most powerful publishing magnate, William Randolph Hearst.

Throughout the twenties Conde Nast's *Vogue* was the market leader, the fashion bible that offered access to untouchable glamour and boasted Paris and

London editions. To try to gain an equal footing, Hearst introduced a rival British *Harper's Bazaar* in October 1929, proclaiming in advertising that it was the 'most magnificent Society periodical ever produced in this country'.

Despite being launched at the same time as the Wall Street Crash of 1929, it became an important tool during the recession for encouraging the rich to spend. In the words of its American editor, Carmel Snow, hired in 1934 to turn around its fortunes, its mission was to serve 'the well-dressed woman with the well-dressed mind'. It also reflected the ways the upper classes were forced to tighten their belts, while also being somewhat oblivious to the hardships facing the rest of the population.

Throughout the thirties, *Harper's Bazaar*, with its editions aligning with the American mothership, was the place to see the latest Paris couture, glimpse the guests at the most glamorous parties and to read essays and stories by the most esteemed writers – Evelyn Waugh, Virginia Woolf, Nancy Mitford, Somerset Maugham, J.B. Priestley and Dorothy Parker. The vibrant illustrated covers were modernist pieces of art, reflecting the Surrealist, Cubist and Futurist art movements, with designs by noted artists like Alexey Brodovitch, Erté and Salvador Dali.

Inside the magazine, there was fashion photography by Man Ray, Cartier-Bresson, Richard Avedon and Cecil Beaton, and glamorous portraits of London society ladies, who played a notable role in the magazine's success. As Penelope Rowlands writes in her biography of Carmel Snow, *Harper's Bazaar* was, like *Vogue*, staffed by 'the usual underpaid society girls, stunning receptionists, imperious white-gloved editors'.[34]

When the British edition first launched, with P. Joyce Reynolds at the helm, the offices were located in a flat in Stratton Street, Mayfair, with its small team writing and setting the layouts on the Art Deco furniture in its living room and bedrooms. The fashion editor, the rather grand Lady Cherry Poynter, set up her desk in the bathroom, but with the Ritz Hotel just around the corner, it became the unofficial gathering place for the team.[35]

It was the editor of the American *Harper's Bazaar* who oversaw the decisions on the cover design and fashion illustration for its British sister, with images from Paris packaged up and sent to New York, set on plates and then shipped back to London. Only during the Second World War, with the Atlantic blockade hindering consignments, did the London edition, with Frances as editor, decide on its own cover.[36]

P. Joyce Reynolds could only steer the inside features, which she tailored to reflect an upper-class British lifestyle. She aimed to create a magazine by society for society, reflecting the fresh-from-the-showings Paris fashions and the cultural trends in London which, in turn, also appealed to the middle classes for the aspirational insights it offered. To provide knowledge of the latest restaurants and tips for weekends away, she hired Frances, writing under the name the Hon. Mrs James Rodney.

One of Frances' first pieces, in June 1933, advised on the best stately countryside retreats that offered an escape from London. Her words summed up the dreaminess of that period between the wars, when people had more leisure time than ever before, took motor cars for long weekends away and where the sharp edges of modernism were softened by a desire for comfort and history:

> We all 'know a place' nowadays – a place half an hour, or three-quarters, or an hour, from London, where it is pleasant to loiter on warm evenings, the car pleasantly parked out of sight, and only a vista of river and meadow, flickering trees and populated swimming pool, before us as we dine, dally and dance.

She described the country club at Poulson as serving food of 'Ritz standard' and Heatherden, near Slough, reminding her of 'an American millionaire's luxurious modern home on Long Island'.[37]

She reported on life as part of the smart set, with weekends in September spent sailing on the Isle of Wight, where the yacht clubs in Cowes bustled with multimillionaire yachtsmen and sailors, and where she went for cocktails at the exclusive Royal Yacht Squadron and dinners on board famous yachts, like newspaper magnate Lord Camrose's, owner of the *Amalgamated Press*. The official end of season was marked by Royal Week, as the king's cutter, *Britannia*, was moored in the bay alongside yachts and ships from all over the world. One of these was James' yacht, *Afrika*, and during their time sailing at Cowes, they crossed the water to the mediaeval manor Beaulieu House for a party held by its owner, Lord Montagu.

Modern women like Frances were more active than ever before, taking part in sailing events and embracing the possibilities of flying, and they needed the wardrobe to match. She instructed her readers that the essential outfit for sailing was well-cut navy serge trousers, a white, blue or scarlet pullover and a beret or cap.[38] In a *Harper's Bazaar* article in August 1933, she was photographed in Cowes by Clarence B. Mitchell in a navy reefer coat, gold buttons and yachting cap, as she gazed out to sea with a cigarette casually in hand.[39]

She also reported on the latest dining trends in the city. In the February 1932 edition, she promoted the latest 'snack bars', such as the Cutty Sark, inspired by the nautical decorations of the Duke of Westminster's famous yacht, and Punch, situated on Waverton Street, which had a 'long filling station' as a buffet. She also heralded The 500, a cosy club in a basement of Leicester Square, which would throb with Battle of Britain flying aces during the Second World War (in which 600 Squadron played a major role), and which she said, 'represents the very essence of our restless "let's help ourselves" age'.[40]

She described the new fashion for snack bars at home, with Mayfair hostesses setting up roast chestnut vendors, buffets of hors d'oeuvre, hot consommé, sandwiches of every variety and 'sticks of such goodies as kidneys, stuffed olives, bay leaf and bacon and sausages'. She was invited to one such party at the Grosvenor Square home of art collector Jack Courtauld, followed by a cinema party at Ealing Studios to watch a charity screening of footage from his brother, Stephen Courtauld's expedition to the North Pole:

> Cinema parties are definitely more amusing than those solemn, smart theatre parties which one once attended. Two and sixpenny seats are every bit as chic as those more expensive 'Royal' reserved affairs. In fact, the cheap dark seat at the back of the balcony has lost its exciting 'no-one-will-know-us-here' attraction. There is certainly democracy to-day. Chauffeurs, maids, mistresses and masters may be seen nightly jumbled at the 'movies'![41]

Frances captured the essence of youthful energy in her writing, where informality was a reaction to the belt-tightening of the thirties. They gave up entertaining in expensive restaurants, with fish suppers washed down with beer or coffee replacing the oysters and champagne from a few years before. The ethos followed Cecil Beaton's decree:

> One is still grand, but one is poor – the new poor. It is vulgar to be rich and extravagant, and it is bad taste to give a large party, even if you can afford it. Even if you haven't lost money, you must pretend you have.

For the summer 1932 season in London, she was alongside the fashionable Mayfair set watching the famous Jack Harris Band at the Café de Paris, going for dinners at Malmaison and Sovrani's and all-night parties where, she said:

> To be chic one must be original, and all that is formal and conventional has been banished sternly by ultra-chic young Mayfairers … To-night is

our night, for London's artificial lights look down upon such a round of festivity as no other capital can out-shine.[42]

These years were when Frances came into her own. She was in love and content in marriage, with a calendar filled with opening nights and social events as dictated by the season. In 1933, she had been promoted to a fashion editor at British *Vogue* and was present at the collections in both London and Paris. There were also invites for weekends away at country estates, whether that was flying in via James' aeroplane or travelling by motor car to the Home Counties. When she and James accepted Leander McCormick's offer to come and stay at his Hampshire retreat in December 1933, how could she have known it would be a decision that would have such devastating consequences.

Chapter Eight

As the winter sun rose slowly over the Hampshire countryside, it revealed the skeletal remains of the Heronry, framed by the criss-cross of bare branches. The grounds around the blackened ruins were now caked with a hard layer of ice after the gallons of water that had been sprayed onto the blazing house by the fire service were frozen by the plummeting temperatures in the early hours of Saturday morning.

Throughout the day, as Frances lay in a hospital bed, her body encased in a stiff plaster shell, she continued to ask for her husband. She couldn't understand why he hadn't come to see her; why he wasn't there to hold her hand as the doctors assessed the damage to her body. Despite the burns and cuts, he hadn't appeared seriously injured, but with the nurses refusing to answer her questions, it only made her more frantic with worry.

Back in London, the Saturday night crowds were gathering in the packed West End restaurants, and as news of the fire filtered through it was the topic of conversation at the fashionable spots. At Quaglino's, on Bury Street, the 'It' restaurant for the 'It' circle, Sir Hugh Seely and Ivor Guest were spotted by one society columnist chatting to Captain and Mrs Edward Compton, who had just arrived in London from a week's shooting at Sandringham House with the king. The columnist reported that as they exchanged hellos, the expressions on their faces became sombre. They could only have been discussing the fire that had killed both Ivor's cousin and the Duke de la Trémoille.[1]

Frances' physical condition was stable, but with the doctors worried that her anxiety was hindering her own recovery, it was decided that she should be told the truth. It was James' uncle, Freddie Guest, who quietly sat by her bed and broke the news.[2] A report in the *Daily Telegraph* stated that she took the shock 'extraordinarily well and the doctors were surprised at her fortitude'.[3] She was described in the *Daily Mail* as 'the beautiful London hostess', and the tragedy 'has broken this ideal partnership – for Captain and Mrs Rodney were known as a most devoted husband and wife'.[4]

The fire had been of huge interest to the press in Britain, Europe and America, and during the inquest in Whitchurch, a week later, witnesses arriving at the Church Hall were confronted by cameras and reporters. The County Coroner was tasked with bringing in a verdict for the two deaths.

Edward Grinsted, the butler, gave evidence, telling the inquest:

> I was called soon after 2 a.m. I sleep in a cottage about 200 yards from the house – by the chauffeur's wife. When I got over, the house was like an inferno. The firemen were hampered by the fact that the water sprayed on the house was freezing when it reached the ground, and made it very slippery for them. Shortly before four o'clock the roof fell with a terrific crash. A shower of flames and sparks shot up into the sky and made the scene as light as day.[5]

The doctor who had attended to James on his arrival at hospital, Dr Day, gave evidence on what the likely cause of death was. He noted there were burns on Rodney's left hand and forearm and slight burns on his face. There was an abrasion in the palm of the left hand, filled with dirt from having broken the window with his fist. Two hours after his arrival at hospital, Dr Day treated James for shock by administering nitrous oxide gas as an anaesthetic. It triggered a response in his body and he died only ten minutes later, at 6.20 a.m.[6] Despite his apparent lack of injuries, he had, it was reported, suffered from heart weakness due to war wounds, which had 'lowered his vitality' and the shock of events when the fire broke out, followed by his exposure to the bitter weather, proved too much for him.[7]

As the only two members of the party to escape injury, Mr and Mrs McCormick were both suffering from acute distress at the deaths of two of their guests, and while Frances recovered in hospital, they were resting in bed under medical attention at the house of a friend in Newbury. It would have been of scant comfort that a few pieces of furniture and the curtains had been saved from the inferno, although the valuable paintings had all been destroyed.

Mr McCormick made himself available to give evidence at the inquest. He stated that he thought the likely cause of the fire was down to a fault in the electric wiring. Reports in the *London Sunday Dispatch* also said that the empty room had been prepared for a visitor who did not arrive and a fire left burning in the room had spilled live coals on the carpet. The guests were hindered in their escape by their unfamiliarity with the corridors, steps and short flights of stairs that connected the various rooms.

Frances was too ill to attend her husband's funeral, which took place on 13 December at St Mary the Virgin Church, Old Alresford, Winchester, the resting place of the 1st Baron Rodney. She requested that it be a quiet event, with close family and friends and members of 600 Squadron, who James had developed a close bond with.

Rather than the planned whirl of social events for the season, Frances spent Christmas in Winchester Hospital, now widowed and immobile in bed from her plaster of Paris encasement. James' family flocked around her, with Corisande and Freddie Guest as frequent visitors. She underwent another operation on her back on 28 December, and spent the next few months bed-bound and unable to move. She had lost her dear husband and was now in a hospital bed in a restrictive brace, facing months of rehabilitation and uncertainty of whether she'd ever be able to walk again. Despite the negative prognosis, Frances wouldn't accept what they were telling her. As she later said, 'For months I lay in plaster casts and was told by the greatest specialists that I would never walk again. But I fooled them.'[8]

The press continued to ask for an update on her progress, and Corisande Guest told inquiring reporters at the end of January that 'Mrs Rodney will be brought to London as soon as she is well enough to be moved. This will probably be in a month's time. She can read now and receive visitors, and is very cheerful and courageous.'[9]

As the Hampshire grounds defrosted, and the spring flowers pushed through the once-solid ground, Frances was given the news she could be moved out of the hospital and back to London. The doctors had been encouraged by her progress in being able to sit up in bed for short periods of time, and they were hopeful that she would eventually be able to gain full movement.

Cameramen and reporters were waiting outside the Royal Hampshire Hospital on 19 March 1934, when Frances was carried out on a stretcher with nurses by her side and placed into an ambulance. An official at the hospital told the media, 'Mrs Rodney's improved condition is remarkable in view of her grave injuries. It is so satisfactory that we expect her to be restored to full strength within a few months.'[10]

She was driven into London by ambulance, where she was staying at a nursing suite in an apartment at Orchard Court, Portman Square.[11] The modernist brick block of flats, later the home of the Special Operations Executive during the Second World War, was just round the corner from Orchard Street, the original location of Paul Caret, the salon that had helped establish her place in society as a young, vivacious and fiercely independent American.

She was back to her beginnings, having to start over again, and now that she was away from the stark but cosseted hospital environment, she was hit by the realisation of all she had lost. All those months, when she had been so stoic and so brave, had finally caught up with her, and she couldn't hold all those emotions in any longer. As was reported in the newspapers on 23 April, 'She bore her sufferings courageously, but a few days ago Mrs Rodney's nerves broke under the strain of trying to forget her terrible ordeal'.[12]

She was expected to lie on her back for most of her day, trapped in a steel brace and wrapped in grief. She was fighting to fix her body and her mind, but as well as the emotional setback, she had also contracted blood poisoning, and was put under immediate medical supervision.[13]

Frances' remarkable story of recovery was featured in a *Sunday Chronicle* special in June 1934. 'What would you do if fate struck you down when in full health as a sequel to a disaster which robbed you of all that you loved most?' teased an advert for the exclusive interview. She was pictured propped up on pillows in bed and spoke of how she was able to walk a little but had to spend most of her time on her back in a steel support brace. She hoped to leave London soon for the country and had ambitious plans to go abroad.[14]

At the beginning of August 1934, Frances' younger sister Mary married Edward Wyllis Scripps, the chairman of the Scripps League of Newspapers, which published the *Seattle Star*. Their intimate wedding took place in the Oldham home in Seattle, with just family in attendance. While she had been making progress, Frances was still recovering from her injuries and was unable to travel the distance to attend the wedding, particularly as it involved a seven-day journey by sea to New York and then a transcontinental train ride. In her absence, she sent a cable expressing her joy at the news and her wishes of happiness to the newlyweds.[15]

Rather than an arduous journey back to the States, Frances chose to go on a twenty-three-day cruise of the Mediterranean and Adriatic on SS *Orford*, with stops including Palma, Majorca. After months of recovery, an unnamed friend revealed to the *Daily Mail* that she was 'now almost her old self again'. She boarded the ship at Southampton, swathed in tweeds, but she wasn't quite ready to be the social butterfly, and instead kept to her own quarters. She and her companion were seen very little by the rest of the passengers, except at mealtimes, and even then, they ate at a table in the corridor rather than in the dining room. The friend also told the newspaper that 'she is looking as lovely as in the days before her tragic experience and now has a wide blonde streak in her dark hair'.[16]

Slowly, as she became more accustomed to being out in public again, she began to make more appearances at society dinners and receptions, always dressed in black to reflect her mourning. The opening night of the winter season for the fashionable Sovrani's restaurant was on 12 October, and it was a typically glittering affair. Frances was in attendance, alongside Ivor Guest, Lord and Lady Carnarvon, Cecil Beaton and Lady Cunard, and in the company of her friend Lady Latham were the McCormicks. It was the first time Frances had come face to face with the couple after the fire, and the atmosphere between them was said to be uncomfortable.[17]

A gossip item in November 1934 noted:

[The] Leander McCormicks are back in London for Autumn and are seen occasionally at Sovrani's and other fashionable places. It has been stated that Mr McCormick is rebuilding on the site of the Heronry at Whitchurch, Hampshire, which was destroyed in the terrible fire. The McCormicks are indignant at the version of that disaster attributed to the Hon Mrs James Rodney. Mrs Rodney, in widow's weeds, is frequently seen at the Ritz and other places frequented by the McCormicks, but the gossip writers have reported that no signs of recognition pass.[18]

This article was likely referring to an insinuation in American newspapers that the McCormicks had abandoned their guests to escape the flames. Leander was adamant they did all they could, and that he was the last one out of the house, writing in a response, 'Thinking over the events of that fearful night a thousand times, my wife and I still cannot see how we could have saved our guests as the circumstances occurred'.[19]

Frances craved work, not just for money, but for her soul, and she'd heard there was a position available at *Harper's Bazaar*. Lady Poynter had resigned as *Harper's Bazaar*'s fashion editor and Daisy Fellowes, the controversial socialite and Singer sewing machine heiress, had been hired for both the British and French editions. French-born Daisy, one of the most fashion-forward and privileged women in Europe, had a take-no-prisoners attitude and a daring sense of style which could instantly set trends. She was a favourite muse of Elsa Schiaparelli, as she fearlessly embraced the Italian designer's most surreal creations, including the lamb chop hat and the shoe hat, a black velvet creation with a shocking-pink heel.

Daisy attended the September collections as part of her duties for the magazine, filing her report via cable:

> I have sat through the collections for the first time in my life. I have sat with the Press for two-hour stretches on specially-constructed, cast-iron backless stools in airless rooms, and all for your benefit!

Carmel Snow, *Harper's Bazaar*'s American editor, may have declared Daisy's tenure a 'sensation', but to take on the role full time would not have been an attractive proposition for temperamental Daisy, whose active social life meant she tended to phone in her articles rather than carefully writing them up herself. She'd receive American buyers in her Chinese silk pyjamas, while lying on a chaise longue on the terrace of her mansion on the outskirts of Paris.

Since she had been appointed as editor-in-chief in 1934, the Irish-born Snow had turned around the fortunes of the magazine by freshening up its look. She brought in art director Alexey Brodovitch in 1934, who streamlined the Art Deco sensibilities with white space and double-page spreads. Diana Vreeland would also be Snow's discovery, hired as fashion editor for the Paris edition to replace Daisy in 1936. 'She was a genius at picking other people of genius,' said Carmel Snow's niece, Kate White.[20]

In the meantime, the wheels were in motion for Frances to be appointed as fashion editor for the British edition. Whether or not Carmel Snow handpicked Frances, she may have had some involvement in the decision. Carmel and Frances had a few things in common. They were both immense fun and possessed a naughty sense of humour. They were similarly meticulous about their fashion choices, possessing boundless energy and discipline, and both could be described as 'a feminist before feminism'.[21] They had a lifelong desire to seek out the best, looking to discover and champion new designers or writers who could be provocative and inspiring.[22]

Frances was introduced in the October 1934 edition, with the headline, 'Nothing Succeeds Like Success'. It featured an image of her in action, coming out of the Mayfair restaurant Isobel's with a black cap on her head, like a nun's wimple, and a giant fox stole draped around her neck. She wrote in platitudes of London as 'the most exciting city in the world', where this year's fashion collections were even grander than they had been before. They required invitation cards, and the 'very exclusiveness of these openings gives them the coveted air of private receptions'.

It was a thrill to be experiencing the collections once more, and Frances, like Carmel Snow, possessed the quick judgement required for these events.

Carmel had a photographic eye for fashion, just as Frances had an impeccable memory – important qualities when reporting from the couture shows, which in those days were held in each designer's salon. The models, with their cardboard numbers, walked quickly, and a good editor needed to have an instinct for which design would create a sensation.[23]

In the December 1934 issue of the magazine, which featured Evelyn Waugh's short story *On Guard*, she wrote breathlessly of London in the lead-up to Christmas, with Bond Street sparkling with seasonal lights and the buzz of opening nights at restaurants. She spotted actress Merle Oberon in white ermine and a Peter Pan collar ('this year's insignia') and Lady Veronica Hornby 'sweeping down the stairs of the Café de Paris in a skin-tight satin'.[24]

In late December 1934, Frances' brother, Robert Oldham, came to visit her in London to check on her health and to keep her company over Christmas, just a year on from the fire. They spent their time going for bracing excursions in the countryside, and he reported back to the *Seattle Times* that she was 'recovering her health and is very much thrilled over her job'.[25]

The *Seattle Times* article, entitled 'Walk a Little Faster', hailed her remarkable recuperation from the tragedy:

> Frances Oldham Rodney has shown them how to 'come back'. A year ago the former Seattle girl was lying critically ill in a London hospital, after a country house fire which took the life of her husband, Captain James Rodney. There was a broken back and there was the mental anguish that follows such a tragedy. Today she is skipping about London, visiting cafes, gown shops with photographer or artist or both as fashion editor of the London magazine, Harper's Bazaar. Always interested in writing, Mrs James Rodney wasn't out of her invalid's chair before she began publishing a few articles in London magazines and no sooner was she able to walk than this intriguing job presented itself, a job that keeps her feet and her mind and her clever hands busy every minute, from early morning to late at night, except for weekends when the country calls her.[26]

Chapter Nine

In the January edition of *Harper's Bazaar*, Frances listed her New Year's resolutions for 1935. She was determined to move on from the tragedy, and these would serve as a manifesto for how she wanted to live her life going forward:

To choose my corsets, belts, bust bodices and undies *before* spring fittings begin.

To consume plenty of orange, grapefruit and lemon juices both for figure and complexion.

To eat regular and simply prepared meals.

To get at least seven hours of sleep out of twenty-four.

To decide upon my colour schemes for day and evening before launching forth to buy.

Never to wear flowers and feathers together.

To concentrate upon having all my accessories complete before venturing forth in a new get up.

To drink milk and eat vegetables both raw and steamed.

To see every collection of models before selecting.

To keep my ermine always at pristine whiteness.

To say and listen only to the kind things about my friends and acquaintances.

To see more cinema and plays.

To drink Vodka with caviar, champagne or hock with oysters, meats or chicken, claret or burgundy with game or red meats. Basosky, Kümmel or brandy as a liqueur.

To weed out and give away articles of clothing I don't want once every season.

To keep my troubles to myself.

To keep my own conscience clear.
To help others to prosper.
Not to interfere in other people's affairs or take sides in quarrels.
To encourage enterprise.
To give only constructive criticisms.[1]

As part of these new beginnings, she moved into a new apartment in Belgravia at 35 Lyall Mews. She still felt the overwhelming sadness at the loss of James and of being a widow in her early thirties. She'd also been informed by her doctors that if she were to marry again, she wouldn't be able to have children.

It was a further blow, and to honour her grief, she chose not to have anything around her that wasn't black and white. She decorated her apartment in monochrome, with black carpets and white walls, and her wardrobe was filled with black Molyneux dresses and Schiaparelli business suits and intriguing hats. It was a choice that not only reflected her inner life, but was elegance personified at a time when Art Deco was the dominating movement. It synchronised with the magazine's own proclamations for monochrome. 'The Modern Polar Effect of Dead Black over White', said one headline.[2]

This display of mourning continued into her office at *Harper's Bazaar*, where she served tea in her black Wedgwood tea set, and her visitors came close to tripping up over her black dog resting on the black rug.[3] 'Sometimes she wore white, but everything around her was black,' says her daughter Marybelle:

> My father's story was going to see her in her offices before they got together, and it was a nightmare because you couldn't see her black Pekingese against the carpet. The chicest colours at the time were black and white, and so she chose it because it was elegant, and it suited her job, but it was also because of Jim. She definitely loved him a lot.

While the American edition, under Carmel Snow, led on the overall content, Frances proudly stated that every fashion editorial was 'entirely thought out by me and represents my own particular taste'. After jotting down details of her selected fashions from the shows, she worked with the artist or photographer to plan the illustrations for each article and then guided the designer on how they should be arranged.

She was finding her place back in society by making the Ritz her second home from home, meeting friends there in the afternoon and observing the comings and goings of the finely dressed patrons who passed through the lobby. Notable faces flickered into sight, offering glimpses of red taffeta, sable capes and gleaming silver.[4] She brought dynamism into her writing with embellished descriptions of some of the famous women she spotted:

> Mrs 'Jerry' Portman in a divine green velvet corduroy coat and skirt in Bond street, enchanting Julie Thompson dancing in golden brown tulle at the crowded Blue Train, Princess Alexis Mdvani with black varnished nails to match interesting shadow under her eyes.[5]

May 1935 marked twenty-five years of George V on the throne, and for the first time in British history there were official Silver Jubilee celebrations and a bank holiday planned. Frances wrote in her editorial that month:

> Never since the war has London so bedecked herself, opened long-closed portals, sounded trumpets, brought out jewels, shined up silver, donned her finest uniforms, approved of, nay, encouraged subjects to make their most costly display at entertainments in honour of Their Majesties the King and Queen.

She recommended Molyneux as 'definitely right' for State occasion gowns, and Schiaparelli's saris for the woman who wants to be the centre of attention.[6]

Her writing and fashion editorial reflected not only what was happening in cosseted society, but also the mood of the country. After a glittering Christmas, the country was plunged into mourning when King George V unexpectedly died on 20 January 1936. As a woman who had only worn black in mourning for her husband, she had advice to give to Britain's citizens, who were expected to wear mourning alongside the royal family:

> You'll want to express your personal sympathy for the nation's great loss through the only medium you can – the choice of the clothes you choose from the season's collection. You'll obviously want to wear black – dead black to begin with – gradually changing to any of the greys or mauves. In choosing remember that black is the one colour that must be good – must be new – nothing is so drab, so gloomy as a bad black.[7]

She wasn't just the widow of a baron's son, she was an influential figure in London in her own right, and the invitations for exclusive events arrived on her doorstep throughout the summer of 1935. In June, she attended the first London exhibition of the artwork of the American cartoonist Percy Crosby at the Arlington Galleries, Old Bond Street.[8] The following month, she was a guest at a charity tennis ball at Grosvenor House, alongside the Duchess of Westminster and the Marchioness of Londonderry, which featured that year's stars of Wimbledon, including the men's British Champion, Fred Perry.

She attended a women's lunch organised by Rosemary Hope-Vere (known at that time by her married name, Mrs Quintin Gilby) and Jean Donaldson (Madame Paul Dubonnet), an American considered to be one of the best-dressed women in Europe. Frances was described as 'looking sunburnt and well after her quite miraculous recovery', following a weekend as the guest of American-born Olive, Lady Baillie at Leeds Castle, Kent, whose house parties were renowned in the 1930s.[9] There was another reason for visiting Leeds Castle, as a companion of hers, a Scotsman called Charles Gordon was assisting Lady Baillie at the castle and living on the grounds in a charming medieval manor, Battel Hall.

In October 1934, at a reception at the Egyptian Legation, it was noted that Frances was in attendance with Captain Charles Gordon.[10] It was the first mention in the papers of her connection to a man who would help to bring her back to life following the tragedy. Charles was, according to their daughter Marybelle, the understanding shoulder that Frances needed to lean on in those difficult months and years following the fire.

Like James, Charles was tall, dark-haired and sported a distinguished moustache, and was tanned from his years spent farming in Kenya in the twenties. He had a relaxed, almost too relaxed, attitude and a way of listening to a woman to make her feel important. He was pleasant and undemanding, and exactly what a woman missing love needed. Idina Sackville-West had felt it when she first met him too.

Charles Gordon, the second son of Alexander Gordon-Cuming-Skene of Pitlurg and Ada Wilson, was born in 1888 in Aberdeenshire. The family moved to Devon, but tragically his parents were killed when he was 6 years old, and when his brother Jack was 8. Rather than being placed in the care of close relations, they were sent to Harrow boarding school, and for holidays with maiden aunts. 'It was a simply terrible upbringing,' remembers his daughter Marybelle.

When they came of age, the boys inherited a home, Park Hill House in Dyce, but neither felt a connection to the house or had the urge for responsibilities, and so they sold it to fund their lifestyle. They celebrated their newfound freedoms by living the London high life. When the money eventually ran out, Jack contemplated going into the Church, but both entered the diplomatic service.

With the advent of the Great War, Charles served as a captain in the armed forces. When the conflict came to an end at the end of 1918, he settled in London, where he entangled himself in the hedonistic, bohemian circles that gathered at the flat of performer Olga Lyn. It was here he met Idina Sackville-West, the cousin of writer Vita Sackville-West. [11]

Idina was described by *White Mischief* writer James Fox as being the 'high priestess' of Kenya's notorious Happy Valley set. She married and divorced five times, elevating her reputation to that of a wicked man-eater. Happy Valley gained further notoriety following the murder of her third husband, Josslyn Hay, 22nd Earl of Erroll, in 1941.

Idina was known to light up a room when she walked in and could wear clothes like they were a second skin. Her friend Rosita Forbes described her as 'tireless and gay' – words that could be applied to Frances too. When Charles first met Idina, she was married to her first husband, a rich and handsome Scot, Euan Wallace. He was a charming philanderer, and she was madly in love with him, but was tormented by his frequent absences. Charles may have been almost penniless, but where Euan was inattentive, Charles was present and loyal, and she hoped to find happiness with him. [12]

After they married in April 1919, the newlyweds travelled to East Africa to establish a farm in the fertile valleys and mountains. The British Government was raffling land to war veterans and Charles was awarded a 3,000-acre farm in the Highlands region. But by the summer of 1921 the marriage was over as Charles was too relaxed for Idina, and she was too much for him. As he later told Frances, 'Idina was a nymphomaniac'. [13]

After their divorce, Charles Gordon married a friend of Idina's, Honoria Adeline Malcolm, a niece of Lord Ruthven. They moved back to Kenya, on land next to Karen Blixen's coffee farm and the Danish writer of *Out of Africa* would be godmother to their daughter, Lukyn. Honoria struggled with her mental health, falling into periods of depression, which were referred to at the time as 'nervous storms'.

They returned to England in autumn 1928, where they moved into a charming cottage with gables and sloping roofs called Swiss Cottage, in Boxhill, Surrey. A year later, it would be rented by John Logie Baird, and was where he carried out experiments to invent the television.

In April 1929, Honoria died in a tragic accident, leaving Charles in distress and grief. She was just 35, and the circumstances around her death made the national news. [14]

Charles returned to live in London, where it was said he was working in a shop in Regent Street and living in Gloucester Place Mews, where the

Rodneys lived. It is likely they had met previously through their similar connections in society, or from having lived near to one another. Charles, because of, or despite, the tragedies in his own life, was drawn to saving people. He also had first-hand experience of losing a spouse in a tragedy that had hit the headlines. Coupled with his tendency to want to support broken people, he was able to give Frances the care she needed, and his presence would mark a new chapter in her life.

Chapter Ten

In August 1935, Frances' portrait was featured on the society pages of the *Bystander*. She was wearing pearl earrings and a three-strand pearl necklace that gleamed against her black top, her hair in a smooth pageboy cut and a beauty mark to the left of her eye – an enhancement she liked to place in different positions. The regal image, taken by esteemed photographer Dorothy Wilding, heralded her as one of the important 'social faces', and the caption described her as possessing 'a dress-sense to match her good looks, and a turn for journalism'.[1]

That same month, she travelled to Paris to report on the most significant time of the year for fashion – the September collections. She checked into the Ritz Hotel, on Place Vendome, where Coco Chanel was now living permanently. Elsa Schiaparelli had recently opened her new boutique on Place Vendome in January 1935 and, with Frances in such close proximity, the two would share hurried greetings over the next few weeks.

It was a welcome return to the Paris shows after an absence of three years, and it was a significant moment in demonstrating how far she'd come. She was feeling especially receptive to the exhilarating atmosphere of fashion journalists with their 'enormous loose-leaf notebooks, pencils and glasses of iced Evian water', mixing with fashion buyers, artists and photographers as Paris hummed with chatter about the collections and 'nothing but the collections'. There were lunches at the Ritz and refreshing cocktails at 5 p.m. to cool down from the simmering urban heat and to discuss that day's shows, and then, after the evening collections, an outdoor supper at one of Paris's exclusive restaurants, interrupted by urgent copy being filed and telephone calls coming in.

'Not even a meal is finished in peace – there is the telephone, an anxious editor demands instantaneous news for his daily, a wire, a director wants to know prices from his already overwrought buyers,' she wrote.[2] She enjoyed the animated discussions about the Lanvin gowns, in stained-glass window colours, and the latest Schiaparelli designs, featuring violet evening gowns, white Grecian tunics with pearls with gold sandals and 'knobbly leather bags big enough almost for a week-end'.[3]

Frances thrived on the hectic activity, with the rewards of long, cool drinks with fellow editors and fashion buyers. Carmel Snow also lived for this time in Paris, when she would be running on boundless energy, moving from collection to collection and party to party. The two editors were snapped together by photographer Roger Schall at the 1937 collections, where they were discussing the hottest fashions as they gathered at a restaurant table. Frances was, of course, dressed in black, her head topped with a veiled hat.

These events fired up her passion for fashion journalism. She brought fun to her writings with her descriptions of the must-have pieces. In September 1936, she hailed 'gorgeous Gauguin colours, putting a flaming orange evening coat on top of an electric blue gown', and described a smoke-blue Siberian lamb coat by Paquin as being wrapped in a blue bear.[4]

She conveyed her own unique sense of style to her readers, and with her image appearing in society columns, she showed how to wear the clothes of the season – but with a twist. She described:

> [The] woman who arrived so late at the Castle, in a Moroccan white wool looking like Persian lamb (its native hood will withstand even a snowstorm), and the girl in a kilt on the Scottish moors; or at tea in the 'shires after the day's hunt, the mushroom-pink hand-crocheted gown with its square train – long, loose sleeves gathered in at the wrists by wide, hand-made Majorcan silver bracelets.[5]

Frances had always loved fancy-dress parties, which had become increasingly popular in the thirties. She had her own selection of clothing that she collected on her travels, with Spanish shawls, Romanian peasant dresses and lambswool sweaters and embroidered blouses from Majorca, and in the Christmas 1935 edition, she encouraged readers to get into the Christmas spirit with a masquerade ball. 'To masquerade is one of the privileges of the party season. What is merely rank folly the rest of the year is the right thing to do,' she said.[6]

In 1936, she took the opportunity to visit the United States for the first time in several years, as part of a work trip. She boarded SS *Bremen* in Southampton on 26 February, travelling with Maude Monell Vetlesen, a wealthy New Yorker who was renowned for her precious collection of Chinese jade statuettes. As her travel companion, Frances was invited to stay at Maude's apartment at 3 East 84th Street, just off Fifth Avenue and close to Central Park.

Frances' sister Mary and her new husband came out to meet her. This was the first chance for her to catch up with them since their marriage, two years before. Her arrival in the States even warranted a mention in the *Seattle Daily Times*:

> Of tremendous interest to Seattle society was the news today that the honourable Mrs James HB Rodney of London, arrived in New York City for a three-weeks visit there. Mrs Rodney, one of Seattle society's favourite and most talented daughters, last visited Seattle in 1928 with her husband, the late Captain James HB Rodney. For the past few years she has served as fashion editor of Harper's Magazine in London and is a very popular and brilliant figure in Mayfair. Her unusual apartment being the gathering place of social and cultural leaders in London.[7]

After two weeks in New York, visiting the *Harper's Bazaar* offices, she then travelled down to Palm Beach to stay with Freddie Guest and his wife, Amy Phipps, at Villa Artemis.[8] Named in honour of their daughter, Diana, with Artemis being the Roman equivalent of the Greek goddess Diana, the mansion was one of the most renowned in the Florida enclave, a symbol of Palm Beach splendour among so many other luxurious villas. It was built in 1916 after the Guests commissioned architect F. Burrall Hoffman to create a retreat from the ground up. With its large pool framed by white Grecian-inspired stucco columns and looking directly on the azure ocean, it was the height of resort chic between the wars. The villa and its languorous pool would be captured two decades later in a famous photograph by Slim Aarons, featuring Lucy Douglas 'CZ' Guest, second wife of Freddie's son, Winston Guest.

Frances and James had visited in 1930, but now that she was on her own, she was treated as a guest of honour by Freddie and Amy. There were lunches with Prince George of Russia and invitations to Casa de Suenos, a pink-tinted Mediterranean revival estate, and to the exclusive Everglades Club of which Amy Guest was a member. Here she enjoyed dinners with some of America's most influential businesspeople, who chose Palm Beach as their status symbol, and where they received invitations for luxurious events at Mar a Largo, the splendid estate owned by Marjorie Merriweather Post.

Not long after this visit, in April 1937, the Guest family suffered another tragedy when Freddie Guest died suddenly, at the age of 61, from pleurisy following a cancer diagnosis. Frances attended his memorial, and was listed as a relative alongside Corisande, Lady Rodney. The two had remained close, with Frances often staying with her mother-in-law at her home in Lymington, and later, with Corisande staying with Frances during the war.

Frances returned to Britain in June 1936 and she was pleased to be reunited with Charles Gordon, still acting as her companion in London. They were pictured at the International Polo Match at Hurlingham, where she earned praise from *Women's Wear Daily* for her chic grey flannel suit and hat. The article said: 'Her dotted blouse and dark red carnation seem to complement Captain Charles Gordon's bow tie and button-hole'.[9]

They also appeared in the pages of *Tatler*, as well-heeled guests for the opening of the Café-Chantant at the Ritz. Frances was dressed in a stunning silver gown with a matching turban, which was becoming her signature headwear.[10]

Frances was, at this time, considered one of the most popular society women in London. Her apartment was a gathering place for fashion figures like Schiaparelli, Madame Dubonnet and Irene Dana, a Swedish fashion designer, also known as Countess Heiden, who worked as 'directrice' of Schiaparelli's London salon in the late 1930s. Frances was a familiar figure at the Ritz, where her image was captured by a newspaper artist in January 1936, wearing a black Schiaparelli hat. The illustration appeared in the *Daily Mirror* with the caption:

Good-looking, dark-haired, pale-skinned Hon Mrs James Rodney – sketched while lunching at the Ritz. Her arched eyebrows are strikingly out of the ordinary. She was wearing an original hat in black felt. Rather like an undergraduate's cap. Mrs Rodney said she felt she ought to have a diploma. If diplomas are awarded for charm and originality I certainly agree.[11]

★ ★ ★

Following his succession to the throne in January 1936, there had been great excitement in the lead-up to the coronation of King Edward VIII, which was planned to take place in May 1937, with little understanding that he would give it all up so he could be with an American divorcée, Wallis Simpson. Despite whispers and discussions in the American press throughout the year on whether he would marry her, most of the British public were shocked by the announcement of his abdication in December 1936.

The news of Wallis Simpson may have been covered up by the British press, but fashion editorials quickly embraced the dramatic changes. Carmel Snow had, in fact, won the first scoop when she heard whispers of the love affair and a portrait of Wallis Simpson, taken by Man Ray in Paris, appeared in *Harper's Bazaar*'s pages in March 1936. It was further evidence that the magazine was continuing to outpace *Vogue* in popularity.

The planned coronation for 12 May still went ahead – but now it was for Edward's younger brother, Albert, who would be known as George VI. In the lead-up to his coronation, Frances, in tune with the mood in the country, declared white to be back in fashion, which 'should look rich and ceremonial, embroidered in diamond, pearls, and gold'.

The 1938 debutante season was noted as the year that Gogo Schiaparelli was introduced to London society with the help of Frances. The 'coming-out season' was of utmost importance among British society, where the country's upper-class girls were introduced at court and then invited to a dizzying array of balls and tea parties, with the aim of being paired off with eligible bachelors.

Frances wrote of the excitement of the season in her editorial in the June 1938 edition of *Harper's Bazaar*:

Because it's June, the month of debutante balls, picturesque weddings, green polo fields, electric canoes on willow-banked rivers, moonlight nights for romancing ... Everywhere Japanese lanterns are strung on lawns, and gardens are starred with wide billows of fragile lace, crisp white organdies.[12]

Before she established her couture house, Schiaparelli had spent five years in the States with her occultist husband, Wilhelm de Wendt de Kerlor, who abandoned her shortly after she gave birth to a daughter in 1920. Born Maria, she was nicknamed 'Gogo' because of her mother's frenetic energy.

As Gogo said:

A mad socializer, Mummy got all dressed up every night for her umpteen dinner parties, leaving me with a nanny. Dashing out of the door she would always call to me, 'Well, I must go now,' and I would look up and say, 'Go, go, going, go, go.' So I was called Gogo and it stuck. Ironically, it describes Mother's maternal pattern perfectly.[13]

Gogo was ill with polio as a child and, to recover, she spent several years in a plaster cast. By the time she was 18, having been schooled in Switzerland, she had blossomed into an accomplished young woman. She was also a tiny thing, just 5ft in height, and still walked with a limp, which may have been something Frances sympathised with, having fought against the odds following her back injury.

Gogo thrived as a debutante. She drank martinis, smoked cigarettes in long holders and wore daring dresses designed by her mother. 'Gogo was lovely,' says Marybelle:

> My mother chaperoned her during her debutante season, because she was great friends with Schiaparelli. She was a very difficult woman, Schiaparelli, but she was gutsy and beyond. But at the same time, they were close friends, and she and my mother would go on trips to Morocco together in the thirties.

The year 1938 was also when Kathleen Kennedy, sister of future president John F. Kennedy, was named debutante of the year. Their father, Joseph Kennedy, had moved the family to London when he was appointed US Ambassador, and their home at the American embassy at 14 Princes Gate was known for its vibrant parties.

A coming-out ball was organised by Rose Kennedy for their two daughters, Rosemary and Kathleen, and mingling in the ballroom, to the sound of Ambrose's band, was Prince Frederick of Prussia, Deborah Mitford and Frances with Gogo.[14]

Frances also accompanied Gogo to the Park Lane coming-out dance held by Lady Moncrieff for her daughter Elizabeth. The dance floor was a cloud of pink organza and tulle, but Gogo wore a daring blue organza gown decorated with a shocking-pink sequined heart. Frances also shone among the young girls in a white sheath dress and a white turban wrapped around her head, with white orchids that had been delivered by aeroplane from Holland that same day.[15] 'Frances Rodney has piloted Schiaparelli through a London debut. She has been a success and is said to be most attractive,' wrote a society columnist in August.[16]

Despite the parties and balls, there were signs of disquiet across Europe. Hitler annexed Austria in March, then threatened war if he wasn't ceded the Sudetenland region of Czechoslovakia. To appease him, Britain, France, Germany and Italy signed the Munich Agreement in September 1938. It had been hoped the Great War would be the last global conflict, but this was seeming more and more futile.

There was a sense of forced optimism in the air, of dancing in the face of the headlines, with fashions screaming in violets, reds and oranges to mask the growing fears. Frances suggested to her readers in July 1938 that they buy:

[A] superb grey Bentley for the run to the South of France, the West of Hungary, the North of Sweden, or the East of Italy, or you'll have a new aeroplane, any of the latest designs painted blue to match the skies, and fly off to Venice, to Brioni, to Le Touquet, to some fairy island on the Dalmatian Coast, to Tunis.[17]

'Remember that boom times are here,' she added in September 1938:

Have your vanity case twice the ordinary size, a diamond onyx monogram set in the centre, with an antelope case cut to show it. Try corn-bread sticks in place of toast for breakfast. Twist your pearls into a rope close up to your throat, more for bracelets diamond clasped.[18]

For business reasons, she continued to use the professional name Mrs James Rodney, but in her private life she was now Mrs Charles Gordon, having agreed to quietly marry Charles in late 1938 at a registry office in Surrey, near where she was staying in Kingston upon Thames. 'She was happy living independently,' says Marybelle:

But my father was kind, gentle and supportive. She needed someone to take care of her, not for his money, because he didn't really have any, but for comfort. If you had been ill as she was, without family around her, she needed to be cared for.

There was also something else that Frances had reason to be excited about – and fearful of. In the autumn, she discovered she was pregnant. After the fire and the long and painful recovery from a fractured spine, she had been told by her doctor that she shouldn't have children because it would aggravate her injuries.

Having thought that their warning was more that she couldn't, rather than she shouldn't fall pregnant, she was thrilled when it was confirmed. The doctor advised her that she and the baby might not survive through pregnancy and childbirth, and she would have to wear a back brace as her body would not be able to cope with the extra stress.

Because of the dire prognosis, she chose to keep it a secret from everybody except her closest confidantes. She had moved to Kingston upon Thames so she could rest away from the bustle of London and she would stay occasionally with Schiaparelli when she needed to be in London. 'I didn't tell anyone I was pregnant,' she later said. 'Fortunately it was winter so I simply wore huge fur coats and huge fur hats and started a vogue for black beauty spots worn between the eyebrows to distract attention.'

At Schiaparelli's November 1938 show in her Upper Grosvenor Street salon, Frances used an elaborate hat to take attention away from her growing belly. As one fashion observer wrote, 'We were all busy awarding full marks to Mrs James Rodney's very original helmet trimmed by cascades of coq feathers sticking out in all directions.'[19]

She gave birth via caesarean section to a girl in May 1939, naming her Marybelle in honour of her late mother, Mary Bell:

I cannot help feeling that having produced a healthy nine-pound baby in defiance of my doctor's orders, my elation must be a little more intense than the average more fortunate mother's, who can have many children normally and with comparative ease.[20]

The doctors may have been proved wrong in some ways, but the physical changes to her muscles and joints as a result of her pregnancy had been damaging to her back, and it would be another year before she was able to take off the brace. 'She was told she couldn't have children, but she didn't take advice,' says Marybelle. 'And my father was there in the background, a pair of arms when she was feeling awful.'

Chapter Eleven

As newspapers throughout 1939 reported on Germany's aggression and displays of power, there was a real sense that the storm clouds of war were gathering once more over Europe. The Munich Agreement had offered temporary relief that a conflict had been averted, but warnings were heightened when Hitler claimed all of Czechoslovakia and set his sights on invading Poland. In the face of this uncertainty, Britain stepped up its armament. As well as a call to join the armed forces, there was a recruitment drive for volunteers to sign up to the Air Raid Precautions (ARP) wardens' service, to protect civilians from the possibility of air attacks if war was to be declared on Germany.

In the fashion world, life continued as normal, and even into 1939, fears were masked by flamboyance and carnival. Schiaparelli had launched her Circus collection in early 1938; it was a riot of colour and whimsy, of prancing horse and acrobat motifs to be worn as if there were no cares in the world. Frances wrote:

> Although we were all so gay in 1938 and having such a good time, there may have underneath been the feeling of doom and the feeling of enjoying as much as we could before war descended. In 1939 the feeling in general was this question of uncertainty. From a business point of view I found that people did not want to place their money, or make contracts, or take houses or flats – nor make up their minds about anything.[1]

Offering a taste of what was on people's minds at the time, Schiaparelli, who as an Italian had watched in horror at the rise of Mussolini's National Fascist Party, penned an article for the March 1939 edition of *Harper's Bazaar* provocatively called 'Cannibals are Kind'. She wrote:

Cannibals are supposed to be fierce. Vegetarians are fiercer. Between them Adolf Hitler and Benito Mussolini eat next to no meat, drink practically no wine. On a diet of noodles and spaghetti they have just changed the map of central Europe. On a glass of cold water they were ready to summon up their vast armies.[2]

In that same edition, it was business as usual for reporting on the latest fashions. It had only been three months since she had given birth and so Frances watched the collections from afar, but one thing was obvious – they were more feminine and dramatic than ever. Chanel's 1939 collection was one of the most colourful in recent years, inspired by flamenco dancers, toreador pants and Gypsy scarves. As silhouettes tended to become more conservative in fraught times, Mainbocher was poised to bring back the corset, with his intricate satin design becoming the subject of one of the most famous pre-war photographs by Horst P. Horst.

★ ★ ★

When Hitler invaded Poland and failed to follow Britain's demands to withdraw, Westminster, on 3 September 1939, declared war on Germany, and there was a collective intake of breath, as if life had reverted to 1914. As Frances recalled, 'Right up until the declaration of war we still hoped and prayed that something could avert it.' But there was also acknowledgement across the country that Hitler's plans for European domination needed to be stopped. The announcement from Prime Minister Neville Chamberlain came over the radio at 11.15 a.m. that Sunday – Britain was now at war.

Frances was spending the weekend in the country with her sister-in-law Diana Guest, and that feeling on hearing the news, and knowing that the world was changing, would stay with her. A week after the declaration was announced, she reluctantly travelled to the grand Knole Estate with Diana to visit its owners, Charles and Anne Sackville-West. Lady Sackville was an American dancer of the New York Follies, under the name Anne Meredith, who became mistress of Knole on her marriage to Charles, the 4th Baron Sackville. 'I did not want to leave my baby and nurse and go on a trip to Kent,' said Frances. 'From the time war was declared we were quite prepared at any minute to be rained with bombs.'[3]

The Sackvilles had already handed over Knole for use by the government, and when Frances and Diana arrived, the couple, like many across the country at that time, were busy rearranging their own living quarters and deciding what they could keep for themselves and what could be left behind.

The world was changing, and the old way of life in the grand houses of Britain would never be the same. The 1930s may have been one of country estate weekends, sailing on the Solent and holidays to the South of France, but that existence would prove to be unsustainable. Only eight minutes after Chamberlain's address, air-raid sirens in London sounded out, causing immediate anxiety. It proved to be a false alarm, yet there were a series of announcements that all entertainment venues would be closed immediately. Windows were taped up to protect from blasts, corrugated-iron bomb shelters were constructed on every street, anti-aircraft stations were established in parks and citizens of all ages were asked to do their part by signing up as air-raid wardens and learning first aid.

By the end of 1939, towns across Britain were awash in a sea of khaki and blue serge as men and women enlisted in the armed forces. With the immediate introduction of the National Service (Armed Forces) Act, men between the ages of 18 and 41 were asked to register for the army, navy or RAF. Whether they were Mayfair socialites, fresh out of school or working as a secretary or chambermaid, women from all walks of life rushed to sign up to the Auxiliary Territorial Service (ATS), Women's Royal Naval Service (Wrens) or Women's Auxiliary Air Force (WAAF); they took jobs in factories for vital munitions work, or went to work on farms as part of the Women's Land Army.

Conscription for women wasn't introduced until December 1941, but in these early days voluntary services would be vital for the war effort. Most popular with married and older women was the Women's Voluntary Service for Civil Defence (WVS). They set up mobile canteens and respite centres for bombing victims, organised the Government Knitting Scheme and, during the Blitz, helped to evacuate 1.5 million mothers and children from the cities to the countryside.

At the offices of *Harper's Bazaar* at 28–30 Grosvenor Gardens, initially, the policy was to carry on as normal as much as possible, even if black-out curtains blocked out the windows and the bomb shelter was being reinforced in the basement of the building. Frances said:

Girls in the office were also given the choice as to whether they would like to take first aid. Apart from that, literally, from the point of view of the magazine, we went on as if there were not at war.

The September issue had already gone to print by the time war was declared, and with its front cover hailing Paris openings and the editorial praising the 'revolution in corsets' and 'Magnificent evening materials, brocaded velvets as in a Velasquez portrait', it was if there was no threat of conflict at all.[4]

You wouldn't know from the cover that, in only a short time, many of the couture houses would grind to a halt, and Coco Chanel would close her fashion line for the next fifteen years. Mainbocher fled Paris for the United States, to relocate his business, and the day photographer Horst P. Horst took his famous image of the Mainbocher corset, he would abandon his apartment to board the last passenger ship from France to America.

While her editorials proclaimed business as usual, Frances was concerned at the situation. She had a baby to worry about, and she also had a sense that her role of fashion editor was almost too frivolous for the situation the world was now in.

Her fractured spine was causing increasing pain and mobility problems as she recovered from her recent pregnancy, but she thought deeply as to what her contribution to the war could be. She said:

> Like every human being in Britain I wanted to make a real contribution to the war effort. Everybody was searching himself to see where his particular qualifications would be most valuable. I began to wonder what I could do with my physical disabilities.[5]

It was incredibly frustrating to her that her injuries impacted on how she could serve the country, but she was warned that donating blood would likely weaken her, and she could end up in hospital from the strain if she volunteered as an air-raid warden. She contacted the heads of the women's auxiliary services, offering her qualifications alongside her medical history to see if there was a particular position that would suit her. In each case, she was turned down because she would not be able to pass the strict medical exams, and the long hours of being on her feet would become unbearable from the pain.

Not one to give up on finding her role in the war effort, she went to the Ministry of Information and the Board of Trade, where she was sure she could put her journalistic and public relations skills to work. Again, she was told that there was nothing suitable for her, as the hours were too long and they didn't think she would be able to stick at it. Instead, a new opportunity at the magazine came her way. In November 1940, Miss Joyce P. Reynolds left *Harper's Bazaar*, and in her place Frances was named editor, alongside Alan McPeake, art director at the magazine.

So, she began to look to at the pages from a completely different point of view: that of how to use them as a rallying cry for women. In this way, as wartime fashion editor, she could still serve the country. Rather than showing 'the newest and smartest' clothing, she selected what would be the most useful to women:

> I tried and, think succeeded, in showing that the flamboyant style was not going to be the most attractive – that the simpler and better cuts with more lasting qualities in fashions, were going to be the right ones.[6]

It was these editorial decisions that helped to shape women's fashion into more utilitarian, practical styles over the next five years. 'The shops, with regard to clothing, followed our lead to a tremendous extent, in ordering better quality,' she said:

> We obviously had to take a line, already in 1939, about evening clothes. I made it our policy that we would continue to show dinner dresses as I felt it was extremely important for all the women in the numerous services to change into something very simple but feminine when they were off-duty. But we stopped anything to do with the so-called ball gown or very dressy evening dresses.[7]

Above all, the message from the magazine was that it was patriotic to order clothing and to live as normal a life as possible. The first wartime edition – a two-month issue for October and November 1939 to help conserve paper supplies – was splashed with the headline 'Fashion as Usual'. The 1930s covers of *Harper's Bazaar* were typically Art Deco works of art, but for the first time, a black-and-white photo was used. It featured a model in a white raincoat, skirt and heels, holding an umbrella, while two sailors with cigarettes dangling from their mouths glance admiringly in her direction. It reflected a new sense of realism that would now mark the next five years.

An article entitled 'It's Up to You' described the 'new order of things', encouraging women to continue to pick their way over the sandbags to their favourite shops. It offered a reassuring message that all the big stores were equipped for air raids, with Debenham & Freebody featuring its own decontamination squad and fire patrol.

While *Harper's Bazaar* had a three-year supply of paper, it was still important to conserve all valuable commodities, so the magazine slimmed down with a reduced pagination. Despite the concerns that fashion magazines would become redundant and irrelevant in these troubling times, wartime circulation increased to 25 per cent above pre-war figures as women sought a form of escapism, and an encouraging cheer, to keep going in the face of hardship.

In the months after war was declared, life seemed to continue as normal. The air raids didn't materialise, there were no chemical attacks, and this period of relative calm would be referred to as the 'phoney war'.

Even food shortages didn't have much impact on daily life. 'Our whole food situation was so gradual that you really hardly noticed when you got less and less,' Frances wrote at the time:

> From a domestic point of view, there are practically no servants and of course it takes much longer to prepare food … The prevalent idea now is that everybody tries to be self-sufficient in every way and you cannot ask anyone to do anything for you – it's really contemporary to be extremely able to look after yourself and not expect service of any kind.[8]

Harper's Bazaar was always a magazine that catered to debutantes, featuring fashions and advice for each year's presentation, but during the war many opted for war work instead of their coming-out parties. 'One deb I knew who could have come out, had taken a course in cooking and went in as a cook in a hospital – she was only 17,' said Frances:

> Now she's 18 she's going into the WRENS. Coming out really means meeting the boys in the services and going to little private parties that are given for them in the country. The debs that I know have much more fun – they have a different kind of independence – the boys are in uniforms and it's a more exciting life. The fun of getting out of their uniform and putting on a pretty dinner dress is again something, because of the contrast.[9]

With the evacuation of Dunkirk in May 1940 and Italy declaring war on France on 10 June, the war moved into the next, more terrifying, phase. Suddenly, the possibility of a German invasion of Britain seemed all too real, particularly when German tanks rumbled into Paris on 14 June. The government had been forcibly relocated to Vichy, and in advance of the occupation of the city, 2 million of its citizens fled. In only a matter of days, a swastika was fluttering from the top of the Eiffel Tower.[10]

It was a sombre editorial for the first issue after Paris was occupied:

Dear reader, This issue of Harper's contains a number of pages from Paris, the last to reach us before the fall of the city. They are presented as originally intended without alteration or apology. They represent the work of our Paris staff, editors, artists, and photographers, at its best, because of the circumstances in which that work was done, mostly in a few hours of special leave from more serious duties.

Despite the sleepless nights and jangling nerves, the mood of the nation was one of defiance – refusing to accept the possibility of a German invasion of the British Isles. 'We all lived on our radios in those days – at that point you were practically waiting for every single news bulletin,' said Frances:

If anyone started about 'if the Germans should occupy England', they would be practically hit over the head. Every single man, woman and child could not conceive the idea that England would be taken.[11]

In July 1940, the Luftwaffe punctuated the sky with daylight air raids over London, and as the RAF were mobilised to counter-attack them, people watched the dogfights play out overhead from their gardens and balconies. 'I remember having tea about six one evening – suddenly a terrific crash and we looked out of the windows and there were the most terrible goings-on,' she recalled.[12]

With this new threat, and the fear of a possible invasion, Frances took the difficult decision to send 1-year-old Marybelle to New York to be cared for by an American guardian. Children had been evacuated from the city to the country as part of a non-compulsory scheme before the Blitz, where they would leave their parents to stay with volunteer families, but this now ramped up.

America, at this time, was considered a land of safety because of its neutrality in the war, and Frances believed it was the best option for her child. She penned an article for an American newspaper in 1941 in which she explained her decision; perhaps as a means of encouraging other families to take in evacuated children who, like Marybelle, held dual citizenship:

Trying to make up my mind as to what was the right thing to do with my baby was one of the most difficult decisions I have ever had to face.

The idea of parting with her for an indefinite period aroused every possessive instinct in me. I argued and fought with myself for weeks. What
was my real duty toward my child? Ought I not to keep her with me in
spite of the present danger and unknown future? In common with every
mother, I was convinced (quite erroneously, of course) that nobody else
could possibly give my baby the care, the love, the understanding, the
sympathy that I could give her and that as my child she was entitled to.
My heart had a bitter struggle with my common sense … All around me
I saw mothers making this heartbreaking sacrifice. Mothers of all creeds
and classes, rich and poor alike, were saying good-by to their children,
not knowing if they would ever see them again. And I knew that I must
send Marybelle.[13]

With the £50 fare provided by her mother-in-law, Corisande, Lady Rodney,
on 7 July 1940 a nurse carried Marybelle on board SS *Washington*, which was
making the journey across the Atlantic from Galway to New York. It was
the same ship on which the daughters of Lord Louis Mountbatten, Pamela
and Patricia, were travelling, having also been sent to find safety in New
York. Similarly, Gogo Schiaparelli fled Europe for New York, boarding
SS *Manhattan* from Genoa in June, alongside 3,300 evacuees.

It was the toughest decision for Frances to make, to send her daughter
across the ocean, without knowing how long they would be apart. She was
reassured that Diana Guest was in New York, and she was there to meet
Marybelle and her nurse on their arrival at the port, before handing the baby
to her new carer.[14] Marybelle would remain in the relative safety of America
for the next few years, staying with a woman who had volunteered to take in
evacuees, Mrs Franklin, in her home in Northampton, Long Island.

'I remember the nurse I had,' says Marybelle:

I remember a sandpit and the huge tree in the garden in Northampton,
and I had a dog apparently, but I don't remember it. I can remember
when I severed my toe on a climbing frame, and I can still see the room
with all the toys when I was in hospital.

Mrs Franklin appeared very old to me, she was a widow and had
her hair back in a bun. She was not like most American women, but
I liked her, and she was very kind to me. I had good memories from
my years there, and so I went back to see her when I was twenty. It
was very strange as everything looked so different, and not as big as I
had remembered.

Throughout the summer of 1940 German air raids ramped up from daytimes to evenings and into the night, and by September Hitler launched Operation London and Operation Sea Snake, to decimate London and other industrial cities. At the height of the Blitz, the Luftwaffe were carrying out bombing raids almost every evening, leaving the population shattered from nerves and lack of sleep. Frances recalled:

> They were very German in that they were always on the dot – they used to come about seven, sometimes earlier. At first people stayed in and did not make plans to go out to dinner much because bombs would fall and fires would start and everything was very difficult. After a time we found it meant for such terribly long evenings – from 7 until about 6 in the morning you did not sleep much.[15]

Lady Rodney was staying with Frances in St John's Wood, and they would sip glasses of brandy to calm their nerves during the raids, punctuated by terrifying noises – the warning sirens blasting out, the foreboding sound of the German engines approaching, the anti-aircraft fires and the thuds and vibrations from the blasts of bombs:

> The night would be simply horrible because you'd hear these terrible crumps, sometimes very near you, sometimes far enough away so that it sounded like an earthquake. When it was very close to you your whole house shook – you'd feel every morning when you woke up that there could not be a house left – you'd get up every day and find a great number of places gone and in a terrible shambles. You'd find lovely looking young girls, who had been up all night, helping to dig up bodies. They were quite amazing.[16]

Frances experienced the terror of being caught outside during an air raid as she walked her Pekingese back to her office one afternoon, after visiting Charles at the private gentlemen's club Guards Club on Pall Mall. Charles had warned her about the dangers of not being allowed into a bomb shelter with a dog, as they were known to get so terrified from the noise that they would lash out and bite people.

As she heard the foreboding wail of air-raid sirens, she looked up to see a mass of planes soaring above. She walked briskly in the direction of Grosvenor Gardens to find a suitable shelter. With the sirens wailing and the roar of engines in the distance, she sought safety in the closest place, Claridge's, where, like many of the luxury hotels in London, a bomb shelter had been established in the basement. The hotel was deserted, as all guests and staff had gone below on hearing the sirens, except for Leslie, Lady Doverdale, who was seated in the bar with a stiff drink to calm her nerves while the nurse was in the basement with her children.

As Frances recalled, her friend often 'had quite a few little drinks to keep her spirits free from being shattered'. During one bomb raid, in which the hotel was almost hit, Lady Doverdale slept so soundly that she didn't hear the alarms going off in the hotel. The management phoned every room to ensure all guests were evacuated and placed on buses to be taken to the Savoy. As Frances recounted, 'The next morning Leslie rang a bell and rang for coffee, and the waiter practically dropped dead – they had overlooked her, and she was the only one in Claridge's – she had slept right through it all'.[17]

London's luxury hotels were refuges for the wealthy during the war, not only because of their solid steel and concrete reinforcements. For those who had lost their homes, or who were without servants due to the call-up for the services, hotels like Claridge's, the Savoy and the Ritz helped them maintain the quality of life they were accustomed to, where food was in plentiful supply. The exiled King Peter of Yugoslavia moved into Claridge's in 1941, and Leslie told Frances of seeing the *Daily Express*'s society columnist, Viscount Castlerosse, in the bomb shelter in 'wine-coloured pyjamas' and 'a puce-coloured face'.[18]

The satirist Michael Barsley referred to it as 'Ritzkrieg', as opposed to the *Blitzkrieg*, where the wealthy fought the war through spending. As Matthew Sweet wrote in his book, *The West End Front*: 'For many, the indestructibility of the social life of London's grand hotels was evident of Britain's indomitable nature, proof that Hitler was not sufficiently powerful to disrupt the rituals of cocktail hour.'

Despite this, Frances observed that the war was ultimately revealing that 'the greatest social changes take place without internal revolution, with a very short time, and without any complaints'. No longer were the great houses in England only for private use. Historic piles like Knole were handed over to the government as barracks or to house ministry staff. The war was the great leveller, with the working classes and upper classes often experiencing the very same hardships – seeing their homes destroyed during air raids and coping with the rationing of essential items.[19] In her partially written wartime memoirs, Frances reflected on the new neighbourly spirit where people helped those who they may not have had much contact with before:

Everybody helps everybody else. The woman opposite me in the Mews, who used to be our housekeeper, Mrs. Hipper, whose husband was chauffeur to a friend of mine, is so cooperative that when she's going one way to buy fish she always asks if she can get us some, too, and when we go the other way with our string bags we always make enquiries of what we can get for her small grandchild.[20]

The fashion magazines may have become skinnier, but they delivered the message that war could be fought through beauty and fashion. One of the roles of *Harper's Bazaar* in wartime was to encourage women to keep making an effort with their appearance, as it was considered both a morale booster and a patriotic duty to look their best. In an article that promoted Elizabeth Arden's lipsticks, women were advised there was a shade for every emotion:

To use lipstick in moments of danger, of emotion, of desolation, or despair, is woman's gesture of courage. With a steady hand, applied to unsmiling lips that do not tremble, this sometimes frivolous gesture shows the resolution and defiance of a brave heart. For one tense moment a lipstick carries with it all the splendid significance of the 'Thin Red Line.'[21]

Frances penned an article that offered practical advice for women on what they could do in an emergency, so they were 'ready to appear fresh as a daisy, anywhere, any time'. She wrote a detailed list for her readers on what was required if they needed to flee their home at a minute's notice:

Be sure to have a box of a hundred cigarettes and matches handy. A flask or two containing brandy, cherry brandy or whisky is useful. Sal Volatile and Valerian should be included in the emergency case, so should a miniature spirit lamp and kettle, a tin of Sedebrol which can be melted into a delicious broth in hot water, and a favourite tin of biscuits. Bicarbonate of Soda is another useful packet for the 'Dash' case, so are cotton-wool, toilet paper, sanitary towels, face tissues, methylated spirits, precious personal photographs in leather frames and with talc instead of glass; all these should have been packed long before the necessity of evacuation. A Thermos and cup can be invaluable and a hot-water bottle a life-saver. A small leather writing-case should be included.[22]

Staying inside night after night during the Blitz became untenable, and so Londoners carried on as normal, dancing away their troubles as best they could in throbbing nightclubs and restaurants. The West End, which had once been illuminated by flashing neon, was now plunged in darkness, with taped-up windows and sandbagged monuments, and the Art Deco department stores on Oxford Street ripped open by bombs. 'People constantly ask me whether it really isn't a horrible thing to live in London now, but you can become adjusted to bombs and discomfort and make your life accordingly,' Frances told a *Seattle Times* reporter in February 1941.[23]

When she had time between meetings, she enjoyed the lunchtime concerts and one-act Shakespeare plays held at the National Gallery, where people could stop during their lunch break for sandwiches and coffee. The gallery also hosted a canteen for full-time war workers, which was organised and run by society and businesswomen. One of the cooks there, Mrs Kirk, had been known as 'Madame Poppy', one of the seamstresses who worked for Maison Schiaparelli in London.[24]

Going for dinner in restless Soho and Covent Garden on a moonless night in the blackout, it was difficult to see anything at all, and with very few taxis about, there was a risk of being caught in an air raid and having to seek shelter underground. 'I sometimes went into the tubes,' Frances said. 'It was incredible – you used to see people at four o'clock in the evening with their children, blankets, and food, going into the tubes.'[25]

If Frances was dining at a hotel like the Dorchester or the Savoy, she would stay the night there, paying for a room to change and bath in, and then sleep in the bomb shelter in the basement. Some hotels had organised partitioned sections with beds to give their guests a degree of privacy:

At the Savoy, they had a room downstairs on the embankment side – it was really a sort of night club – you could go over to one side and make merry and dance, then retire and sleep on the other side. Old dodoes who could not stay in their rooms would have to come down and lie with gay young things dancing to music.[26]

During the height of the Blitz in autumn 1940, Frances spent time with Frank O'Driscoll Hunter, a First World War flying ace from Savannah, Georgia, who had been sent by President Roosevelt to Britain to carry out observation work at the Office of the Military Attaché. Known as 'Monk', she described him as 'a very attractive Southerner with a tremendous personality, great moustache, pitch-black eyes, and a devastating way with the women'.

They arranged to meet at Covent Garden's Restaurant Boulestin, considered one of the finest in London, for dinner one night, arriving at nine o'clock, when bombing raids were underway. The basement-level restaurant was packed, and over a meal of oysters, grouse, crepe suzette, and Veuve Clicquot 28 champagne, their conversation flowed. They had much in common, not only both being flamboyant Americans but with a shared experience of having fractured their spine. In Monk's case, he had damaged his back when his plane came down during air combat in the First World War.

With so much to talk about, by the time they finished dinner it was late. As they emerged onto street level, it was pitch black outside and neither had brought a torch. Unable to see their hands in front of their faces, with no sign of any taxis and the sound of bombs in the distance, rather than find a bomb shelter they retreated to the 400 Club.

The basement nightclub was a popular spot for those in the RAF, and its packed dance floor was the place where many of the Battle of Britain flyers could be found burning off their stress. Some of the men there may have been from the 600 (City of London) squadron – and it must have been poignant for Frances to see the new generation of brave pilots who had trained under the legacy of James. It wasn't as busy as usual that night, and after ordering some wine, Frances and Monk decided to take to the dance floor to see, as she joked, 'whose broken back did the best dancing'. They felt the floor vibrate under their feet, heard a shudder in the walls, and they were hit by a cloud of dust and the smell of gas. A bomb had struck the building above them.

The club was evacuated by the fire service, and with the sounds of further explosions around them and no transport available, they decided to go back to Monk's apartment on Grosvenor Square, which he was sharing with a friend. As they sat in the living room, sipping brandies, the walls and floor shook from the reverberations caused by nearby anti-aircraft guns. Finally, once the sirens had given the all-clear, she made her way back to her home in St John's Wood, still in her evening gown, but offering a cheery greeting to Charles when he arrived home from the night shift working for the Royal Air Force Volunteer Reserve.[27]

During one particularly severe raid, her home came dangerously close to being destroyed when a time bomb went off in the garden. She and Charles were staying with friends in the country, and when they came home, they found that other buildings on their street had been blasted apart. It was this devastation that led them to leave London for the relative safety of Buckinghamshire, in a cottage on the Latimer Estate, owned by Lord Chesham. He'd given his house to the War Office and was staying in the rectory. 'We borrowed a bed and some chairs and black out material and moved in as soon as we could,' she said. [28]

Still working in the city, Frances would either sleep in her office, or travel to and from the city with Charles. Early in the morning they'd drive to London to go to their respective offices, taking detours when the roads were out of action and passing through villages where homes had been destroyed. They'd head back to the country in the early evening, seeing the orange flares from explosions in the distance, feeling the vibrations in the road beneath them. With their car lights dimmed due to the blackout, they struggled to see their way through the darkness, and the car crept very slowly along the road. By the time they arrived home, tired and exhausted, they took a late supper, and then went to bed, to wake early for the drive into London the next day. Even in the relative safety of the country, Frances and Charles would often be woken in the night, hearing the roar of planes sweeping overhead, and with bombs falling unnervingly close by.

The night of 29 December 1940 became known as the Second Great Fire of London. The Germans dropped around 100,000 incendiary bombs across the city, and with the water mains having been fractured, firefighters struggled to draw water to be able to put the fires out. St Paul's Cathedral was hit by twenty-eight bombs, and after one broke through the famous dome, Winston Churchill gave the edict that it must be saved.

Frances said:

You always went up to London with a feeling of looking to see if the things you loved were still there. We came up once and found the Guards Club had no light, no gas, no phone. Charles had to arrange for oil burners, and they cooked lunch out in the back. Everybody took to the bottle rather a lot in those days – sort of nerves – even I who didn't drink much, used to be practically never without a Pimm's No. 1.[29]

A teenage Frances with her father, Robert Oldham, in the beautiful wilderness of Washington state.

Frances' mother, Mary Bell Strickland, in the early 1990s.

23-year-old Frances was the epitome of the stylish young flapper in Europe in 1925.

A portrait by celebrated photographer Madame Yevonde, 1928.

The coq feather hat was a paticular favourite of Frances' in the 1930s.

An illustration of Captain the Honourable James Rodney, Frances' first husband.

Frances in the 1930s in a shimmering turban – a dramatic accessory that she would favour for the rest of her life.

Frances was a favourite subject of illustrators in London in the 1930s.

Frances' second husband, Captain Charles Gordon, in his Royal Air Force Volunteer Reserve uniform.

Posing for the cover of *The Sketch* in June 1933.

MR. CHARLES GORDON AND THE HON. MRS. JAMES RODNEY

A photograph of Charles Gordon and Frances at the Ritz from *The Tatler*, October 1937.

Frances' father Robert with her daughter Marybelle in New York in early 1941.

Frances modelling the polar bear coat for *Harper's Bazaar*, which she took to New York in 1941.

On her Second World War trade mission to New York, Frances took part in many radio broadcasts.

Adjusting the dress of a model during her trade mission to New York in 1941.

A portrait of Captain Alwyne Farquharson during the Second World War.

The Farquharsons (by the door) in the Auld Kirk, Braemar, after it was transformed into a theatre.

The Laird and Frances Farquharson in the Great Hall of Invercauld, watching a Highland dance performance with piper Norman Meldrum, *c.* 1966.

Piper Norman Meldrum playing for guests at one of Invercauld's lavish dinners, *c.* 1966.

The Queen Mother at Invercauld Galleries in the late 1950s, with Frances' daughter Marybelle to the right.

Frances and Alwyne outside Braemar Castle in the 1950s.

Frances by the entrance to Invercauld in the 1980s, wrapped in her Farquharson wool cape.

Frances at Invercauld in the 1980s – her beloved home for over forty years.

Chapter Twelve

As a fashion editor, Frances hadn't felt satisfied that her contribution to the war was as impactful as she would have liked. The government's departmental ministers may have turned down her offer of help, but she set out to create a role for herself, using her influence in the textile industry and those marketing and sales skills which she had honed over the years.

There were two immense pressures facing Britain during the war: the military fight and the economic push required to support the country. Britain liquidated over $1.5 billion of its overseas assets to fund the conflict in its first years, and its export trade had plummeted. The American dollar was vital for Britain to be able to buy up all the essentials – guns, bullets and aeroplanes – needed to hold out against the enemy.

While the major commodities before the war had been ships and steel, these had to be converted to war production. Frances believed that British textiles held the key to raising money by selling them overseas. Convinced that there was a case to be made through the power of fashion, she sourced France's pre-war export figures to discover that clothing and textiles had been the country's most lucrative export, ahead of wine and champagne. When she studied Britain's current wool sales under the Board of Trade, she found there was scope to increase them, even with the pressures on industry. She also knew that with the threat of German U-boats and *Kriegsmarine* prowling the Atlantic, American buyers who were unable to travel were crying out to source British textiles and designs.

American style was famously relaxed, yet they looked to the sportswear traditions of Britain, studying the pages of British *Vogue* and *Harper's Bazaar*, and seeking the expertise of fashion editors like Frances, to find the 'right' clothes for countryside pursuits. Before the war, fashion buyers frequently travelled to Scotland to discover quality tweeds from Borders mills, which were threaded with a sense of prestige. Frances had met many of these buyers in Paris and London, and they had bombarded her with questions about what British women wore:

> Americans were always extremely interested in detail, so they would ask the reason for a piece of leather on the shoulder, or the raglan cut of the sleeve, or the loose weave of a particular fabric. I was convinced that there was a general and a genuine interest from America in our sports clothes and fabrics.

With first-hand experience from her American friends and family and her time spent at Palm Beach, the epicentre of a casual Anglophile style, she knew they were willing to pay high prices for quality sportswear, as it was known that British outdoor clothing lasted longer and looked better as they aged. 'It sort of mellowed', she said.

Having gathered as much background detail as possible, she drafted a plan to present quality British merchandise to American department stores. She knew that if she convinced the Board of Trade that these commodities could be sold to the United States for much-needed dollars, the government would then have the power to insist upon the manufacturers supplying the quantities needed.

As part of the Board of Trade's Export Council, a meeting was held on 30 May 1940, where it was pressed that 'Unless we expand our export trade we are sure in the end to be defeated'.[1] They were aware that there was a need to increase exports of cotton and wool, despite the raw materials being required to make uniforms, but a full proposal hadn't been formulated.

The men who worked in the governmental ministries were typically dismissive of a woman in business. They were particularly unappreciative of fashion, which they considered frivolous, superficial and overtly feminine, with all the negative connotations that went with it. But Frances was quite insistent that they sit up and take notice. She said:

> Let it be quite clearly understood that the Board of Trade did not seek me out to do a job for them, but that I was so determined that this was a way I could serve both America and Britain, that I made it my business to go before the manufacturers and the Ministry at the Department of Overseas Trade, Harcourt Johnstone, and present my case.

Harcourt Johnstone, known as 'Crinks', was a personal friend of Frances and, she said, a man of 'tremendous vision', and over several long lunches they discussed her proposal. She asked the minister to arrange a meeting with the important woollen manufacturers at the offices of the Board of Trade to persuade them to focus on selling goods to America.

With Harcourt Johnstone as chair, twelve British manufacturers gathered around the large mahogany table in the wood-panelled boardroom, with their sceptical eyes trained on Frances. She was the only woman in the room, and she had made sure she was dressed for business, in her custom black suit and hat. Seated next to her, in faultless tailoring, was the reed-thin English designer, Edward Molyneux, who she had invited to give his first-hand experience of building a successful couture house through the power of American purchases.

Despite her preparation, it proved to be a hostile first introduction. The manufacturers made it clear they felt that the meeting was a waste of time, and they evidently saw no benefit in taking advice from a female fashion editor. 'They looked at me as if I might have come from Mars,' she said. And they were also condescending to Molyneux, despite his position as the most successful British designer of the last twenty years; the go-to couturier for every fashionable woman in the twenties and thirties.

Molyneux had been hired as an illustrator for Lady Duff Gordon, the couturier known as Lucile, in 1910, but following the outbreak of war in 1914, he served as a captain in the British Army. He was severely injured during the Battle of Arras, resulting in the loss of an eye, and was invalided out of the army. He returned to work for Lucile, but after they had a falling out, he set up his own fashion salon in Paris's rue Royale, and quickly developed prestige as an impeccable but unpredictable couturier to duchesses, princesses and queens.

He opened salons in Monte Carlo, Cannes and London in 1932, but kept his headquarters in Paris. When France fell to the Germans, he was forced to leave behind all he had built up over the last twenty years and make his escape on a coal barge. British *Vogue* described the moment where, among the confusion, his former batman and butler of twenty years emerged in a white jacket, 'carrying a tray with glasses and a shaker of Martinis'.[2] He was devastated that his life in Paris was over, and he was also, according to Frances, 'an extremely ill man at this time'.

Despite suffering from poor health, when he arrived back in England he was desperate to do what he could to support the war effort. 'Everything to do with women's clothes – couture – he felt was beside the point,' said Frances. He accepted the commission to design the uniform for the Women's Royal Naval Service, known as the Wrens, and the sharp navy tailoring embossed with gold buttons became the most coveted of the women's services.

Whenever Molyneux felt disheartened at the loss of his home and business in Paris, Frances would pick him up with words of encouragement. She convinced him that his knowledge of exporting to America was exactly what made him valuable to the war effort. Americans had lapped up his woollen sports clothes and tailored suits, which were made in Paris, but from British wool. It took all her influence for him to agree to come along to the meeting, but it was demoralising to see his work being dismissed by the manufacturers. She noted:

> In England, as Captain Molyneux would be the first to say himself, the type of man who has made a success of the manufacture of materials for which Britain is justly famous, is the type to look upon a man who makes women's clothes as not good enough to spit on.

Judging by their hostility, she was sure that the meeting had been a futile effort. They couldn't see past the fact that she was an American woman talking to them about feminine fashions. She made the journey back to her house in the country feeling deflated. Charles was waiting for her with a bottle of champagne and poured her a glass to help her relax after what had proved to be a tiring and disappointing day.

She rang up Harcourt Johnstone the next morning to tell him that perhaps it was best they give up on the scheme. 'I was extremely discouraged and felt that none of the people who could make it possible were willing to do so,' she said.

'You're not the sort of gal who drops it after the first dreary meeting – what are you going to do now?' Harcourt Johnstone replied.

Those words were enough to encourage her to try again, using a different approach – one inspired by the champagne she had been drinking the night before. Instead of Molyneux, she went armed with data. She handed out typewritten sheets that provided financial information on what the French fashion exports market was worth in comparison to the other major French exports such as food and drink.[3]

Seeing these figures in black and white – that the fashion industry generated more income than champagne – triggered their interest:

> They were apparently staggered by what the French had been able to make out of a women's fashion industry. It was only then that they

began to look upon me with new eyes as somebody who brought them a real exchange possibility and not just a fancy tale.[4]

To further boost her scheme, she planned to go to the United State herself, where she would call in personally to the owners of every department store in New York to encourage them to buy British, and tap into her media connections, such as Carmel Snow at the American *Harper's Bazaar*, and Edna Woolman Chase at *Vogue*, to help drive publicity.

It would be a huge undertaking, and there were many logistics to factor in, including the troubles of travelling to the States in wartime. The Board of Trade provided her with all the help in leaving the country, but she still had to convince the directors at Hearst Publishing to grant her time to go overseas. She explained how important it was, and the prestige to the magazine of their editor undertaking 'such a vast program of exchange'. She had anticipated that the job would take six weeks – and ultimately it took six months – but it would generate many thousands of dollars of publicity for *Harper's Bazaar* and a boost in advertising for the magazine from the textile manufacturers. 'Going to America was a serious thing for her, it was a huge coup, and it was in a different sphere as to what anyone was thinking,' says Marybelle.

In January 1941, Frances made the perilous decision to cross the Atlantic to embark on her trade mission. Only the bravest souls made the journey from Europe to America at that time, given the threats in the Atlantic – passenger ships risked hitting mines or being torpedoed by enemy submarines.[5]

But often it felt like it wasn't much safer in Britain. The night before she was due to leave, there was an explosion unnervingly close to the house. 'I got dressed because I had to get my clothes together as I was going to America,' she remembered:

My maid got up, in the dead of winter, and we started to pack. The air raid wardens told us it was all right and we could go to bed – we had hardly gone to bed when they said there was a time bomb in our garden and we had to go out. So we started packing again, as I said I had to go to America on a very important job regarding wool.[6]

After a treacherous journey by sea, she arrived in Manhattan and was greeted by her father and stepmother, who had made the long trip from Seattle to stay with her for a couple of weeks. The trip allowed her to be reunited with her daughter, who was now 2 years old, and who met her grandfather for the first time. 'I have come to America to see Marybelle,' she wrote in an article explaining her decision to be apart from her child:

> Oh yes, I know I've come over for a great many other reasons, too. It is true that as editor of British Harper's Bazaar I have business over here connected with fashions. British wools and British exports. But first and foremost I have come to America to see Marybelle. Of course we had to make each other's acquaintances all over again. And, although I was dying to grab her in my arms and hug her, I restrained myself with a fortitude that I felt was worthy of the Victoria Cross, and greeted her in a casual, friendly manner, knowing that a pleasant relationship was all I could hope for until she grew to know and trust me. My patience was rewarded, and Marybelle is my own little daughter again.

Squeezed into her luggage were a number of eccentrically thrifty pieces that she had designed herself for the trip, following the 'Make Do and Mend' ethos. One of the items was a polar bear coat (this was at a time when fur was acceptable to wear), and it would become infamous when she carried it with her to Invercauld, years later. It wasn't, however, the type of garment she could sell to American markets, rather she was more interested in pushing the practical British cottons and soft wools that suited their preference for casual styles. While the pervading trend at that time was for simple black and white suits, she planned to convince them of the merits of smart tweed suits and bright tartans. An article in the February 1941 edition of *Harper's Bazaar*, entitled '*Bon Voyage!*', hailed her trip to the States:

> Our Fashion Editor, the Hon Mrs James Rodney, has gone to America with the blessing of the Board of Overseas Trade, on a goodwill mission on behalf of British Fashion industries. Mrs Rodney has designed many of the clothes she will take with her … For the chill winds of a New York February – a snowy white polar bear coat. Almost any type of hat can be worn under the enormous hood, which is detachable.[7]

She found being in the United States, without the enforcement of a black-out, to be thrilling, 'especially in a city as gloriously dazzling and bright as New York', and after months of rationing, what she really craved, she told one interviewer, was an enormous steak. There wasn't much time for entertainments, though. Working with a tireless, single-minded focus, she set up meetings with the managers, sales and publicity people at every department store in New York, such as Bonwit Teller, Bergdorf Goodman and Saks Fifth Avenue, who she persuaded to stock British clothing, and to buy some of her own designs. She fully understood the way they operated – that they were more direct than the typical British reserve – and there was a certain hustle to doing business there. She was plain-speaking and forthright, which went down well in fast-paced New York, and on top of this, she smoothed the hustle with diplomacy and charm.

She also used her friendship with some of the most influential business-people, including Miles Trammel, President of the National Broadcasting Company, and William S. Paley, Founder and President of Columbia Network, whose future wife Barbara 'Babe' Paley was fashion editor at *Vogue*. She took part in dozens of press interviews and was bombarded with questions from curious Americans at trade luncheons and dinners, and in taxis and lifts as to whether British women were actively taking part in war duties, how they coped with rationing and whether they could still get their hair set in permanent waves.

In a letter dated 28 April 1941, Carmel Snow, American *Harper's Bazaar* Editor, wrote to her with encouragement:

> I have been so interested in the work you have been doing here, espe-cially all of the contacts you have made with the wholesale and retail stores, as well as with magazines and newspapers. The very fact that you yourself have come over here in these times, is one more impor-tant proof of the future trend of trade relationships between our two countries, and a further example of the indomitable spirit of the British people...you have proven by your own outlook, as well as through the pages of the British Harper's Bazaar, that quality in British goods is what Americans desire and need.

As well as speaking with journalists from *Good Housekeeping* and *Ladies' Home Journal*, she appeared in dozens of radio broadcasts, including one with Janet Flanner, former Paris correspondent for the *New Yorker*, model and actress Julia Hoyt, and the artist James Montgomery Flagg, where they discussed American fashions and the situation in Europe.

She was so persuasive that, for a while, every department store on Fifth Avenue had a 'buy British' window display. The pinnacle of her trip was a fashion show held by the Women's Fashion Expert Group of Great Britain in July. With an audience of 2,000 buyers, celebrities like Gertrude Lawrence, and members of the fashion press, gathered on the rooftop of the Astoria

Hotel, with the Empire State Building as a powerful backdrop. Together with Lady Dorothy Onslow, wife of the British Ambassador Edward Wood, 1st Earl of Halifax, she made an introductory address, explaining how the British designers were carrying on with typical stoicism, despite the air raids and threats of invasion.[8]

Afterwards, she received a telegram from Bruce Gould of the *Ladies' Home Journal* in New York: 'There will always be an England as long as there's a girl like Frances to put her across.'

The *New York Herald Tribune* lauded some of the simple British designs that were displayed in the windows of Bonwit Teller. 'They wave no banners about being gay, subdued, feminine, classical or patriotic. They are just clothes – lovely clothes. They are easy and elegant, and seem to belong to a world of pleasant living.'[9] There was also a campaign to encourage American women to wear white silk armbands emblazoned with the Union Jack and the slogan 'Britain delivers the goods'.

As part of her promotional tour for both *Harper's Bazaar* and the Board of Trade, she met with Joan Younger, a reporter from the *Seattle Times*, who hailed her as the 'beautiful and talented' editor who had made a 'brilliant "comeback"' from the fire that killed her husband. She was described as 'tall and slim, with her hair in a short straight bob' and wearing 'a coat she designed herself and made of mink tails' and 'a pencil-slim, gray jersey dress'. Joan reassured her readers that Frances was showing 'no signs of strain from the seven months of London bombardment she has experienced'.[10]

Frances used her interview with Joan as a means of delivering a message of resilience to her American readership, and she spoke of how she was convinced Britain would win the war:

Hitler's deadliest weapon is propaganda, and the English are having none of it. We Londoners go right on dressing for dinner and most of us have a pact that we won't talk about the war at home. Our aim is to live as normally as possible.[11]

'Fashion work for England is my own war work,' she added:

Because of the fact I broke my back some years ago, I can't drive an ambulance, so I'm trying to be a sort of one-woman expedition to find out what the Americans want in the way of British producers and inform the British Trade Council when I return.[12]

Once she'd carried out her rounds of publicity in New York, Frances further lifted British textiles by helping to organise a South American collaboration for *Harper's Bazaar*, for which Molyneux travelled among a convoy of designers. The magazine published a Latin-American edition in Spanish, Portuguese and English, which highlighted several of Britain's textile firms. 'That is the kind of work Mrs Rodney is doing and that is why the beautiful and plucky former Seattle woman is international news,' wrote the *Seattle Times*.[13]

After arriving home, she reflected on the ambition and success of her trip:

> I had no idea when I first decided to come to the United States what an enormous job I was taking on. I have not only had to keep appointments all over new York every hour of every working day, but my luncheon and dinner hours have been devoted to business meals with different store executives and out-of-town buyers. ...I have exerted every ounce of my vitality towards ingratiating British goods with American merchants and I know that my work has been recognised and appreciated – several British merchants have told me – 'You have done the biggest goodwill job for us that has yet been done.'

Despite receiving many job offers in New York, she declined them all, and after six months in the States, she decided it was time to return to her home. She made the journey back to London in August 1941, travelling by Pan Am clipper to Lisbon, then on to England. The clipper was an exclusive flying boat, which took off and landed by sea, and shuttled wealthy passengers between New York, Lisbon and London. It was limited to thirty-four passengers per flight and they were flown in relative comfort, with a lounge and dining room which, before the war, featured top chefs serving six-course meals. Tickets were expensive and hard to come by during wartime, and tended to be reserved for top government officials, movie stars, aristocrats and important businesspeople, such as Frances.

Now that she was back in Britain, she was determined to continue her mission to encourage Britain's textile industry. She planned trips to visit textile manufacturers across the country to explain to them all that she had achieved in the States. She took the train to Manchester in early October 1941 to meet the manager of the Cotton Board, so that, in her words, she could:

> ... assure the Lancashire cotton people that their material is welcomed in the highest fashion circles of America. It is unlike their own. They

pay more for it, but they love to think it has been imported, which, they say, makes their dress distinctive and unusual.

As part of this trip, she visited Manchester's theatres and hotels to observe what the average woman was wearing as part of her research for *Harper's Bazaar*. She still had a job to do at the magazine and now that she was home, she was conscious of reflecting practical, real fashions for wartime women in its pages.[14]

Chapter Thirteen

When Frances sailed into the office after months away, her focus as editor was to completely revise the concept of *Harper's Bazaar* to be a wartime magazine that could serve as a useful tool to contribute to the war. She was determined that 'any members of the staff who still had the pre-war conception of the magazine as a purely luxury product must go'.

Under her direction, there was to be no waste – of time, energy or vital supplies, such as paper, pencils and camera film. 'Every single thing that it took to make up a well-produced magazine was going to have to be strictly curtailed,' she said. The photographers would no longer be able to choose from dozens of prints and instead would have to learn to use as little film as possible without the need for expensive retakes.[1]

She made a point of speaking with each member of staff to see if they were aligned with her vision for the magazine, and those who weren't willing to make practical changes, she let go. The staffers combined their magazine jobs with part-time roles as fire-watchers or members of the Home Guard, and a woman in the advertising department, Miss Joyner, kept her tin hat on while at her desk to ensure she was always prepared. These women lived and breathed the war, travelling to the office each morning despite the reduced transport links, and not knowing if they would make it home safely at the end of each day.

One of the staffers who found themselves out of a job at the magazine was a woman who declared that she didn't even know how to boil an egg. Frances had long considered this a rather pathetic admission, even writing about it in the early thirties, and had little tolerance for women who were unable to do such a simple task for themselves. Combined with her unwillingness to even open the shutters in the office, as she believed that was the office cleaner's job, her future at the magazine was not looking promising. 'That in itself made me realise that she was not going to be an effective member of the organisation,' said Frances, who could be tough when she needed to be:

> I told them all that there would be no more getting one person to do telephone calls – that if you had a telephone beside you and you had a number to ring, ring it yourself – don't expect anyone to do it for you.[2]

The conscription of women to the auxiliary services or industry meant the magazine faced a shortage of typists and receptionists who, before the war, had typed up the handwritten notes of the magazine's journalists. Now, they were expected to type their own copy, answer their own telephones and fill their arms with couture to transport them across town by bus, in lieu of the pre-war messenger boys. Frances expected them to 'have a camaraderie and willingness to step into any breach – whether to clean the floor if the charwoman was not there, empty the ashtrays and do the technicalities as well as their own jobs'.

The most important thing in her mind was that the magazine should be useful and serve a purpose as a guiding arm for the reader to navigate their way through the regulations and restrictions in place:

> We, in other words, were going to have to get down to earth – that we had lived a long time in the clouds and what we called a glamorous world, but now was the time that we would have to carry our weight.

The clothing featured would be selected on a practical basis – it was to represent quality and simplicity. The illustrations could still be attractive and aspirational, but there would be no languorous shots on the Riviera or models reclining in long satin gowns. They would be active, wearing the right clothes for the right job or for off duty. The models would be pictured riding on bicycles, going into offices with their briefcases or taking part in voluntary canteen work.

Under her direction, *Harper's Bazaar* was a guiding example to women across the country. It had such a positive reputation that *Time* magazine, in May 1941, lauded both *Harper's Bazaar* and British *Vogue* as a 'wartime publishing phenomena', where 'instead of withering as peacetime luxuries, both magazines have done well and made money'.[3]

As a friend of many of the ministers, Frances arranged individual meetings with each one to offer them British *Harper's Bazaar* at their disposal. From now on, the magazine would coordinate its messaging by showcasing utilitarian clothing and help to translate the strict wartime codes into attractive options for women. Every issue, she created a page called 'It's the Fashion', which provided a series of rules that the *Harper's* woman should live by if they were going to make themselves useful during the war.

In June 1942, she used the column as a call to arms to women to do everything they could to help the war effort. It suggested that the fashionable woman of 'today' was the one who 'asks herself every day if anything has been wasted in her home', and 'spends every spare moment knitting for the Forces'. She was 'proud of looking well-groomed in old clothes' and 'learns to do all small repair jobs about the house herself'. This was opposed to the woman who 'lives improvidently, extravagantly, sees no need to save; Thinks choosing a new hat more important than sowing a row of carrots; Expects her friends to share their rations with her when she is visiting'.[4]

The *Harper's Bazaar* woman was encouraged to do everything she could to help the war and, of course, there was an outfit for every moment of self-sacrifice. A black wool dress for broadcasting an appeal to the Red Cross, a soft wool topcoat for going to work at one of the ministries and a versatile country suit in plaid checks. The magazine became a part of the circular economy, as older issues could be recycled and pulped to be made into bullets. The editorials encouraged readers to ensure every piece of scrap paper, iron and tin was collected and recycled, and with paper shortages, it advised:

Please arrange to share your 'Harper's Bazaar' and all new books and papers with a group of friends – who may in turn share them with groups of their friends. This will make more use of the diminishing supply of paper.[5]

As she continued to support British textiles, Frances held discussions with Diana Vreeland and Carmel Snow to try to push more British products into the pages of the American *Harper's Bazaar*. In return the American editors asked for high-quality photography, alongside human-interest stories on what fashion life was like for British women – whether they were now hatless, like Americans, and whether they were wearing old clothes or keeping up to date with fashion.

In December 1941, Frances received the news her father had passed away in Seattle, just months after having been reunited with him in New York. For the last two years of his life, Robert Oldham had been financial director for the Democratic Party in Washington and represented his state for the January

1941 inauguration of President Roosevelt. As a long-established member of Seattle's bar, his death was considered a big loss, and in tributes, he was acknowledged for his 'kindly impulses and his devotion to his friends'.[6]

On 11 December 1941, the same day as hundreds gathered to say goodbye to her father at the Bonney-Watson Chapel, Seattle, the United States declared war on Germany, three days after announcing it was at war with Japan. It officially marked the beginning of the country's participation in the global conflict.[7] While it offered hope to the Allies that the might of America was on their side, it was also a terrifying indication that life was going to get tougher in Britain. It also meant that the United States was no longer a safe haven for Marybelle.

Chapter Fourteen

Britain's wartime rationing system had been expanded to include clothing in June 1941, and with the United States now entering the war, this would be tightened further.

Frances had long been a proponent of frugality, and she came up with ever more inventive ways of recycling her clothing to make new pieces, such as transforming a Majorcan white lamb rug into a magnificent ankle-length coat.[1] She rummaged through her wardrobe from the 1930s, converting lamé and velvet evening gowns into blouses and lining her sweaters and coats with fur trimmings for extra insulation. With her fashion connections, she could ask her designer friends like Edward Molyneux or Norman Hartnell to help remake these flashy pieces into something more practical, and she suggested that those who had bought from couture houses do the same. Her favourite garment to dine in at home was a pair of wide, white woollen trousers and she buried her feet in fur-lined shoes to keep them warm, particularly when staying in cold country homes without modern central heating.

Initially, everyone was allocated sixty-six clothes rationing points a year, with a certain number of points assigned to every item, such as eleven points for a dress, five for a pair of shoes and two for a pair of stockings. This was cut to forty-eight in 1942, thirty-six in 1943 and twenty-four in 1945–46. To further support the rationing system, she ensured that *Harper's Bazaar* offered sound advice to readers on how best to look after their garments. These included tips on removing wine stains with salt, ink with warm milk, grease with French chalk, and lipstick marks with eucalyptus oil. It was also advised never to wear street clothes in the house, to always brush and shake them and never let them dry by the fire.

She praised the way people looked much more groomed than they had in the previous decade:

What has been done away with is all the silver fox coats, messy pearls, the kind of chi-chi muddles – the messy look has gone – no more dripping foxes. Women in England today look better than they have ever looked in their lives, because they wear the clothes that suit them – a good coat or suit of good wool fabric, tweed, or west of England worsted, man tailored.[2]

Because soap was rationed, it was courteous for a guest to bring their own when visiting friends. 'I went for a weekend to what used to be an enormous house, they live in one wing now but comfortable,' said Frances. 'I found I forgot my soap and was frantic. I rang the bell and asked the maid for soap but was terribly embarrassed.'

It was considered good manners to supply one's own rationed foods for a weekend in the country, and Frances would arrive armed with her own coffee machine, coffee grounds and sugar, even her own bacon and fat for a breakfast in the morning. 'All I used to ask for is a little hot milk,' she said.

As she reported back to the *Seattle Times* in December 1943, when parties were held in private homes, everyone invited was expected to contribute:

It may be a bit of rationed food, maybe a bit of galantine, as yet unrationed, it may be coffee, or a flask of whiskey, in fact it can be anything that can go to make up the food for the gathering. A few people still give weekend parties in the small wing of a house that has been taken over by the War office or the Red Cross. They are informal, rather cosy affairs and meant to give a little relaxation to hard-working factory girls in the services, who have 36 hours' leave.[3]

Rather than going to dinner parties, she said the phrase was to 'have people for dinner', serving up what could be found in the markets. Her cook, Anna Guadin, was from Latvia, and after escaping across the border and arriving in Britain, she had initially worked for Charles, before being poached by Frances. She came to rely on Anna and her magic in the kitchen, making delicious meals from rationed food, such as beetroot soups, and left-over casseroles. Frances particularly championed cups of vegetable bouillon as an effective alternative to coffee and tea, providing much-needed vitamins and warmth.

Finding a means to make a dessert proved tricky, but Anna would mix chocolate with egg powder for a soufflé and crepes with honey or dried fruit tarts. It became a source of pride as to the unusual combinations that would now be served at dinner. 'I thought the heights had been reached when I asked Crinks to lunch and I could not get white wine, so we had red wine with lobster,' Frances said:

> We all crave wine and we are convinced it has something to do with the lack of fruit. I never have craved it but I cannot wait to get it now. Everyone is the same. Now, at the Ritz, every date has a bottle of wine.

During one important meeting at *Harper's Bazaar*, Frances' secretary peeped round the door to say she had a call, even though Frances had instructed her that she didn't want to be disturbed.

'But it's Anna on the phone – she said it's very important,' she replied.

'I'm terribly sorry, I must talk on the phone, it's about food,' Frances apologised to those in the room. She explained she was arranging a dinner for an important American friend and she wanted to ensure they had enough to feed them.

Over the phone, Anna told Frances she had found some very young grouse, but at 25 shillings (nearly $6 or $7), it was far too expensive. The partridge was 18 shillings, but she managed to source smelts for one and six each.

'All right, you had better get six,' Frances told her.

She hung up and resumed the meeting, but a little while later the telephone rang again, with Anna calling Frances to update her on the dinner. Everyone in the room paused their conversation, waiting in anticipation as to how the menu planning was going. Frances then heard that her friend, Harry Standley, was home on leave, and she invited him to come for dinner too, instructing Anna to make the fish stretch to an extra person. As a thank you, Harry brought a magnum of champagne that he'd been given, and so the off-the-cuff dinner party 'was an uproarious success – in peace time I could not have had a better dinner'.

With the success of *Harper's Bazaar* in delivering the messages on rationing, Frances was asked by other government departments to help with their campaigns. They may have dismissed her at the start of the war, but they had come to realise how effective a woman's magazine could be. She said:

> I think there is no ministry in existence with whom the editorial staff does not have some dealings. The publication of a fashion magazine in wartime is quite something. In fact, I often wonder whether I am putting out a political gazette, since government departments and Board of Trade regulations are so many.

She supported a variety of campaigns, from boosting recruitment of the Women's Land Army and the ATA to encouraging women to ditch Veronica Lake-style hairdos in favour of cutting it shorter or keeping it tied back. There had been examples of farm and factory workers having been horrifically scalped or disfigured after their long hair had caught in machinery. With more women doing active jobs, bending and moving in ways their bodies weren't used to, the magazine commissioned trained nurses to offer advice and advocated the wearing of corsets to offer support. This was something Frances, with her back injury, had first-hand experience of.

As the war continued, people wondered whether there would ever be an end to it, and travel arrangements to the United States were becoming increasingly difficult. By mid-1942, Frances felt that, given the new uncertainties, it would be best for Marybelle to return to Britain. On 16 June 1942, Frances sailed from Gourock, near Glasgow, to New York, arriving ten days later. She spent several months in the city for business, where she stayed at an apartment at 111 East 73rd Street.

When she came to collect her daughter from her Long Island home, Marybelle didn't recognise her at first:

> I think I remember my mother visiting me dressed in black, but I hadn't seen her for so much of this time, so I didn't know who she was. Every time she had come to visit, people would tell me that she was my mother, but I didn't know what that meant.

They crossed back over the Atlantic in November in a small ship as part of a huge convoy, to provide safety in numbers. Ahead of Thanksgiving on 26 November, she wrote an article for the *Daily Mail* on reasons to be thankful, at a time 'when the whole future of liberty hangs in the balance':

> Now I look forward to celebrating Thanksgiving Day here in this country. I shall do so as eagerly and be as mindful of its significance as will all those hundreds and thousands of other Americans serving here and in North Africa.[4]

Back in London, Marybelle was introduced to her father, Charles, as if she was meeting him for the first time. To a small child, he seemed incredibly tall and with an intimidating moustache, and she burst into tears at the sight of him. 'The first time I saw him, I said, "I don't want him for a daddy, he has a moustache",' remembers Marybelle:

He was in the air force and I never really saw him as a child as I was farmed out to different families. I didn't know him and a daddy didn't come into the equation. I only got to know him later when I was married. He was very outgoing, everybody adored him, and was the life and soul of the party. He was good company, and good looking, but he wasn't good with small children, probably because his own upbringing was so appalling.

With London still subject to air raids, and with Frances and Charles working hard for the war effort, Marybelle was sent to stay with different families in Yorkshire and London. In a letter to the *Seattle Times*, Frances described 4-year-old Marybelle as:

> … blue-eyed and golden-haired and full of fun and games. She has grown to an enormous girl and is twice the usual 4 year old size. In fact, I have had to tell her that perhaps California or Arizona or Texas will be about the only places where we might find a husband tall enough for her. As you know she was in America for two years, and whenever French is spoken to her she always looks at me and says Mummy, let's speak American!

The war had helped to find new freedoms as they joined up to the auxiliary services and stepped into the gaps left behind by the absence of men as they fought overseas. Many were reluctant to give up these new freedoms, and Frances picked up on that sense of change in the air. She hoped that there would continue to be opportunities for women, but she acknowledged that many 'cannot wait to get back to the home and the bed and have babies'.[5] She also anticipated a shift in class hierarchies towards a more equal, fair society, as the war had exposed the deep inequalities of life in Britain. Possessing a modern outlook, she felt there was a need to build:

> … proper houses for everybody regardless of income, with adequate facilities, adequate water for baths. I think it will simply gradually become normal for everybody to have decent living accommodations. I think we are all in our hearts desperately ashamed that it should take a war to bring it.

She had ambitious plans for *Harper's Bazaar*. She envisioned that once the war was over, it could be a magazine that connected women around the world, where they could share their ideals, goals and cultures with each other, forging vital relationships in peacetime.[6] Change was in the air as a result of the war, and for Frances, despite these aspirations for her magazine, her life would shift in the most unexpected of ways.

Chapter Fifteen

The vibrant London of the interwar period had been ripped apart following months of heavy bombardment throughout the summer and into the endless autumn and winter of 1941. Once-majestic streets, with their bright lights and neon advertising that welcomed crowds to the department stores and entertainment venues, were now open wounds revealing their steel bones. As people stepped around the piles of rubble where buildings used to stand, it was a constant reminder of what had been lost.

Buried under the ruins of one destroyed home was Myrtle Farquharson, the 15th Chief of Clan Farquharson. She had inherited the title from her father, Alexander Haldane Farquharson, the 14th clan chief, who had served as lieutenant colonel in the Gordon Highlanders in the First World War. Myrtle was a charismatic socialite and a stylish lady-about-town. She was close friends with the Queen Mother in the 1920s and '30s, when she was Duchess of York, and had been a bridesmaid at the 1919 wedding of Dennis Trefusis and Violet Keppel, the socialite and author who was infamous for her long-standing illicit love affair with Vita Sackville-West.

Myrtle had her own glittering wedding, in 1925, to Robin d'Erlanger, the son of a French-British baron, at the Savoy Chapel in Westminster. She was dressed in shimmering silver satin, with her twin niece and nephew, 6-year-olds Alwyne and Mary Compton, beside her as pageboy and flower girl.

She was part of the Ritz set, moving in the same circles as Frances and even penning travel pieces for *Harper's Bazaar*, where she imparted her wisdom on the right clothes to wear for the right occasion. In an article in July 1935, she offered her tips on the wardrobe to pack when holidaying in Scotland. 'Heather tweeds,' she suggested:

Felt Hombergs have ousted berets. Reason – the Duchess of Kent wears them and they keep the rain off the back of the neck! Hand-sewn shoes of softest leather from Norway, Angora wool stockings. At night, severity relaxes. Exotic teagowns stimulate, fur shoulder capes keep us warm. Last good tip – the new long-sleeved nightgowns are a real comfort, north of the Tweed.[1]

Myrtle was widowed in 1933, only a few years after giving birth to her daughter, Zoe Caroline d'Erlanger. Her life changed further when her father died in 1936, and she inherited his title and vast Scottish estate, which included Invercauld and Braemar castles. She changed her name from Mrs Robert d'Erlanger back to Myrtle Farquharson of Invercauld to reflect her new position as chieftain and her pride in this Highland heritage.

When she arrived at Invercauld House on 3 September 1937, she was given a Highland welcome as a homecoming to the new clan chief. Sixty clansmen greeted her and her 7-year-old daughter, who was dressed in a Glengarry bonnet and kilt, with pipers playing an especially composed tune for the bagpipes, 'Mrs Farquharson of Invercauld's Welcome Home'.

Despite the warm reception at Invercauld, the castle, with its vast number of rooms, wasn't the place that she would choose as her home in Scotland. Myrtle's father had lived predominantly at the smaller Braemar Castle, part of the estate, and this was where she and her sister had spent their childhood, running up and down the spiral staircases and exploring the fairy-tale turrets. This became her base when she was in the Highlands for the summer season.

Myrtle ensured she remained very much at the heart of London society, with *Tatler* splashing a glamorous portrait of her as a 'lovely Scots-woman', swathed in furs, to mark her status.[2] She embraced the theatre, arts and society gatherings, and was described as filling every room with 'gaiety, joy and laughter'.

She was staying with a friend in London during the Blitz, when the house next door was struck by a bomb during an air raid in May 1941. Her friend and two servants were pulled alive from the rubble, but Myrtle's body wasn't recovered until several days later. She was just 44 when she died and her ashes were taken to Scotland, where they were scattered in the grounds of Braemar Castle, as her mother's had been. Her orphaned daughter, Zoe, like Marybelle, had been sent to safety in New York during the height of the Blitz, but returned to Britain in 1943, where she was cared for by Myrtle's younger sister, Sylvia Compton. Inheritance laws meant that the title of clan chief was passed to the next male in line, Sylvia's son, Captain Alwyne Compton of the Royal Scots Greys.

Alwyne was born on 1 May 1919, to Sylvia and Major Edward Compton. As well as his twin sister, Mary, he had a younger brother, Robert, known as

Robin, and they grew up in London and Yorkshire, with terms spent boarding at Eton College.

Major Compton had inherited Newby Hall, near Ripon, through his mother's line. In the 1760s, their ancestor, William Wendell, commissioned renowned neoclassical architect Robert Adam to alter an existing Christopher Wren-designed home to create a place of Georgian splendour, where Wendell could display his collection of Roman sculptures and Gobelin tapestries. On his inheritance of it in 1921, Alwyne's father transformed Newby into one of the finest stately homes in Yorkshire, further developing the gardens and the woodland walks, and it was where Alwyne spent a happy childhood.

After Eton, he attended Magdalen College, Oxford, and with his studies in Land Economy, he took after his father in his interest in managing tracts of rural space. But his time at university was interrupted by the outbreak of the Second World War and he enlisted as a cavalry officer in the Royal Scots Greys, Scotland's senior cavalry unit. The regiment was still using its signature grey horses up until 1941, when it upgraded to tanks to fight as part of the Eighth Army in the North African campaign.

Alwyne was stationed in the Middle East when he heard the news that his aunt had been killed, and he had now inherited the title of clan chief, as 16th Laird of Invercauld. While his father had land in Yorkshire and Mull, he hadn't ever considered at that point that he might, one day, be heir to 280,000 acres of moors and mountains. The title of clan chief wasn't merely a formality; it was loaded with the heavy responsibility of being Laird of Invercauld Estate, which included Braemar Castle, and overseeing the wildlife and the economy that came with the vast territory. Its value lay in its deer forests, grouse moors and the rivers teaming with salmon.[3]

For a typical 22-year-old, it must have been a sobering moment, knowing the responsibility he now held. But at that time in his life, he also had a duty to his comrades, as they fought in the Western Desert, seeing off General Rommel at the battle at El Alamein and pushing the Afrika Korps into Tunisia.

In September 1943, the regiment and their American Sherman tanks took part in the Salerno landings in the south of Italy, and as the Axis Powers retreated north, they returned to Britain to prepare for D-Day. Having acted as a troop commander during the Italian campaign, Alwyne was promoted to captain, and it was during the Battle for Caen, on 10 June 1944, that he was severely wounded.

Under a hail of shellfire, he went forward alone and on foot to find out why an infantry battalion was stuck in position. He discovered that five deadly German tiger tanks were holding up the advance. Caught by a shell, and with half of his foot blown off, Alwyne dragged himself back to the radio in his scout car to impart the vital information to his commanders. For this devotion to duty, he was awarded the Military Cross in 1945.[4]

Now out of action, Alwyne was evacuated to Britain to be treated for his injuries and was invalided out in 1944. Convalescing at Newby Hall, he thought about his future, and how he would manage the land once the war was over. He discussed his plans for Invercauld with his father and he realised he had much to do if he was going to help the estate thrive.

With his aunt Myrtle and her father having lived at nearby Braemar Castle, Invercauld had been neglected for many years. During the war it had been used as a storage space for other large houses in the region. Many of these country estates had been acquisitioned by the armed forces to be used as barracks or command headquarters and had been cleared out of much of their furnishings. Invercauld's rooms were now stacked high with old wardrobes and bureaus, paintings and heavy antique frames and a jumble of boxes filled with potential hidden treasures that he needed help identifying. And he knew just the right woman.

Chapter Sixteen

It was during the 1938 season, when she accompanied Gogo Schiaparelli to a series of lavish balls, that Frances first met Alwyne's younger brother, Robin Compton, who was one of the eligible bachelors of that year. She introduced him to Gogo, in the hopes that it could spark a romance. She then met Alwyne, who was one of several young men who were in her circle of acquaintances who mixed at parties in London. At these social gatherings, Alwyne was quite taken with the older Frances and initially a friendship developed between them. She even came to see him at Newby Hall on a couple of occasions. At some point in 1944, once he had received his demobilisation papers, he invited her to visit Invercauld to show her this impressive estate and to ask for her help in sorting through the jumble of boxes and furniture stacked high in each room.

Frances had made trips to Scotland before, having delivered fashion talks in Glasgow in the late 1930s, and she relished the idea of experiencing this castle in the Highlands, which needed some love and attention. This time she travelled by steam train from London, stopping at Waverley Station in Edinburgh and then crossing the rust-red Forth Rail Bridge into the rolling greenery of Perthshire and through the barren ruggedness of the Cairngorms. The countryside was scarred with reminders of conflict, with the silhouettes of searchlight stations and barrage balloons, the military bases still active, and the farmland ploughed to an inch of its life to feed Britain.

She disembarked at Ballater Station, which was the closest stop to Invercauld. After being greeted at the station by Alwyne, they drove alongside the moss and fern-floored forests of fir and birch that edged onto the River Dee until they came to the stone entrance gate to the house. It was here that she took in its immense history and realised the weight of expectation felt by the new clan chief.

Later, Alwyne would discover that overseas descendants of clan Farquharson liked to visit the area and experience the history. 'The whole idea of Invercauld is that it is Farquharson country,' he said in 1979:

> For the future I would always like to think of the house and the estate in that way, the home for Farquharsons all over the world. The whole property is so unique, so magnificent in its scenery, its history, and its wildlife, it's too beautiful to tamper with.[1]

★ ★ ★

Farquharson history is traced back to the fifteenth century, when Farquhar Shaw, fourth son of Alexander Shaw Mackintosh of Rothiemurchus, established himself on land to the south-east. His son, Donald, married Isobel Stewart, heiress of the original Invercauld tower, and their son, Findla Mor, officially founded Clan Farquharson. He chose to raise his family of nine sons and five daughters in the glacial valley overlooking the Dee, where he acted as a watchman for the king's land; a role that involved being part policeman and part bailiff.[2] He was the royal standard bearer at the Battle of Pinkie in 1547, where he was killed on the battlefield.

The clan had a reputation as 'the fighting Farquharsons' and being fierce supporters of the Jacobite cause – to rebel against the ruling protestant Hanoverians and to see in favour of the Catholic house of Stuart returned to the throne. The Jacobite rebellions were sparked by the death of the Stuart Queen Anne in 1714, with Parliament giving the crown to her German cousin, King George I. As clans came together to fight for the return of the exiled James Francis Edward Stuart, Invercauld was a meeting point for the 1715 Jacobite uprising. It was at the Invercauld Arms Hotel, located in the village of Braemar, that the Jacobite standard was raised before going to battle against the Hanoverians.

John, 9th Farquharson of Invercauld, was imprisoned at the notorious Marshalsea Jail in Southwark following his involvement in the 1715 rebellion, and so he chose not to fight at the 1746 Battle of Culloden, which was led by Charles Edward Stuart, also known as Bonnie Prince Charles. Instead, the clan was led into battle at Culloden by Colonel Francis Farquharson. John's Jacobite daughter, Anne Mackintosh of Mackintosh, nicknamed Colonel Anne for her leadership skills and her eagerness to fight, donned trousers as she mounted her horse and rallied an army of warriors. Anne's husband, Angus Mackintosh, Chief of Clan Mackintosh, was a member of the Black

Watch and thus a supporter of the Hanoverian government – and so they fought on opposing sides.

After the Jacobite defeat at Culloden, Anne saved Bonnie Prince Charlie from capture. She was arrested and held by government troops at Inverness but was released six weeks later into her husband's custody. Colonel Francis Farquharson was also captured and faced execution, but he was saved by the Reverend John McInnes, Minister of Crathie Kirk, near Invercauld. He travelled on horseback to London to meet with the Duke of Argyll and plead for the colonel's life. He was spared, but was exiled from Scotland along with other clan 'troublemakers', until he was given a reprieve twenty years later.

In the second half of the eighteenth century, James Farquharson, the 10th Laird of Invercauld, was keenly innovative in agriculture and set out to improve and enlarge his estates. His wife, Amelia, daughter of Lord George Murray, encouraged the local flax-spinning industry. By the time of his death in 1805, the laird was said to have planted some 19 million trees.

The original Invercauld was much smaller than the expansive castle of today. It was initially a tower, built on a late-medieval stronghold, and was rebuilt in the sixteenth century by Alexander Farquharson, the son of Findla Mor, but parts of the original barrel vaulting still survive. It was further developed by generations of Farquharsons in 1674, 1750, 1820 and 1847.

In the 1870s, the 13th Laird, Colonel James Ross Farquharson, known as 'Piccadilly Jim' for his raucous London social life with Edward, Prince of Wales, brought in his London architect, John Thomas Wimperis to remodel the house in local granite. With Queen Victoria and Prince Albert sparking a mania for the Scots Baronial style with their Balmoral Castle, purchased in 1852, he constructed a 70ft tower, battlements and crow-stepped gables to create a formidable mansion. The style was very similar to that of Ardverikie House on Loch Laggan, a paean to the Victorian romanticism as embodied with Sir Edwin Landseer's 1851 painting 'Monarch of the Glen'.

Queen Victoria had been a frequent guest at Invercauld and Braemar when spending time at the neighbouring Balmoral Castle. In fact, in 1848 the Farquharsons sold some of their land to Victoria and Albert when they were establishing the Balmoral Estate. Victoria must have felt quite at home when being entertained by Piccadilly Jim in his drawing room, which was decorated in the Balmoral style of tartan carpets and oak panelling with stag heads and guns mounted on the walls.

Despite the many reconfigurations over the years, Invercauld remained imprinted with a sense of its heavy history. In the exterior stonework above the front door is a carving of the Farquharson shield, with its lion rampant denoting loyalty to the Earls of Fife. It was put there in 1674 by Alexander Farquharson, who had made his own alterations to the house. Hidden in the face of the rock opposite Invercauld House was Invercauld's Charter Chest, where Colonel Francis Farquharson concealed his title deeds before joining up with Bonnie Prince Charlie to fight at Culloden in 1746.

★ ★ ★

Frances and Alwyne searched through the contents together, discovering rare pieces of china and artwork, such as a portrait of 'Colonel Anne' Farquharson by Allan Ramsay, Italian masterpieces and Native American artefacts, collected by his ancestors who had visited the New World in the eighteenth century. One of the valued finds was a trinket box given by Mary Queen of Scots to Findla Mor's second wife, Beatrix Gardyn of Banchory. There were also chests of uncatalogued ancient records, which needed to be kept in a dry place, safe from the damp and woodworm.

As they heaved furniture and separated the good quality pieces from items that could be scrapped or auctioned off, romance began to blossom. Alwyne was enraptured by her beauty, energy and magnetism, and the way she made people feel like they were the most important in the room. She was drawn to his tall, blond looks, his calm nature, humour and sense of duty. He was 26, she was 43, but the seventeen-year age difference didn't seem like anything at all. As Frances later said, 'After a week of sorting out he realised it was a lifetime's work and he had better marry me!'

The reality wasn't quite as simple as that. Frances was still married to Charles, and while she'd found contentment with him and his calm, caring nature, they had drifted apart as a result of the war. They had both been so busy with their own work that there had been stretches of time where they had hardly seen each other, with Frances going on trips to the States and Charles working long night shifts for the war effort. She had leaned on him as he helped her recover from her trauma, but she hadn't felt the same way about him as she had about James. With Alwyne, there was an instant spark, and as they explored Invercauld together, it manifested into true love. They both had an adventurous spirit, a desire to see the world, and he must have reminded her of the passion and excitement she felt during her first marriage.

She returned to London to carry on with her work on the magazine, but Alwyne wanted to do what he could to be with her. She asked Charles for a divorce, and a year and a half after their first visit to Invercauld, she and Alwyne were engaged, although they kept the news as secret as they could.

Marybelle says:

The war couldn't have been easy and my mother was smitten with my stepfather, and they were very happy. My father was very generous, and he would say my stepfather was a most wonderful man. He knew that he couldn't take her to these exotic places that she wanted to go to, as he had other children he needed to support. After their divorce, he would visit them in Invercauld and they remained really good friends.

Having worked tirelessly at the reins of *Harper's Bazaar* during the war and almost single-handedly encouraged demand for British textiles in the United States, there was a new challenge Frances wanted to take on. She felt she'd done what she could with the magazine, so around March 1945 she resigned as editor and Anne Scott-James, former *Vogue* beauty editor and women's editor of *Picture Post*, stepped into her place. Frances wasn't looking to retire, but instead she had her eyes focused on the next chapter of her life, which would take her far from the bustle of London, to a place of great beauty and vast open spaces.

Part Three

Mrs Frances Farquharson

Chapter Seventeen

On 3 February 1949, one year after her divorce from Charles Gordon came through, Frances married Alwyne Farquharson in a low-key ceremony in London. She was a 46-year-old mother and he was a 29-year-old aristocrat with the expectation that he should produce an heir, but despite these constraints, their desire to be together outweighed it all. They knew they wouldn't have children, but what they had was a deep love and respect for one another.

She packed up much of her belongings from her London flat, and with her daughter Marybelle and cook, Anna, travelled north by railway to her new home in the Highlands. For 9-year-old Marybelle, who had spent her early years in the bustling metropolises of New York and London, the dramatic Scottish wilderness was an enchanting wonderland.

'The first thing I saw was what I thought was a forest of Christmas trees,' Marybelle says, reflecting on her arrival in the Highlands:

Having lived in London, I'd never seen a forest of pines, and it was a magical thing. 'Look at all those Christmas trees!' I wasn't impressed that it was a castle, or anything like that, I just adored it. The first years in Invercauld are what made me the character that I am. I just loved it so much. It was a whole, magical world. And I was there until I got married, when I was in tears about leaving to go to London.

Those travelling to Invercauld would take the train to Aberdeen and then switch to the smaller train to Ballater. They then travelled by car along the winding, forest-edged Old Military Road that follows the River Dee until reaching the gates of the estate, near to the Old Bridge of Dee.

A long driveway led to the front of the castle, offering flashes between the trees of the formidable granite with its turrets and battlements standing on ceremony among the salute of tall Scots pines and with snow-peaked mountains as a dramatic backdrop. At night, car headlamps sometimes caught the stags at the side of the road, their eyes glowing red, before turning and retreating into the protection of the forest. The Dee Valley was covered with spruce and larch trees, and its moors and forest were teeming with red and roe deer, grouse, ptarmigan, with its snow-white belly, and capercaillie, a type of forest-dwelling wild turkey.

Braemar is cited as one of the coldest places in Scotland. In February 1895, the temperature plummeted to −27.5 degrees centigrade, and this was repeated almost 100 years later, in January 1982. Over the winter months, when feet of fresh snow blocked the roads, the village was frequently cut off from the outside world. The Devil's Elbow, a challenging double-hairpin bend in the Cairngorms which connects Braemar with Perth, could be closed for several months.

Almost as soon as Frances arrived in her new home she realised there was an immense amount of work to do, including introducing electricity to the estate. She had never lived in a place of such size, but she'd spent much time at the grand homes of her friends, such as Knole Castle and Newby Hall, and these had given her a masterclass in household management.

Spread out on multiple floors, connected with a labyrinth of staircases, Invercauld featured numerous reception rooms, a ballroom, fourteen bedrooms and eleven bathrooms, all in need of attention. The Great Hall, with its stained-glass windows imprinted with the Farquharson crest, was decorated with old swords and breast plates that were once used in battle, and portraits of Farquharson ancestors. When she first arrived at Invercauld, Frances joked that she would need a pair of roller skates to get round it all.[1]

She may have lived with back pain for over a decade, but she put in the hard work to make it homely. She cleared out the antique furniture that was piled up in the dining rooms, drawing room and kitchen, including those left there by other estates during the war. Some of the pieces would be taken to auction, others, where she saw the potential, could be cleaned up and placed in one of the rooms. 'The house was absolutely filled with furniture, and it was a monumental task. I don't know how she did it all,' said Marybelle.

Having acted as a de-facto mother to her younger brother and sister, Frances had learnt from a young age to roll up her sleeves and get to work, and it was this attitude that she pressed on those who worked with her during the war years. 'The women who are really attractive to men these days are the capable ones,' she said in 1942. 'You literally cannot tolerate people who are always grumbling and criticising – one does not have time.'

The post-war period would be markedly different from the days when a country estate was serviced by dozens of staff: a butler, cook and chauffeur, liveried footmen and a handful of maids. After losing their manpower to the war effort, the aristocratic owners of large houses were forced to adjust to making do with less.

As Frances had anticipated, all those who had sacrificed so much in the war wanted a new, more equal Britain. Rather than Winston Churchill and the Conservative Party winning the July 1945 general election as expected, Clement Attlee and his Labour Government swept to victory on the promise of social reform. To help Britain to recover its economy, a programme of austerity was put in place and an increase in estate taxes, from below 60 per cent to 80 per cent, was introduced. It left many upper-class families, including the Farquharsons, struggling under the weight of hefty tax bills.

Frances initially ran Invercauld with the assistance of her cook, Anna, an odd-job man, and the housekeeper, Minnie, who had been there for as long as anyone could remember, having worked for Alwyne's grandfather, Alexander Farquharson. The family lived in a small back part of the castle while undertaking the arduous task of clearing out every room.

The solid Victorian and Georgian furniture was shifted to reveal some of the old features that had been in place during the reign of Queen Victoria. There were the imposing stag heads that had been hung as trophies on the wall, the rifles on display, the heavy old shutters on the windows, the carved lions in the entrance staircase and the Gothic-style fireplaces in every living area.

The old Invercauld kitchen was a huge space that reached two floors in height, featured a large scullery and pantry and was equipped with three old-fashioned stoves and a vast bread oven that dated back to the turn of the century. There was a huge open fire, over which, she said, 'an entire beast can be roasted on its iron spit'. Not wishing to change it too much, as she wanted to retain its charm, Frances preserved all the shining copper pots and pans and the staghorn masks that hung on the walls below the high windows. She painted the walls a 'gay yellow' to complement the chestnut beams.

She enjoyed talking through the menu for the day with Anna. 'She was a character in her own right, and very special,' says Marybelle of Anna. 'She was a miracle worker in the kitchen and would make these wonderful creations. I remember when we went to Paris together, and she whipped up some mayonnaise in the hotel room.'

Soon after Frances' arrival in Invercauld in May 1949, a belated wedding party was held for the new Captain and Mrs Farquharson at the Invercauld

Arms Hotel, Braemar. Over 150 guests gathered for dinner, which was also a celebration to welcome in a new era with Alwyne as the young and enthusiastic laird. The candlelit dining room of the historic inn was decorated with long Farquharson tartan curtains, Farquharson shields and branches of fir, which was the emblem of the clan. The couple were presented with an inscribed silver tea service from their tenants and friends, and after dinner, the organist of Crathie Church, Samuel Page, played music which was followed by storytelling and songs.[2]

In July, Alwyne was officially confirmed as the new chief of the Farquharson clan, in the style of 'MacFionnlaidh', by the Lord Lyon King of Arms, Sir Thomas Innes, at the Lyon Court in Edinburgh. This was the official and ceremonial means of marking the succession to clan chieftainship, where he could now bear the arms of that family.

Just as her husband did, Frances felt the sense of duty towards the immense history of her new home. She wished to support her husband in helping to bring Invercauld back to life and worked tirelessly to make the estate as productive as possible for the tenants, given it was still in a state of suspended recovery from the war. She reflected on the significance of her new title as the wife of the laird and took very seriously the importance of preserving the history of the castles that she now had the task of restoring and maintaining.

Invercauld Estate had 200 properties over its 280,000 acres, which included workers' cottages, farms, tenant farms and houses in the village that were let out. She made sure to introduce herself to the local community, to meet the gamekeepers, ghillies and crofters and all those who made a living on the land.

The villagers weren't quite sure what to make of her at first, this dynamic vision who dressed in ways they hadn't seen before, but they referred to her as 'Madam', and her husband as 'The laird'. 'She was larger than life, and they never would have met anybody like her,' says Marybelle.

By the mid-fifties, she would proudly state that she had helped make the estate cottages so comfortable that she would gladly live in them herself. She may have left fast-paced London behind, but Frances didn't lose her flair for introducing bright colours into her interiors at Invercauld. The grey granite of Invercauld often looked dull over the winter, and so she visualised ways to lift it out of the gloom. She settled on lemon yellow paint for the outside window frames and back door.

She chose tartan carpets for all the staircases and was liberal in her application of pink paint. It wasn't the same shocking pink as invented by Schiaparelli; it was softer, more akin to cherry blossom or candyfloss, and she found it cheering and warm. One of her first refurbishments was to paint the outdoor game larder, built in a pagoda style, that same shade of soft pink. Her husband Alwyne would later comment on how marvellous this looked against the snow.

'She brought her own style to decorating, so that it wasn't like anything else that existed,' said Marybelle:

> We have a climate that tends to be rather grey, and she chose colours that were warm and light, and made you feel cosy when it was very cold.
>
> Invercauld was cold, but nowhere was very warm in those days. That luxury didn't exist. A fridge in London was a luxury, a shower was a luxury. People didn't think about it. You just put on layers of clothing. To heat the rooms they put on a fire that would last through the night. It wasn't exactly warm, but it took the chill off.

The drawing room was given a modern feel, in fresh, light tones with antique chintz curtains and Regency sofas covered in pink-and-white-striped fabric. Another early renovation project inside the house was for the Tartan Room, which was decorated with the Farquharson tartan – including the settees, curtains and tablecloths – with swords, pistols and sporrans on the walls. It was an update of the Victorian Balmoral look, unashamedly embracing the symbols of Scottish romanticism.

Marcia Brocklebank, a close friend of Frances after first meeting her in the early sixties, describes her as:

> … colourful, way out and flamboyant, not a bit conservative, and very, very positive, and productive. If there was one thing I would say, she was colourful. It was the way she decorated her houses, and someone like that, in post-war Britain, must have been a breath of fresh air.
>
> In her flat in London, there was a room that was very vibrant, and I think that might have been her bedroom. It was a strong colour. That was amazing because everything in Britain was either grey or pale green, because they were so deprived that they mixed all the paints that were leftover, together. So the colours were terrible, but I remember Francie's houses were very colourful.[3]

As she had made her London flat a vision of effervescence, with turquoise and pink, and white and yellow colour combinations, post-war Deeside would be her canvas. This way she could express her unique style and vision through the paint on the walls of Invercauld and Braemar. The bright hues she chose seemed to fit perfectly with the changes of the seasons. In autumn, the clear light highlighted the russet leaves, when red deer bounded over the moors. In winter, the nights seemed endless, but during the short daylight hours the landscape glimmered under a thick blanket of fine-as-icing-sugar snow. Over spring and into summer, white-barked birches were in full foliage, blue lupin flowers burst from the granite shingle and centuries-old Scotch firs pierced the dazzling sky.

For Marybelle, Invercauld was an enchanted place, with endless rooms to explore:

> I must have been about nine when we went there, and it was a whole new world. My mother and stepfather would go away a lot, and I'd be left there with a governess. And I'd go around the house and look, and explore, and I didn't find it scary. It was magical.

The main highlight of the calendar in royal Deeside was the annual Braemar Gathering, which in later years was held at the village's specially built pavilion at Princess Royal Park. A society was first formed in the region in 1816, when a group of local joiners and carpenters came together to create social evenings, and they held an annual procession for Highland clan chiefs known as the Wrights' Walk. In 1826 the group changed its name to the Braemar Highland Society, and in 1832 they began offering £5 prizes to the winners of a series of competitions and games.

The event developed further following Queen Victoria and Prince Albert's interest in the region when they first came to stay at Balmoral Castle in 1848. The following year, Queen Victoria, Prince Albert and their children were greeted by the Chief of Clan Farquharson, and it sparked a new custom, that the laird, who was patron of the games, would always welcome them to the Gathering.

In the following years, the castles of Invercauld, Balmoral and Mar took turns hosting the Gathering, until it was given its permanent site on the outskirts of Braemar. Every year, on the first Saturday in September, thousands gathered to watch the processions of pipers, Highland dancers and strongman events like tossing the caber and hammer-throwing. It was a chance for friends and family to meet and celebrate together for this one day in the year.

For many years, the event was opened by the March of the Clansmen, a lengthy procession by three clans – Clan Duff, Clan Farquharson and the

Balmoral Highlanders, but it had been discontinued by King George V, allegedly due to the size of the bar bill at the Fife Arms the night before.[4] The Gathering had ceased to take place for the last eight years as a result of the war, but it returned to the region in 1946 and, with feelings of celebration in the air, 31,900 people made their way to Deeside.

That year was his first Gathering, and Alwyne, who had only recently been demobilised from the army, continued the tradition by greeting King George VI, Queen Elizabeth and the Princesses Elizabeth and Margaret at the royal pavilion at Princess Royal Park. The war was over, and despite the constant rain throughout the day, the crowd were joyful at being able to come together in peacetime.

During her first summer in Invercauld in 1949, when Frances received word that the royal family were due to arrive at Ballater on board their private train, she ensured she upheld the traditions of the Farquharsons by greeting them on arrival at the station. 'We went to meet them because that was polite and correct,' she said, many years later, when speaking with the *Washington Post*'s Joy Billington. 'It's probably always been for centuries that the owners would be pleased that the queen or the king arrived and went to meet them along with the lord lieutenant, and a few people who were important to them.'

She reflected on how this first greeting developed into a long-standing tradition, even after the station at Ballater was closed down in 1966:

Now they come by car so we are [outside] Balmoral when we meet them. As it's been traditional they would be quite upset if we were not there. In fact I know they would be because once I was ill – only once in all this time – and Lord Plunkett, who had been with them all his life, rang me up and said that the queen was very upset. Where was Frances?

Frances made her debut at the Braemar Gathering that same year, which was attended by the king and queen, newlyweds Princess Elizabeth and Philip, the Duke of Edinburgh, Princess Margaret, and the Duke and Duchess of Gloucester. There was huge affection for the royal family at this time, particularly after the November 1947 wedding of Princess Elizabeth and Philip, which was considered a much-needed celebration after six years at war.

In *British Pathé* footage, Frances can be seen standing next to Alwyne and 10-year-old Marybelle as they wait for the royal cars to arrive at the pavilion. She offers warm smiles and curtsies to the royal party, encouraging Marybelle, who is blonde and shy and smiling in a little bonnet and kilt, to do the same. Frances' outfit that first year was quietly chic: a tweed jacket and tartan skirt, a raincoat draped over her shoulders and a tartan bonnet on her head. As the footage focuses on the men taking part in the caber tossing and shotput, the majority of whom would have been recently demobilised from their branches of the armed forces, it encapsulates a sense of post-war optimism, of the men, sun-tanned and rugged in kilts and rollneck sweaters, waiting to take their turn in the games.

The following year, in 1950, Frances upped her fashion choices by wearing a specially commissioned Farquharson tartan cape, jacket and skirt. From then on, she would make unforgettable fashion statements at the yearly Gathering, with a series of spectacular outfits that she often designed herself and which were made by local manufacturers. She sometimes teamed her blue-and-green-checked jackets and skirts with bright colours, combining different textures and patterns and accessorising with enormous scarves and throws.

In January 1952, she ordered a bright yellow wool jacket, Farquharson wool kilted skirt and waistcoat from Christie and Gregor, which she wore with a yellow skull cap. Her locally bought wardrobe also featured a vivid pink mohair coat and skirt, a Farquharson tartan mohair evening skirt and throw from Strathtay originals, worn with a bright green wool jumper from Catherine of Inverness, and a purple and emerald dress from Heather Mills in Selkirk.

'My mother always said that when it came to clothes in Scotland it was hard to beat the men,' said Marybelle. But not even the clansmen in their full regalia could outshine Frances Farquharson in her tartan outfits, turbans and capes. For the 1951 Braemar Gathering, she designed a dramatic full-length cloak in Farquharson tartan, which she swooshed with every step.

'She was remarkable from every point of view,' said her friend, the South African actress Moira Lister:

> She would make you feel you were the only person in the world. I was always a bit surprised one of her husbands didn't say, 'I think your clothes are a bit far gone tonight'. But I think perhaps they were all proud of her. [5]

Her embracing of colourful cloth wasn't new; Frances had lauded Scottish tartans and tweeds since the late 1930s. As fashion editor at *Harper's Bazaar*, she was prescient in describing some of the flourishes that would become her trademark in the Highlands. In fashion advice that mimicked her style in Scotland, she suggested in 1938 to wear autumnal tweeds and tartans and 'evening gowns with harem skirts to enable you to step on and off yachts, wind yards of turban round your head to keep untidy hair from sight', and advocated for capes for both evening wear and outdoor pursuits.[6] On her trade trip to New York in 1941, she had proudly worn a Gordon tartan sash in tribute to her second husband Charles, and had encouraged the uptake of earthy tweeds and bright tartans sourced from Scottish Borders mills.

Now that her life was in Scotland, she threw herself into its traditions. Marybelle remembers:

> She was dressed in tartan from head to foot most of the time. And the boys on the bus when I went to the village school, would say, 'do you think she's wearing tartan knickers too?' And I would be cringing. And it was true. She was usually in tartan! And then she had a shop where she created fashions. But she didn't always wear tartan, she wore Mandarin silk jackets, which she looked amazing in. She invented things, and she would put together her own style. There was no one else like her.

Frances was a proponent of mixing designer labels with items purchased from the high street long before it became a popular combination. Marybelle says:

> Marks and Spencer's went to Aberdeen first before anywhere else in Scotland, and if it sold in Aberdeen it would be a success. And she spotted some of the clothing that they had, before anyone knew about it. She was quite happy to go to Woolworths and buy costume jewellery there. It wasn't a question of what something cost.

When King George VI died in February 1952, his 25-year-old daughter, Elizabeth, became queen. The coronation celebrations in spring 1953 were embraced across the country, as if it was the reward for all the sacrifices made during the war and the tough economic choices that followed.

The new Elizabethan age would mark a shift in Britain's fortunes, with a sense of revived spirit and innovation, and for Frances, she had ambitions for Invercauld and Braemar that would make a huge impact on the prosperity of this remote part of Scotland.

Chapter Eighteen

In the years after the end of the Second World War, the Scottish Highlands were described as being 'a land in a coma'.[1] Its communities, scattered over mountains and moorland, were suffering from a rapidly depleting population, not just from the loss of men during the Second World War, but from the long-term effects of crofters being cast out from their farms in the eighteenth and nineteenth centuries. In a period from 1750 to 1860, which later became known as the Highland Clearances, tenants evicted from their homes were given little choice but to find work in the growing industrial centres like Glasgow, or to seek a better life by migrating overseas to the United States and Canada.

In the twentieth century, the vast and rolling Highland wilderness suffered from a lack of economic investment due to the ongoing conflict and then the post-war recovery, and this had resulted in the overgrowth of heather and a depletion of grouse. The moors could be a sustainable, circular economy for Scottish estates, where the wildlife was both a food source and a means of creating jobs in the area, but it had to be carefully managed.

With heavy rain washing grouse nests away, and with the spread of disease, so few young birds survived in 1952 and 1953 that it had a knock-on effect on the 1954 season, meaning there was less income generated for the estates and their dependents.[2] The deer population had also exploded as a result of a lack of manpower for stalking during the war, and without this management, they ate into vital crops and created an imbalance in the ecosystem.

There was a gloominess to life in post-war Britain – and Scotland, in particular. America may have entered a period of prosperity, with a wave of spending, mass consumerism and ambition that defined the fifties, but life on the other side of the Atlantic was a struggle. Food rationing was still in place in Britain until 1954, with coal rationing continuing until 1958, and the wartime mentality of being careful not to waste anything was still very much in people's minds.

Frances was a lifelong supporter of reducing waste, and this was the ethos she insisted upon in her homes, where she chose to reuse and recycle rather than buying everything new. However, despite the efforts to conserve, like other grand manor houses across the country, it was a struggle to keep Invercauld Estate and its hundreds of farms and properties running. It floundered under the double death duties that were owed from both Alexander Farquharson's and his daughter Myrtle's deaths, made worse with a sluggish economy and a lack of workers to manage the land.

After becoming Laird of Invercauld Estate, Alwyne worked hard to make it financially stable. He wanted to support those who relied on the land for their livelihood as much as he could, but there was still a mountain to overcome in terms of being able to make it sustainable. He genuinely cared about the 2,000 people who lived and relied on the estate.

Having studied agriculture before going to war, he had a keen interest in developing an understanding of how to manage the land. He embarked on a breeding programme for pure-bred Highland cattle, dairy cows and black-faced sheep. He arranged selective forestry and milling and he brought in an electricity service and indoor plumbing to all homes and farms, where possible. As an older resident was quoted as saying in a 1953 article, 'The young laird has done more in five years for Invercauld than had been done in the past 200 years – and his lady is right there behind him every minute.'[3]

Alwyne and Frances were equally invested in the culture. Their focus wasn't just on bringing income to Invercauld; the Farquharsons wished to enhance the use of Gaelic dialect, which was dwindling due to falling populations and a lack of teaching in schools. In a feature in *Country Life* magazine in 1953, it was noted:

> The present laird has enhanced the family reputation, for he and his wife interest themselves in each tenant on their extensive estate, and also encourage the old Gaelic language, which is in danger of being lost in this part of the Highlands.

With the shortage of grouse in the fifties, many visitors to the area were content to walk the moors rather than shoot, and Deeside, with the attraction of royalty living close by, began to experience an influx of tourists over the summer months, as had been the case when Queen Victoria was at Balmoral.

Frances, always with an eye on how she could help make improvements, real-ised there were opportunities to take advantage of this increase in visitors – in particular, those from the United States, who felt strong ancestral links to relatives who had emigrated from the Highlands.

She wasn't the first to take advantage of visitors to the Highlands – there was a line of forward-thinking Farquharsons who had made a difference in the area. Like his namesake, two centuries later, Francis Farquharson of Monaltrie (born in 1710 at Monaltrie House), known as 'the Barron Ban' for his blond looks, had the foresight to attract early health tourists in the eight-eenth century.

As a fervent Jacobite, he was imprisoned in London following the failed 1746 uprising. He was destined to be executed until an unknown woman, believed to be his future wife, Margaret Eyre, paid for his freedom. He spent twenty years under house arrest in Hertfordshire, and in that time, he studied new farming methods in the hopes of one day returning to Deeside. In 1788, when exiled Scottish lairds were finally given the rights to buy their land back, he returned to Monaltrie, and he became an environmental champion by planting acres of trees and raising flax for spinning.

He had heard that the waters of Pannanich Wells had cured a local woman's tuberculosis and so he built a pump room in the small settlement of Tullich. From there, he developed the spa further by establishing the village of Ballater, with hotels and bathhouses, near to his Monaltrie House.

Lord Byron spent his early years in Aberdeen, and as a boy was sent to Ballater to escape a scarlet fever epidemic and to help cure his own ills. This helped to seal its reputation as a fashionable spa resort with its healing waters. A train station at Ballater opened in 1866, with a royal waiting room built especially for Queen Victoria for her arrival and departure from Balmoral.

The Invercauld Arms, just over half a mile from Braemar Castle and within the village, became a tourist destination in the 1860s under the manage-ment of Mr A. McGregor, when it was known as the place where Queen Victoria would frequently stop to change horses as she explored the area. Advertisements boasted that it was 'the finest hotel situation in Scotland', with running water, salmon fishing to enjoy and coaches and horses provided for visitors to take in the beauty spots like the Linn of Dee (with the more adventurous climbing Ben Macdhui) with packed lunches from local suppli-ers. Here, they could breathe in the clear air, which offered a respite from the city smog of the Industrial Revolution. By the end of the century, adverts proudly announced the hotel was fully electric; although it would be many decades before Invercauld Estate caught up.

It was in a gabled stone cottage in the village of Braemar that Robert Louis Stevenson wrote *Treasure Island* during the summer of 1881, further adding to the appeal of the area. Those coming to this hard-to-reach spot at the turn of the century would take the train to Ballater and would then be transported to Braemar by an open, gaslit coach, which took an hour and a half along bumpy, loose-stoned roads. After the Second World War, the horses were replaced by motor cars and buses, making it more accessible and less exclusive, with hotels opening to people on different budgets, but it was the wealthy and connected who more often flocked to the area for stalking, fishing and grouse shooting.[4]

The post-war reconstruction in the region brought with it a renewed sense of cultural recognition, and a key figure would be this American outsider – Frances – who was able to admire the culture, and wholeheartedly and unashamedly embrace it. She had only been in Scotland a few years, yet she had already given her heart to Invercauld, and with typical fortitude, she put her mind to how she could turn the fortunes of the estate, and Royal Deeside, around.

Just as she had devoted herself to increasing textile exports to the United States and waving the flag for homegrown British fashion during the war, Frances utilised her skills and connections to champion Highland artisans, and to establish Braemar as a must-see destination for visitors. In 1949, Alwyne bought a disused church in Braemar and it became one of the first of their cultural projects, working hard to transform the dull grey interiors into a theatre and exhibition space.

Dating from 1832, the Auld Kirk was one of the oldest buildings in the village, and with its spired tower and Gothic gables and windows, it had too much potential to go to waste. As part of the makeover, Frances recruited the local joiner to construct a raised stage, inspired by those of Elizabethan theatre, and she introduced her favourite pink and yellow into the interiors to complement new stained-glass windows which cast colourful light into the space. As a backdrop, she commissioned a young Scottish artist, Jim Spiers, who had been recommended by the principal of Gray's School of Art in Aberdeen, to create three large, colourful murals which depicted the Farquharsons throughout history, including Findla Mor at the 1547 Battle of Pinkie.[5]

The former parish church was completely transformed into a unique space that reflected Frances' tastes, while being true to its historic interest. Rebranded as the Invercauld Studios, it was formally opened on 9 August 1951, with a special pageant named 'The Spirit of Scotland' to showcase Scottish music and dance. Frances recruited Glaswegian poet Maurice Lindsay to devise new compositions and verse for the occasion, which were designed to complement the romantic Highland atmosphere that Frances had created in the new theatre.

In anticipation of developing plays with a local history theme, she and some of the resident performers raided the storage rooms and attics of Invercauld and Braemar Castles to find suitable pieces that could be used as props and costumes for their productions – perhaps a sword and shield that had been kept in the armoury or a plaid owned by a previous laird. She wanted the plays to be of the utmost quality, and she contacted some of the best playwrights around Scotland to contribute. She tapped into the BBC in Aberdeen, where she easily persuaded one of their producers to write an original play for her. Later, one of Scottish playwright Lesley Storm's most successful plays, *Roar Like a Dove*, was performed at the Braemar Festival in the 1960s – it told the somewhat familiar story of an American woman who married the laird of an expansive Scottish estate.

'It is amazing the things we have done over the years,' Frances told an interviewer in 1982:

> We have had huge choral groups, light opera, wonderful singing, orchestras, children's theatres. There is practically nothing we haven't done. And we have had many plays written specially for the theatre about local history.[6]

Her ambitions for the theatre included the launch of a Highland festival which would take place from July to September every year and feature music, dancing, folk songs and recitals, as well as an exhibition of contemporary arts, which she hoped would stimulate and encourage young Scottish artists.[7] It was only a few years since the first Edinburgh International Festival had launched to great success in 1947, and Frances' vision was to create a similar cultural event in the Highlands.

With the recently proclaimed Queen Elizabeth II agreeing to be patron, the Scottish Festival Braemar was officially opened in July 1952. Among the esteemed guests at the opening were Major David Gordon of Haddo and his wife, Beatrice Mary June Gordon, a trained pianist and conductor, who would become patron of the Aberdeen International Youth Festival and founder of Haddo House Choral and Operatic Society.

Some of the Scottish talents Frances persuaded to create original works for the festival over the next few years included Thea Musgrave, who was commissioned to compose her *Suite O'Bairnsangs* as an accompaniment to words by

Glasgow poet Maurice Lindsay. The Jolly Beggars, composers Cedric Thorpe Davie and Hans Oppenheim, mezzo-soprano Jean Alexander, singers John Mearns and John Tainsh, and character actor Moultrie Kelsall also took part.

The *Aberdeen Evening Express*, in July 1953, described the festival as:

[A] magnificent combination of months of imagination, enterprise, and hard work by a comparatively small group of people led by Captain and Mrs AAC Farquharson of Invercauld. The aim of this unique all-Scottish Festival, which is under the patronage of the Queen, is to give a full representation of Scotland's folk music and drama, together with her finest contemporary arts and traditional crafts.[8]

Only a few months after 1953's festival had ended Frances was looking towards the next year's programme. She enthusiastically spoke to the paper about her plans for 1954. 'More productions for children,' she told the reporter, particularly as the puppet show, acting out Scottish stories, had been such a great success. She also had a desire to feature more local artists from the north-east, to give them a platform to lift their careers.[9]

Frances and her theatre soon developed a reputation across the Grampian region for helping to revive Highland arts, which had been neglected for so long, and encouraging the potential in novice performers and artists. It was quite an accomplishment to attract big names to the quiet village of Braemar, but Frances was determined to put her section of Scotland on the map.

To ensure people from across the region could attend, buses were organised from Aberdeen and back, with refreshments provided. In May 1954, the *Aberdeen Evening Express*'s entertainment editor offered their 'bouquet of the week' to Frances, who they credited as being 'the first person outside our immediate drama circles to give encouragement to amateur clubs in the North-East and present them to a wider public'.[10]

As well as the theatre and festival, Frances was integral to introducing a number of new businesses to Braemar, which further promoted local arts. Just as she'd breathed new life into the Auld Kirk, Frances acquired the vacant Victoria Hall, opposite the Robert Louis Stevenson cottage on Glenshee Road, and transformed it into an exhibition space and shop, which she named the Invercauld Galleries. Not only had she spent the war years singing the praises of Scottish heritage fabrics, but she'd observed the interest among the women who came to the Highlands during the summer season.

In her first few years at Invercauld, she noticed how guests to Balmoral, such as Princess Alice and the Duchess of Gloucester, went on shopping trips to source tartans and tweeds from local mills – the Campbells of Beauly or to Captain John McLeod's Inverness showrooms. By creating a space for Scottish artisan goods from across Scotland, not just its fabrics but ceramics, glass, ironwork and jewellery, visitors could experience traditional craftsmanship. The skills that were developed in remote cottages and passed down the generations, such as weaving, glass-blowing, whittling and leather-tanning, were in danger of dying out if there wasn't investment in helping to support them:

> I felt I really must do something with crafts, for there were so many wonderful pairs of hands everywhere, people who could only help themselves in their homes and had no proper outlet for their talents. I was so anxious for young people to understand that it is essential to look at good things because today there is so much rubbish about.[11]

As per her vision, the galleries took the visitor on a journey through the history of Scottish textiles and design. On display were historic pieces, such as a 200-year-old Ross of Balnagowan tartan, believed to have been worn as a kilt at Culloden and discovered at Invercauld, and modern tartans and tweeds by contemporary Scottish weavers. The building was set over two floors, and in the downstairs area, craftsmen and women would be invited to give live demonstrations as they operated the handlooms to weave tartan or to showcase the intricacies involved in lace making. Initially, customers were meant to order directly from the makers, but when Frances found out that the system didn't run smoothly – orders were getting lost or people were receiving the wrong items – she stepped in and managed the orders herself with typical efficiency.

Some of the talented craftspeople Frances invited to Braemar included Hamish Robson, a horn carver who skilfully whittled antlers into knife handles and bottle openers, and James Crichton, a craftsman wood carver, who came to the village with his wife Isobel in the early sixties on the invitation of Frances. The profits from the shop allowed them to carry on with their experimental work over the quiet winter period.[12]

She described in 1955 how she found 'a man in Edinburgh who is making brightly coloured pottery which can be taken from the oven to the table', and how she had inspired a new wave among craftspeople to 'brighten up their products' to create 'more colourful crafts'.[13] When she travelled to Mull, to stay at Torloisk House, she would seek out local craftspeople – the mohair weavers or crofters' wives who handknitted stockings.

She also reinvigorated interest in Harris Tweed, a durable and hardy fabric traditionally made by Isle of Harris crofters in their own homes from wool shorn from the island's sheep and dyed with native plants. The demand for the cottage industry fabric may have exploded in recent years, but it was a different situation in the fifties, when it struggled to compete with the innovative synthetic fabrics that had been invented out of necessity during the Second World War. Many of the skilled home-craft weavers were also pushed out of business by mass manufacturers who could provide tweeds and tartans for less.

By the 1960s, some of the small industries that she supported had found a new resurgence, thanks in part to this attention. Bute Looms, woven at a small mill on a hillside above Rothesay on the Isle of Bute, was being snapped up by haute couture labels from around the world, including Christian Dior, Yves Saint Laurent and Mary Quant, who admired its vivid chevron weaves in the colours of a peacock's neck or orange and post-box-red check.[14]

What Frances was doing was decades ahead of her time – championing home-grown artists, urging people to buy local and helping to promote these textiles in every way she could. Alwyne's kilts were made from tartan woven in the galleries, copied from his great grandfather's kilts which traditionally had a larger sett, or pattern. Some of her friends, like Parisian couturier Irene Dana, 'very sophisticated people who dress in Paris', would snap up smooth tweeds and soft-to-the-touch cashmeres, and Frances would also use the textiles as inspiration for her own fabulously colourful creations, worn to the Braemar Gathering.

Catherine Drummond-Herdman, who assisted Frances at Invercauld when she was a teenager in the eighties, says:

> It must have been such a wonderful ray of sunshine when she first moved up to Invercauld. I know she effectively kick-started the Scottish tweed industry in the post war years and she had some magnificent woven fabrics for sale in The Galleries. I think there were other wonderful Scottish arts and crafts she promoted here. She was a strong believer in promoting local Scottish producers and makers of all sorts, and an early proponent of Scottish is best and local is best.

The Queen Mother was a frequent visitor to the Invercauld Galleries during her time in Royal Deeside. In October 1955, she and her two ladies-in-waiting, Lady Hyde and Miss Iris Peake, were greeted by Alwyne and Frances, who showed her some of the crafts on display. She was reported to have purchased a mohair stole from the Outer Hebrides and Bute tweeds and tartans and placed an order for deerskin gloves.[15] The following year, when she was welcomed to the shop by Frances, Alwyne and Marybelle, she purchased three papier-mâché models of corgis, three white teddy bears and Royal Stewart cotton table mats and tweed.[16]

The concept of the Galleries would expand into the Invercauld Speciality Shop, which opened in 1963 as a dedicated space to display Scottish fabrics and fashions. Visitors to Braemar couldn't miss its façade; it was yellow-and-pink candy striped, and the windows were filled with eye-catching designs. They were the type of outré clothing that Frances favoured in Scotland: the jewel-toned mohair, oversized bonnets, handknitted stockings from Bute and Fair Isle sweaters. It was inspired by the women she knew from Scotland's north-east who, she said, were:

> … very fashion conscious, and who use only Scottish products. They dress in tweed, and wear knitted stockings, and felt hats with a feather. The inspiration of their costume is really from male attire.[17]

As a tie-in with her fashion boutique, she hosted a yearly fashion show as part of the Braemar Scottish Festival. She recruited a selection of local women, including the gamekeeper's wife, Ruth Cameron, who was also a talented singer, to model the confections, such as capes in tartan, anoraks in tweed, ankle-length mohair coats, and tonags – a Gaelic shawl. 'I'm training the girls myself,' Frances told local reporters, who took an interest in the novelty of these fashion shows. 'What we want to show are outfits which will look good in a big house or a small cottage.'[18]

'You have to realise,' says Marybelle:

> … that in those days there was not even a pavement in Braemar. There was a shop and a butcher and a chemist and that was about it. I think the locals to begin with were gob-smacked. But they liked her. Because when we went up there, there were so few shops, and by opening this old church and making it into a theatre, and by opening the gallery and the shop, she brought life to Braemar. The local council even developed a pavement in the village, due to the business she was bringing in.

One of the local girls, Doreen Wood, later a BBC features editor, remembers fondly her time when she was recruited to model the tartans and mohair for Frances at one of these fashion shows:

She was a sensation when she arrived in the village. I didn't become aware of her until primary school, and then as a teenager. She had the fashion shop, and she used to line us all up to act as models. We all thought she was absolutely off her head, but when you look back, she was absolutely amazing. Innovative, and bringing all sorts of stuff here. And of course the pink and the yellow, which was her signature, and which was quite amazing. And who wore tartan in those days? No one, just to do your Highland dancing, and that was the only time you stuck on a kilt. But she got special pieces designed for her, and she wore tartan or tweed a lot of the time.

She was a huge personality, and she was actually not that tall. She was quite small, and when you see her clothes, she had the tiniest of waists. But she filled a huge space, because the arms were always out. She was a big personality, and an American, in Braemar, which was a little surprising. What she did was extraordinary, and totally unappreciated by us lot at the time.

With her background, she understood marketing, she understood what was needed, and she just delivered it in this fantastic setting, and these rich Americans were just blown away. When Alwyne took over, I'm sure the estate would have been fairly run down, and they would have been pretty tight for cash, and she came in, and she said, 'what can we do' – and she brought these rich, rich Americans to Braemar.

The establishment of these new businesses were only the first step in Frances' reinvigoration of Invercauld and Braemar. With her knack for entertaining, her love of bringing new people together and her connections to some of the most affluent people on both sides of the Atlantic, the estate would be further shaken up with an influx of illustrious, and very wealthy, visitors.

Chapter Nineteen

On an extended trip to California and Hawaii in early 1953, Frances and her husband were not only catching up with old friends and her family, who she'd not seen for many years. They were also there for business. There were visits to ranches in California, Arizona and Hawaii to learn techniques in cattle rearing, a tour of Napa Valley's wineries to select the best vintages to bring back home, and an opportunity to speak to the press about their ventures in Scotland.

Since the early fifties, they'd been inviting eight or nine guests at a time from all over the world to Invercauld to stay for a week or two, where they could take part in shoots on the moors. One guest in 1952 came from China – Dr Shu Fan Li, president of the Gun Club of Hong Kong. There were also aristocrats from Germany, Austria and Italy, and there were, of course, Americans.[1]

In *The Evening Standard*'s 'The Londoner's Diary' column in September 1952, it made mention of Invercauld:

From Scotland I hear that one of the most cosmopolitan house parties for the grouse shooting is at the home of the Queen's neighbour, Captain Alwyne Farquharson. This year he has had paying guests to do the shooting.

There was another snippet in the *New York Daily News* in September 1953:

American socialites recently in the Scottish Highlands for the shooting and the annual games 'gathering' have been sending back enthusiastic accounts of a fellow American known as the 'Queen's next door neighbour.'[2]

The Farquharsons had arrived in the States in March 1953, accompanied by Anna, Frances' long-time cook and assistant, to catch up with family in Seattle, revisit her father's 2,000-acre Brown Farm near Olympia and embark on a road trip around California, like the one she had done with her brother and father all those years before.

They flew to Hawaii in May for 'a complete change of environment'. They stayed with a Scottish friend, Peter King McLean, who lived in a house close to Diamond Head with amazing views, before taking in some of the other islands in the archipelago, including Big Island, where they experienced the famous Parker cattle ranch.[3]

Hawaii was an extravagance, but it had been a late wedding present from her family. 'We couldn't have made the trip otherwise,' they told a reporter from the *Honolulu Advertiser*, who referred to them as the 'Invercaulds' and headlined the article with the alliteration 'Hanalei Hideaway for Highlanders'. The newspaper was invited into their motel room in Hanalei, a small settlement on the paradise island of Kauai, where they watched as Alwyne:

> ... deftly wiped dry the last dish from the dinner table and handed it to his Seattle-born Lady of Invercauld, to be placed on a shelf above the electric plate on which skillfully she had cooked the meal in their studio apartment at this modest motel. It was a far cry from the servant-attended ceremony of dining at Invercauld and Braemar.[4]

The press coverage was revealing of the interest in their lives – the Highland laird and his American wife, offering the opportunity for intrepid travellers to experience life in a Scottish castle. The *San Francisco Examiner*, when interviewing them in March 1953, described the Farquharsons as 'two very charming people', and put the call to 'California sportsmen' to visit 'the magnificent domain of Invercauld and Braemar Castle' for the shooting season, beginning on 12 August.[5] They said there were a range of nationalities attending – Chinese, Turkish and Italian – and those who didn't shoot or fish could be entertained with walks on the moors or exploring what the village (and Mrs Farquharson's ventures) had to offer.[6] The article, with some embellishment, related how, 'At dinner his guests gather around the table set with the gold service and the gold candelabra, while fifty pipes march around the banquet table. Hunters and fishermen exchange reports of their skill'.[7]

After Hawaii, they made a stop in Arizona, before hurrying home in time to finalise the Highland Festival, which was set to open on 17 July under the patronage of Queen Elizabeth II. They would also be busy preparing the house for their guests.[8] One of their American visitors in 1953 was San Francisco's Darthea Powell O'Connell, who arrived in Britain to attend the coronation. She had such a good time at gala parties in London that she extended her trip, making time to visit Invercauld in August.[9]

Opening up Invercauld House to paying guests had proved to be an effective means of bringing in much-needed money for the estate in the mid-fifties. Darthea was one of several well-to-do Americans with deep pockets, who enjoyed the invigorating outdoors and wished to discover the romantic Highland experience. Mostly, they heard of Invercauld House and 'Francie' Farquharson's parties through word of mouth, and they would come for exclusive week-long retreats over the summer and autumn seasons.

In the post-war period, many of Britain's country estates were struggling under the weight of inheritance taxes and the costs of upkeep, and there were only a few options to stay afloat. Some of the houses that had been acquisitioned by the government during the war had been so neglected by their military residents, with their leaking roofs and broken windows going unrepaired for so long, that they would never again be habitable. *Country Life* magazine in 1945 featured a series of articles on 'The Future of Great Country Houses' and declared that 'without some form of relief or subvention, many of the more artistically and historically important cannot be maintained much longer, if at all, for their original purpose of a family home'.

The most tragic of these were the hundreds that were bulldozed after the war as their owners couldn't afford the upkeep, despite their clear historical interest. Others were handed over to the National Trust, which could accept the gift of an estate, free of tax. In 1946, the National Trust had eighteen country houses and by 1961 it had acquired another sixty.

For the more forward-thinking estate owners, the answer was to open their doors to day-trippers. The 11th Duke of Devonshire and his wife, Deborah Mitford, were one of the first when they opened Chatsworth House to the public in 1949, and the Duke of Bedford followed suit with Woburn Abbey in 1955, proudly accepting 300,000 visitors each year. 'This is the day of personality,' acknowledged the duke. But few were ready to have paying guests staying overnight, let alone for a week or two.

Frances' innovative concept dated back to the house parties of the past. For over a century, Scottish country estates had offered a relaxing retreat for guests from London and overseas, where they could immerse themselves in nature and outdoor sports. The 1860s saw a phenomenal spread of shooting lodges across Scotland; a trend that was triggered by Queen Victoria and Prince Albert's interest in Balmoral.

In the early 1800s, few people thought of visiting the Highlands, but 100 years later, a network of new railways and roads helped to breathe new life into country lodges and castles. There was a dark history to this sudden surge of interest, as crofters had been forcibly removed from their homes in what became known as the Highland Clearances, and with this land now taken up with shooting lodges.

The fashion for Highland escapes reached its peak in the Edwardian era when King Edward VII and his decadent friends, such as his mistress Alice Keppel, would make frequent trips to Balmoral for weekend shooting parties, and the king and his group would often call in at Invercauld for drinks and dinner with the laird, Alexander Haldane Farquharson of Invercauld, Myrtle's father.

'The doors of Highland houses always stood open,' wrote the Marchioness of Aberdeen in *Musings of a Scottish Granny* in 1936, and as Frances filled Invercauld with her convivial personality, she also wanted to see a return to the fabulous house parties of the past. The world that existed before the war with homes being staffed by butlers, housemaids, housekeepers and footmen was gone, and instead country estates were typically run by a reduced staff. For the summer and autumn seasons, Frances would bring in over a dozen temporary assistants to help manage the housekeeping and extensive catering that was required to ensure her guests were well looked after. Frances told Joy Billington of the *Washington Post* in 1985, as they were seated in Invercauld's Tartan Room:

> It's really kind of a rhythm you get into. When I interview them, I explain that I expect them to work very hard and to remember that they are the host and hostesses as much as we are. They can make their stay happy and comfortable or they can make them uncomfortable.
>
> Scots are notoriously very hospitable and in these days it's nearly impossible for them to open house as they used to without contribution. In our case I don't know whether we would ever come to it but for our sport. We started taking people for a week at a time, sometimes two weeks, for the shooting, and staying with us as a house party.

She described the paying guests as 'mostly friends or friends of friends', and her parties were a gathering of people from all over the world – those who could afford the many thousands of dollars it cost to attend. Over the years, there would be members of America's wealthiest families, including Nelson 'Rocky' Rockefeller and his second wife, Margaretta 'Happy' Large Fitler,

William duPont and Willard Rockwell Jr, of Rockwell International, the primary financier of the Space Shuttle.

Because it was word of mouth, the initial guests had connections to their hosts and would be recommended by friends. They were expected to be mutually compatible – to fit in with the intimate family circle – but because Frances was so magnetic, had friends far and wide and made such an impression on all those who met her, it was easy to fall under this category. 'If people stay with you, they know about you and your way of life and they stimulate you enormously too,' she said. The du Ponts' New York State home, for example, was purchased by Freddie Guest and his wife Amy Phipps in the 1920s, and Frances may have met them while staying at Villa Artemis in Palm Beach.

★　★　★

The Highlands had always held an appeal to those on the other side of the Atlantic. In the 1930s, wealthy Americans sailed to Britain to participate in grouse shooting on the Scottish moors. The Duke of Windsor had inspired an appreciation of the aristocratic way of life, and his country sports style of durable tweeds, Fair Isle sweaters and plus fours shaped the burgeoning Ivy League look. The concept of leasing a Scottish home for the season appealed to businessmen like Herbert L. Pratt, and financier J.P. Morgan, who rented the Earl of Dalhousie's Gannochy Castle in 1939.[10]

Following the end of the Second World War, there were increasing numbers of American tourists taking advantage of cheap airfares to come to the 'Old Country'. Some had been stationed here during the war, others were interested in tracing their ancestry. In 1950, 127,830 made the trip, and by the end of the decade, it had increased to 356,540. With these numbers, there was no shortage of visitors willing to be welcomed into the warm hospitality of Invercauld.

Famed Minneapolis food writer Virginia Safford visited Invercauld in October 1957, and enthusiastically reported on her experience. She described Frances as 'possessing a great deal of talent and energy, as well as charm', and 'from early spring until late fall, this castle offers a fascinating experience to anyone who comes to this wild and beautiful Scottish highland country'.[11]

Whether they were film stars or maharanis from India, Danish royalty or American businessmen from the Midwest, Frances sought to make their stay incredibly comfortable and relaxing, and she loved nothing more than throwing disparate guests into the social melting pot. 'I have never found anyone who won't mix,' she once said, and she followed the ethos of the Queen Mother, 'There is no one who is really boring – if you find someone so, it must be because of you'.[12] She believed that she could arrange a party where everyone, no matter how diverse their lives, would get on well. The key was in the seating arrangements. 'Americans would never have had the chance to meet some of the people who were at these dinners,' says Marybelle. 'There were people from India and China, and the guests came for the opportunity to meet such a wide range.'

Frances' friend Marcia Brocklebank, an art historian from Michigan, who moved to Suffolk after her marriage in the 1960s, said:

> She charmed everyone she met because she was such a flamboyant dynamo, and she was attractive. She attracted people. People were really enthralled by her. She was delightful. And also, being not an east coast American, but a west coast American, the Brits could sense that she was different, and that might have helped her in a way. I'm from the Midwest, and we're more straight talking, more straight up, and not a bit European really.

As vibrant groups of guests came and went, the house was alive with activity, fulfilling the purpose it had been designed for. The entrance halls bustled with the hum of different accents in the air, with people leaving their muddy boots and waterproof jackets by the door. After a day spent on the bracing hills, shooting, walking or fishing on the Dee, they would pile indoors, pulling off their boots, handing over the guns to be cleaned, and then to their rooms for hot baths, after which they would change into their finest gowns and suits for a dinner.

Frances used her experience of dining in extraordinary surroundings, such as at Marlborough House in the twenties, Villa Artemis in Palm Beach in the 1930s, or with the Queen of Romania at Peleş Castle in the Carpathian Mountains, to host an evening like no other they had experienced before. These events breathed life back into Invercauld, and instead of meeting the fate of other country estates that had to be sold, or were abandoned into disrepair, it would thrive under the organisation of Francie Farquharson, the most dynamic hostess this region had ever seen.

Chapter Twenty

When a private jet touched down at Prestwick Airport, a tiny airport in Ayrshire, David Geddes, a local Braemar lad who served as electrician on the Invercauld Estate and petrol pump attendant at his grandfather's petrol station, had been sent by Frances to collect the new arrivals. Stepping onto the tarmac was William du Pont Junior, the famous businessman, racecourse designer and horse breeder.

David Geddes, president of the Braemar Royal Highland Society from 2011, was born in Braemar and grew up in the area, with his mother's side of the family traced back to the 1700s. He had know of Frances since he was a teenager:

> I first met Mrs Farquharson when I was working for my grandfather's petrol station in the village, when I was about fourteen or fifteen years old. She would come in with her Morris Minor traveller for fuel, and she needed everything done. So did everybody in those days, but she needed her tires done and the oil. We always knew who she was, and we were told, when we started working, to show respect, as these are important people, and good customers. So I was a little bit in awe at the beginning. I had met her before that, she used to run the Invercauld Festival Theatre, and I was involved there, with Highland dancing. Everyone knew that she was to be called 'Madam'. She was a force to be reckoned with, there's no doubt about that.
>
> I was also the electrician and would do work for them at the big house. When you went there, you had to be prepared not to be back home until late that day. Because she'd have you moving furniture, she'd have you preparing this and that.

David was tasked with chauffeuring du Pont the 140 miles to Invercauld to begin a week-long vacation where they would be fully immersed in the Scottish Highlands. Du Pont, known as Willie to his friends, suffered from respiratory problems, according to his wife Margaret Osborne, and the crisp Scottish air may well have been soothing to his lungs. David Geddes remembers:

> Often the guests would fly into Prestwick Airport, some would come into London and then Aberdeen, and we didn't have taxis at that time, so we used to pick up them from Prestwick. And there was a chap, William du Pont, who I used to pick up, who came twice a year, for the grouse and for the stags. Mrs Farquharson would phone me up, and the question was always the same, 'You're picking Willie up tomorrow, tell him he must phone me to say if he's coming for lunch.'

They arrived at the entrance to Invercauld in cars loaded down with suit-cases, packed with all the clothing required for a week in the Highlands. There were the sturdy tweed jackets and waterproofs, the woollens and thermals, and for dinner, the gentlemen needed to pack their smartest dinner jackets and black tie, and the ladies, a different evening gown for each night.

Once all the suitcases were unloaded from the cars, they would be shown to their sleeping quarters – perhaps one of the rooms at the top of the tower, which offered breath-taking views over the pine trees to the River Dee or the Cairngorms. 'One greets them when they come and I hope they feel that they're just coming home,' said Frances to Joy Billington in 1985:

> Now in the grouse season, [my husband] greets them at the front door, enormous numbers, and there's boys with all their luggage, which is huge, because all the things to do with the shooting are very cumbersome. They come into the library and have some tea and we discuss everything.

Minneapolis Food writer Virginia Safford, who was the Nigella Lawson of the Midwestern city at that time, was invited through mutual friends to spend time at Invercauld as a relaxing final stop following a two-month tour of Europe. 'There could have been a no more glorious end to what has been one of the best trips I ever have taken abroad,' she said:

I wish I could give you a real picture of this great graystone castle with its towers and turrets and the six stories rising from the center part. As I saw it in the distance, looking across to the other side of the River Dee, with its back up against the wooded Cairngorm mountains, it appeared dreamlike. Yet, this is a place that is loved and lived in.[1]

Guests could have their breakfast brought to their room on a tray or they could go downstairs to the old kitchen, where they would gather around the long wood table, and help themselves to the buffet. There were ladles of porridge, with milk or cream, grilled tomato and sausages, toast, marmalade and pots of hot coffee, all designed to set them up for a day spent in the surrounding hills.[2]

As Frances described it herself in a brochure for her guests:

It is here in this great hall kitchen that next season's guns and their families will be welcomed to the traditional Scottish breakfast – wooden bowls round the sizzling porridge pot. You may eat it with salt like the Scots, or perhaps with black treacle or brown sugar and home farm cream. So help yourself and roam around eating it as you lift the pottery lids to see whether it is those succulent kippers or the equally delicious 'smokies' or finnons with their golden covers – of course there will be Dyce-cured bacon and home farm eggs – the butter will tempt you to Scottish scones or oatcakes and bannocks. The coffee specially blended and home roasted and ground ... great loaves of whole meal bread and fluffy rolls, the big knives providing every possibility of making your choice of sandwich for the day. You are warm, you are well fed – what a sound beginning to the sport of the day.

Alwyne was responsible for organising the shoots with his gamekeeper and ghillies, and he would lead the guests across the moors as their tweeds brushed the heather and their boots protected them from the peat bogs. If they didn't like the idea of shooting, the guests could simply walk, taking in the panoramic views and breathing the crisp mountain air or exploring the surrounding forests, on paths softened with pine needles and scattered with cones. Virginia Safford wrote:

The men come in to tell of their day's adventures hunting in the highlands for grouse, or ptarmigan or perhaps another favourite game – mountain hare. Or they may have been out 'stalking deer', as they say in

Scotland. The women at tea time appear fresh and radiant after a brisk walk through the woods. To appreciate this country, one should be a walker, even a climber. The panoramas one delights in from the higher areas are magnificent.[3]

A hamper filled with a hearty picnic lunch was brought out to the guests on the moors and they would tuck into it while sitting on blankets on the ground. Invercauld's own garden supplied the fresh vegetables, with salad greens picked only an hour before they were to be eaten. They also grew many of the Scottish berries that were included in the menu, such as cranberries, strawberries and loganberries. There was a dairy in the grounds of the house, which provided milk and heavy cream, which in turn made cheese and butter. The grouse, venison and partridge came from the moors, salmon from the Dee, and 'smokies' from the North Sea, which were served as hors d'oeuvres with sour cream. There would be sausages from the local butchers and bread baked fresh from the ovens of Invercauld.

As Virginia Safford described:

It's surprising what big appetites can be acquired here by lunch time especially if you have enjoyed a brisk walk through woods or meadows. One luncheon menu: rare roasted venison delicious with a tossed green salad; a heavenly dessert, which I was told was the Duke of Edinburgh's favorite. It could easily be my favorite now: a torte made with meringue to which had been added ground hazelnuts. The filling was heavy cream, whipped, flavoured strongly with coffee infusion.[4]

In the guest brochure, Frances described with her characteristic flourish how they might host a traditional feast on Sunday nights in the old kitchen. A deer could be roasted on the open fire with guests and ghillies taking turns to rotate the spit. Frances described the evening as 'so feudal':

[with the] keepers in kilts giving butlers a hand until charred by birch wood outside and juicy red within. Then everyone has a cut of the joint; guests, hosts, ghillies and staff eat at the great tables, exactly as they all used to do 200 years ago.

Frances would sometimes join them for lunch outdoors, but she wouldn't come out onto the moors for the daytime activities, as she was averse to the idea of killing for sport. 'I don't do any killing at all and I don't really like it,' she said in 1985. 'I always laugh, I must love my husband very much to be where a great deal of the economy is based on killing and I don't believe in killing a fly.'[5]

The Invercauld Estate possessed fishing rights on 24 miles of the Dee, and much of this was rented out to other estates. The section they used for guests, known as the 'Private Water', on both banks of the Dee and close to the castle, was considered the prime spot, particularly in May and June. On these waters, Invercauld's guests could fly fish from the banks or wade into the crystal-clear waters. As Frances said, 'A great number of the big rivers you can't see the bottom, but with the Dee, except in a storm, you can see every pebble in the bottom. It's rather special.' While one salmon a day was considered a good catch, Alwyne reflected on his golden day in 1973 where he and three guests caught fifteen salmon in six and a half hours, which had the combined weight of 150lb.

One of the stories Frances enjoyed amusing her guests with was that of an American woman who was casting on the bank of the river, close to the castle. The Queen Mother, who was staying at Balmoral, appeared on the other side of the river, setting up her rods for a day of fishing. The American woman, on looking up between casts, suddenly spotted her and, flustered at the sight of royalty, tried for a curtsy. As she dipped down in reverence, her wading boots filled with water and she lost her balance, tumbling into the river. She was only saved from floating down stream by a ghillie who stepped in to catch her. That evening, the Queen Mother called Frances on the telephone at Invercauld to ask after the woman and check she had recovered from her fright.[6]

The daytime dress code was comfortable, with warm sports clothing, such as tweed jackets, wool jumpers and walking boots. For the evenings, when the laird and lady dressed for dinner, their guests were expected to change into their most dazzling gowns and dinner jackets and gather for pre-dinner cocktails in the Upper Hall. Alwyne made his entrance just before 8 p.m., wearing his dress Farquharson kilt, one of his velvet doublets, a fur sporran and *sgian-dubh* tucked into his long brightly coloured socks. ('The *sgian-dubh* is just for a bit of show. I probably couldn't open a letter with it,' he said.)[7]

Frances would dress in chic evening gowns, often with a turban wrapped around her head, perhaps designed by Dior, Schiaparelli (before she closed her couture business in 1954) or by another good couturier friend of hers, Irene Dana. Sometimes, she would wear a silk Mandarin coat, cinched at the waist with a belt. She adored drama in her clothing – the vibrant clashing oranges and pinks, purples and greens, or abstract monochrome designs that immediately attracted the eye.

At 8.30 p.m. dinner would be served, and guests were led down the stairs to the wood-panelled dining room, where a long table, and another smaller table if needed, was set with huge silver candlesticks, fine china and heavy silverware which had belonged to previous generations of Farquharsons for their entertaining. After dinner, and with their expectant faces glowing in the candlelight, the guests would hear the bagpipes played by Norman Meldrum. 'It all looks very pretty and then in comes the piper looking magnificent because he's in full regalia and it's marvellous. I take a lot of trouble because I'm interested in food and presentation,' said Frances.

Norman Meldrum was the Farquharsons' personal piper, while also serving as the estate's plumber, a dual role he performed for many decades. As Frances told Joy Billington in 1985:

> This particular piper we have is very special. He came here to be our plumber so he could study with the queen's piper who is a very fine piper. You see, you have to have a job and earn your living and then at night he has a good time. He pipes by day and he pipes by night! [8]

Norman and his wife Stella lived in Keiloch, a hamlet close to Invercauld, which locals referred to as 'the big house', and which was home to the sawmill and the estate workers' cottages. With 200 properties across the estate, a live-in maintenance squad was required for upkeep, including a stonemason, joiner, plumber and electrician.

It wouldn't just be for the dinners that he piped; in 1952, when Frances was invited to launch a new North Shields to Oslo passenger service, called the *Braemar Castle*, he performed an accompaniment on his pipes. In August 1953, he piped 'The Standard on the Braes o' Mar' during a ceremony to unveil a new plaque at the Invercauld Arms Hotel to commemorate the raising of the Standard opposite the hotel on 6 September 1715. [9]

His daughter, Norma Sudworth, who worked in Invercauld's estate office in the 1970s, says:

> My father was from Forfar, and he came to Braemar in 1947, about the same time as the Laird, because of the piping scene. He wanted to learn from Bob Brown, the Queen's piper. My dad was a very well-known piper; he started a pipe band in Braemar, and the Laird then asked him to be the personal piper. The first time he piped the guests after dinner, he played the Invercauld March, and the Laird asked him, 'Meldrum, what tune is this?' and when he told him, he said, 'well, I've never heard

it played like this before.' The others in the village had tried, but they couldn't play like my dad. The Laird, and Mrs Farquharson, were both fond of him.[10]

Norma Sudworth's mother, Stella, would often come to Invercauld to carry out tasks for Frances, such as mending and adjusting her clothing, or upholstering the furniture. She remembers:

My mother used to do all sorts of things for Invercauld, painting and decorating, or repairing the soft furnishings when they were shabby. Mrs Farquharson used to buy lots of dresses from London, and my mum used to take them in for Mrs Farquharson, as she was very petite. During the school holidays, my mum would bring me to work with her, so I spent time in Marybelle's room, reading her books. Invercauld was incredibly awe-inspiring and it was very grand. But she and the laird were very nice people and very down-to-earth. Mrs Farquharson could be a forceful character, she had loads of personality and she liked to get her own way. But it was very good for Braemar.[11]

Norman would walk around the table twice, before performing in the passageway outside the room. He was then invited by the laird to share a Gaelic toast to good health over a dram of whisky. 'Sometimes the guests will ask him questions,' said Frances. 'If they're musical or interested in bagpipes he'll come back after we've had coffee in the drawing room and play up and down this passage.'

Marcia Brocklebank, who treasured her times in Scotland, would often attend dinners at Invercauld in the sixties and seventies, and was struck by the splendour of the occasions, which she was sure were designed by Frances to attract Americans:

Invercauld was baronial, and it was big, and I did get the impression that she, with Alwyne, ran it beautifully. All the flamboyant things, like being piped into dinner, and having the piper walk around the table, and you were seated at dinner, I knew perfectly well were her ideas. That's rather American, to love the pipes. I got the feeling that other people didn't love it, but I loved it. I adored it. Because he didn't just pipe you in, he then walked around the table a couple of times.

As a child, Norma sometimes came along to these dinners with her father, and because she was a Highland dancer, Frances would ask her to perform as

after-dinner entertainment. She danced the Highland fling in the Great Hall
in front of amused and charmed guests, while her father played the pipes as
an accompaniment. Norma says:

> They had a lot of money and she gave them a unique experience. There
> would be big ballgowns, and the piper piping them in, all the beautiful
> settings. The guests really enjoyed it and she was a very good hostess,
> she did it in style. It was mostly Americans who would come and visit,
> and she was very good in how she organised them.[12]

Virginia Safford travelled around the world to experience some of the most
fabulous dinners, and her time in Invercauld left a huge impression. She
wrote:

> Probably no place in all Scotland can exceed Invercauld in the elegance
> of cuisine. Mrs Farquharson cleverly works out the daily menus with
> Anna who is much of an artist in her kitchen as you'd find the masters
> of their paints in the Louvre.[13]

In great detail, Virginia described the exquisite dinners cooked by Anna that
she received during her stay. Salmon roe or red caviar as an appetiser, wood-
cock grilled over a birch wood fire, capercaillie stuffed with oatmeal, onions
and herbs and lightly roasted, grilled mountain hare and jellies from locally
sourced cranberries and loganberries.[14]

Virginia continued:

> White-gloved butlers placed a steaming hot borsch soup at our places,
> especially good because it was made from the stock of venison bones,
> A castle speciality, piroshkies – flaky pastry filled with bits of meat, or
> cheese and herbs – piping hot were very tasty with soup. Then we had
> grouse that had been brushed with olive oil and cooked quickly over a
> hot birch wood fire so it appeared almost black on the outside, yet was
> underdone and juicy red. A bread sauce went with the game as well as
> rowanberry jelly. Browned potatoes, greens, and a tossed salad were
> served. For dessert we had a creation – a mound of puff paste, glazed
> with sugar, centered with gobs of ice cream swirled in spun sugar. And
> with this went a hot foamy sauce. Strange as it seems, the lord and lady
> of the castle are slim as rails, yet they go on the theory that nothing is
> too good for their guests.[15]

As Marcia remembered:

> The dinners followed the general pattern. I think we left the men
> behind, after dinner, just for a little while, while they drank port, and
> the girls went into the drawing room and waited. Dinners were pretty
> formal, they followed a set pattern, and they were beautifully done. The
> butler drifted around and poured the wine. There was no wine on the
> table – the butler did that – and for food, I'm sure we had grouse. There
> was a wonderful game cellar at Invercauld.

Also arriving as a guest in 1957, a day after Virginia Safford said goodbye, was
the Maharani of Indore and her teenage son, Prince Richard Holkar. She was
an American-born socialite, also known as Lady Fay Holkar, who had married the Maharaja Yashwant Rao Holkar II in 1943.

Another American writer, from Cincinnati, was amazed at the names in
the guest book when looking through it during his visit. Dave Roberts, a
reporter for the *Cincinnati Enquirer*, who was visiting in August 1962, was
searching for any fellow Cincinnatians who had visited previously, when he
came across the names Elizabeth R, Philip and Margaret, handwritten in its
pages – and realised royalty had attended very recently.[16]

He had arrived at Invercauld on his return from a work trip to Moscow,
where he and his companions switched off from Cold War reportage to fish
for salmon and walk the moors, and where he found he was just one of several
visitors from Cincinnati:

> It was Cincinnati week at the great, grey stone castle, standing bold on
> a wooded benchland high above the river … None of us had met before
> – nor did we know the others would be there. The guest who arrives at
> Invercauld for the first time is struck, immediately, by the graciousness
> of the host and hostess and by the immensity of the lands they own.[17]

Sharing the table that week was Lemuel Boulware, vice president of General
Electric, and a New York lawyer, J. Franklin van Duren. Dave Roberts
described the dinner of salmon served on the finest china and the heaviest,
brightest silver, and sipping delicious wine in the 'great, candle-lit dining
room', where he 'estimated that some 50 guests could be seated and served
without being crowded'.[18]

The fabulous dinners at Invercauld were all about forging connections, and one of their guests, who had a home in the Bahamas, invited the

Farquharsons to visit her for their winter holidays. The American woman, who was incredibly rich and wore enormous diamonds, would come to Scotland on numerous occasions, and the large amount of money she, and the other guests, spent contributed to the cost of running Invercauld.

'The money raised helped to keep the roof on,' says Marybelle:

This was long before anyone dreamt of inviting paying guests to their homes, and in fact turned their noses up at it, as it was just not done. When people attended the shoots, they would send checks because she got a theatre going in Braemar, and a shop. Sometimes you would find these large checks left as a bookmark. Money came in, but she wasn't business-like in this sense – she wasn't money oriented as such.

As well as their days spent on the moors, the guests would visit the village, where they would make stops at Braemar Castle for a private tour, the Speciality Shop to buy soft-to-the-touch mohair, tweeds and tartans, and to the Galleries for paintings and hand-blown glass, brilliantly coloured pottery and antler and bone carvings. The money would also come into other businesses in the village as the guests would need to fill up their cars at the petrol station or buy items from the chemist.

As Norma Sudworth remembers:

The rich Americans came to the theatre and they bought things from the Speciality Shop, so they were spending money, and brought a lot of income into the village. Without these influences, it's unlikely the estate would have continued. She was very frugal, she was all about make do and mend, and it seemed like a very happy marriage.[19]

David Geddes remembered Frances' natural talent for selling the products in her shops, where she would easily flatter her guests into parting with their money. Whatever they were looking at or trying on, she told them it looked absolutely marvellous on them, that they simply had to have it as it would be a great reminder of their visit. These were the sales skills she had developed when working for the Cassini salon in Florence and Paul Caret in Paris and London, helping to encourage well-heeled customers to buy the latest fashions.

Marybelle was around 12 years old when Invercauld first opened up to paying guests in the early fifties, and growing up with the vast castle as her playground, she was actively involved in the house parties. 'I didn't know it was so unusual then. They would go out to dinner and leave me, aged fourteen, to host the dinner party. And of course, everyone was terribly kind to me.'

While Frances loved nothing more than a party, Marybelle was more introverted:

> I remember she said once to me, 'darling, I wish when we went to someone's house you'd say something to them'. And I said, 'but by the time you use every adjective that exists there's nothing for me to say, except to be a parrot.' Because always she saw the best, and I was left with nothing to say because it had been said.

Part of the appeal to guests at the parties was that they were meeting people from all parts of the world and were brought together by Frances' exuberance to share their experiences over dinner. They'd discuss the day's events, as well as their own lives back in the States, in the Middle East or in Europe. With people from completely different backgrounds sitting together at the table, it was, for Frances, a means for them to find common ground in a polarised world.

As an American in the Highlands, Frances wholly appreciated the romanticism of its history and traditions, and this, in turn, inspired her visitors. As she wrote, in a piece entitled 'Highland Hospitality' in the 1950s:

> It is the feudal, in its very best sense, atmosphere still surviving in the Highlands, in an otherwise highly industrial atomic age – which enchants our numerous visitors – for enchanted they certainly are, with the gay kilts, with the pipes, with the games, with our Scottish Festival of revived 18th century drawing room dances, as well as the country variety danced to the age old fiddlers' music by candlelight in the Invercauld Theatre.
>
> I cannot stress too strongly the genuine appreciation overseas guests express for the possibility of this opportunity of seeing and hearing typical Scottish artistry by entering into the life of the people of the community; of being in our big family atmosphere which embraces them one and all.

One good friend who often visited Invercauld, although not for the shooting parties, was the New York photographer, Toni Frissell. With Frances' encouragement she took a series of photographs that captured clan chieftains in their natural habitats – on the moors or posed by their mantelpieces in full regalia.

Another close friend who frequently came to Scotland to spend time with Frances was Moira Lister, the South African-born actress who had starred opposite Audrey Hepburn in one of her early London stage performances, and then worked with Ealing Studios and BBC Radio. She became Viscountess of Orthez following her marriage to the Belgian-French Jacques Gachassin-Lafite, the Vicomte d'Orthez.

Moira recalled that when Frances would walk into the room 'it would literally light up'. She was also struck by the daring outfits that Frances frequently wowed her guests with. 'If you ever wondered who wears the sort of clothes some designers model on the catwalk, well, that was Frances. She was the only person I knew who would wear those wild extravaganzas people like Schiaparelli designed.'

Not only did Frances wear Schiaparelli, but the two remained good friends, with the designer visiting Invercauld on a couple of occasions and undoubtedly taking an interest in the special fabrics that Frances had sourced. Like her contemporary, Coco Chanel, Schiaparelli was a champion of quality tweeds for her collections, and in the thirties, she often visited textile manufacturers across the country to source them locally. 'I became intensely interested in British textiles and visited all kinds of factories in England and Scotland,' she wrote in her autobiography, *A Shocking Life*. She described how a trip to the Isle of Skye in the 1930s, inspired by the frequent visits by the Duke and Duchess of York (later King George VI and Queen Elizabeth), remained 'vividly in my mind'.

It was here that she stayed with Duncan MacLeod at what she called 'Skibo Castle', but really meant Skeabost Castle, where she was delighted by the children in their 'gay kilts' and the 'striking tweeds' and 'beautiful tartans' in every colour – pink, periwinkle, grassy green – worn by the whole MacLeod family, over thirty of them, who entertained her for dinner. As well as being dazzled by their 'joy of living', she found them to be 'artisans', who taught her much about textiles. Schiaparelli was fascinated by her days spent at the mills, choosing the wide variety of colours and patterns and learning about the different herbs and plants that created the dyes.

During this trip to Skye in the thirties, Schiaparelli was invited to meet Dame Flora MacLeod at the MacLeod seat of Dunvegan Castle. The designer noted how the elderly matriarch was 'dressed in a large black bombazine dress and wore old Cairngorm brooches'. Flora MacLeod was known for her embracing of tartan, and following her influence, Schiaparelli was inspired to use tartan-patterned tweeds and Cairngorm clasps in her designs. For her autumn 1938 collection, Schiaparelli designed a robust tweed suit which featured a sporran, traditionally worn at the waist by Highlanders.

Decades later, she kept her affection for Scotland in her heart, and would visit Frances at Invercauld whenever she had the opportunity. By the time the designer was writing her memoirs, published in 1954, she was about to close her business, and perhaps, as she visited Frances in Scotland and saw all the wonderful textiles that were on display in the Invercauld Galleries, it helped spark her memories of those happy times in Scotland in the thirties.

Marybelle says:

Schiaparelli came to Invercauld to stay for a couple of nights. She was a very eccentric lady. She was very tiny. I was terrified of her. She wouldn't come to do shooting, or when other guests were here. She would visit my mother for a couple of days, and they would go walking, or visit the shops in the village.

Another fashionable friend who Frances invited to Invercauld was Irene Dana. She had been assistant to Edward Molyneux and Jeanne Paquin, before being hired to be 'directrice' at Schiaparelli in 1938 and by the 1950s she had launched her own fashion line, and regularly sketched bespoke gowns for Frances.[20] She was a frequent visitor to Invercauld, sourcing her fabrics from local mills, and Frances would champion her friend by wearing Irene Dana designs and encouraging her friends to do the same.

For the 1954 Braemar Festival, Frances invited Irene to showcase her creations as part of a French fashion show, one of the first of a series she would hold in the village. As a piece in the *Observer* on 18 July 1954 noted, 'Mlle Irene Dana, so well known in the couture world, will bring over from Paris to Braemar, as soon as the coming Paris collections end, models made there in local handwoven Scottish tweeds'.[21]

Chapter Twenty-One

American guests, used to their homes being equipped with thermostat-controlled central heating, had to adjust to the temperature of Invercauld, where a lack of central heating meant that every room could be chilly, with the exception of the kitchen, which was warmed by its stoves. Frances had by now become well accustomed to the castle's draughty stairways and would layer tweed jackets and skirts with Shetland wool and cashmere sweaters and cover her head with her signature bonnets. But she would worry about her guests and, to make them more comfortable, she placed electric heaters in every room and hot water bottles in their beds, and ensured fires were lit throughout the home. The cheery, homely décor also helped, so that those staying there hardly thought about it at all. As Virginia Safford wrote, following her visit in autumn 1957, 'There are great halls at Invercauld where at the moment you might find a slight chill. But the drawing room has its modern feeling for light fresh colors, old Chintz and Regency sofas.'[1]

It wasn't until a few years after King George VI died in 1952 that a decent hot water boiler was finally brought to Invercauld as a gift from the Queen Mother. She had asked if she could lease Invercauld while she was carrying out extensive renovations on her Highland home, Birkhall House. Frances recounted:

> They knew we were going to stay at Braemar Castle that year so she asked could she rent Invercauld and my husband said, 'You cannot rent it, ma'am, but we'd love to lend it to you'. She was very thrilled at this and came to me and said, 'Now I want to give you a present. What will we give you?' I said, 'Nothing at all.' She offered all sorts of lovely things and finally I said, 'I know what you can do, ma'am, you can give us a boiler for hot water because the one we've got is in a very

dicey state. At any moment it could completely collapse and it would be awkward for you if you had guests.' She was very amazed by this but pleased to do it. Ever after that whenever people tell us what staggering hot water they have, I say, 'Well, you must write a note to Queen Elizabeth. She is the one who provided it.'

Birkhall, located on the Balmoral Estate, is a stone-built lodge dating from 1715, which features beautiful gardens that look out over the River Muick. While the Queen Mother found it cramped and quiet in comparison with Balmoral, others considered Birkhall one of the warmest and most comfortable Highland retreats, where rooms were filled with the aroma of juniper and lavender twigs burning in the fireplaces. In 1955, Birkhall underwent extensive renovations to build a new wing, and while this work was being carried out, the Queen Mother moved into Invercauld.[2] She already leased the Corndavon Moor from the estate, and by living at the castle, she would be able to continue her Highland rituals of summer shooting parties and fishing on the River Dee.

'The Queen Mother moved into Invercauld, and lived there in great style,' remembers Marybelle:

> She invited me to dinner, even though I was very young, and we sat in the middle of the table, not at the end, with me sitting opposite her. It was such an honour that I adored her from then on. She was the most remarkable woman.

★ ★ ★

While the Queen Mother was at Invercauld, the Farquharsons moved into Braemar Castle, which was a very different experience. With its narrow, winding staircase and turrets, it was the sort of place imagined in the most romanticised of Scottish history. The castle's construction included a round central tower with a spiral staircase, barrel-vaulted ceilings and a massive iron lattice gate, or 'Yett', to be drawn to keep enemies out. Its unusual and distinctive features included an ominous underground prison, with the narrow entrance a bar-covered drop through the stone floor, and its eighteenth-century, star-shaped defensive curtain wall, which reflected its history as a garrison.

The original construction, the tower and staircase, was built in 1628 by John Erskine, 18th Earl of Mar, primarily as a means of keeping a watchful eye on the Farquharsons, as he considered them to be becoming too powerful in the region. This tower was described by a contemporary as a 'great body of a house, a jam and a staircase',[3] and it also proved to be a convenient hunting lodge as it was close to Braemar's thick forests which teemed with deer.

The Earl of Mar was a supporter of the Protestant King William III, while the Farquharsons were Jacobites determined to see the Catholic Stuarts reclaim the throne. In 1689, Braemar Castle was attacked and burned down by John Farquharson of Inverey and Balmoral, so that he could prevent it falling into the hands of government troops. Also known as the Black Colonel, he was a ferocious figure, who was said to have been in the habit of summoning his servants by firing a pistol.

After its destruction, Braemar was slowly rebuilt, and in 1732, John Farquharson, the 9th Laird of Invercauld, acquired it. When the Jacobites were defeated at the Battle of Culloden, the laird leased it to the government, doing exactly what the Black Colonel had been desperate to prevent. In 1748 it was restored by John Adam, brother of the renowned architect Robert Adam, and it was further used as a barracks to house government troops.

By the time Queen Victoria first visited Deeside, Braemar was still a garrison, but a few years later, the 12th Laird of Invercauld transformed it back into a family home. From then on, Braemar was often rented out to a cast of colourful characters.

In 1897, it was home to another Frances – a British woman who had become a Russian princess through marriage. Frances (Fanny) Fleetwood Wilson, the daughter of a wealthy industrialist, was one of the moneyed Marlborough set, the group of extravagant friends of Edward, Prince of Wales (later King Edward VII). In 1898, at the age of 50, she married an exiled prince, Alexis Dolgorouki, and divided her time between living lavishly in Mayfair and spending tranquil summers in Deeside, when she leased Braemar for the next twenty-five years.[4]

Another tenant was Marie Corelli, the Italian novelist and daughter of Scottish poet, Dr Charles Mackay, who wrote some of her books while renting the castle. In 1902, she wrote to the editor of *The Gentlewoman* complaining that her name had not been included in a list of guests who had attended the Braemar Gathering that year. In response, she was informed by the editor the omission had been intentional, due to the derogatory comments she had made about those who appeared in puff-pieces about society events.

In recent years, Braemar had been rented to Lord Tweedsmuir, son of the novelist John Buchan, and his wife, Lady Tweedsmuir, Conservative MP for South Aberdeen, following their marriage in 1948.[5] When the Tweedsmuirs moved into their own home in Balmedie in 1952, Alwyne had advertised for new tenants, but with the Queen Mother temporarily at Invercauld in 1955, he and Frances chose to live in Braemar themselves for the first time.

With its narrow, winding stone staircase leading to the different rooms on many different levels, Braemar was cosier than Invercauld, yet it could also be freezing over winter. 'Braemar Castle was very charming, but it had low doors, and I had a headache from ducking to get under,' Marybelle recalled of her time spent at Braemar:

> The windows leaked like sieves, and the ceilings were so low I often hit my head. Mummy took it in her stride, 'I'll just climb the rocks', she said going up the stairs. The fires were lovely but it was very cold, and we had snowdrifts blowing inside. I decided the Christmas I was there, to give everyone thermometers.

In anticipation of temporarily moving into the smaller castle, Braemar became a renovation project for Frances in 1955, and she gave it a makeover in her own inimitable style. Braemar's exterior was of thick granite coated in rough grey harl, and in the outside courtyard, which connected to the kitchens, was an old cheese press, a hollowed tree trunk with a mortar and pestle and a mountain ash to ward off witches as stipulated by the local folk traditions.

The ground floor reflected its former use as a garrison. Its stone-vaulted rooms, once used to house ammunition, were now home to a collection of stuffed trophies, a seventeenth-century French gun and an oil-burning lamp that had been used to light the courtyard. Its upper floors were quite different, revealing its cultivated history as an Edwardian family home. Frances used her eye for interior design to lift and enhance these rooms with liberal splashes of paint and new curtains, while ensuring she preserved the period characteristics.

She painted the walls of some of these rooms in either pink or yellow, her favourite colours, which had been used to effect in Invercauld, on the mural in the theatre and on the outside of the Speciality Shop. When she suggested to Alwyne that they should colour the outside of the castle pink, it was perhaps one step too far and, on this occasion, he didn't let her convince him otherwise.[6]

'All I did was paint it,' she said simply, when asked about the transformation. But the daffodil yellow morning rooms, candy pink bathrooms and tomato red dining room gave the entire castle a lift and looked charming with the antique furniture. The drawing room was particularly vibrant with its pink walls, chintz curtains and candy-striped furniture. When she entertained her visitors in the morning room, they would be immediately cheered by the yellow décor, as they enjoyed afternoon tea served with napkins woven in Farquharson tartan.

Every room was filled with interesting pieces of furniture that quietly told the story of the residents who had come before. The dining room held a Robert-Adam-designed sideboard and a 1799 grandfather clock designed by John Gartley of Aberdeen. The drawing room was filled with French and Dutch furniture collected by Alwyne's grandmother, Persian rugs dating to 1800, a painting of Braemar by Gustave Doré to mark his visit in 1873, and in the shutters, the engraved names of the soldiers who had been garrisoned there in the eighteenth century. The bedroom on the third floor featured an eighteenth-century four-poster bed, a Queen Anne tallboy and a Hepplewhite chair covered with deerskin from the Invercauld Estate.

Frances was a woman who was always on the move, and she threw herself into the transformation of Braemar. She may have now been in her mid-fifties, but she still possessed the energy of a woman two decades younger. 'She never stopped moving,' Marybelle recalls. 'When we moved from Invercauld to Braemar, there was so much to do. I collapsed, but she had so much energy, even with the broken spine.'

After spending a year at Braemar, they moved back to Invercauld and the smaller castle was rented out once more. One of the famous figures who leased it as a holiday home was controversial politician John Profumo and his actress wife, Valerie Hobson, a good friend of Frances'. The Profumos were staying there with their friends, Lord and Lady Balfour of Inchrye, in September 1960, when a fire broke out in the kitchen. The flames spread to one of the bedrooms, but luckily the fire brigade was able to bring it under control. It was a near miss, as it could easily have destroyed so much history, and it must have been a stark reminder to Frances of the fire that she had survived twenty-seven years before.[7]

By 1961, given the increase in tourism to the area and the number of visitors who were fascinated by the sight of the intriguing castle on the edge of the village, Frances decided to open Braemar to the public. 'I was always showing people over it and running back and fore and in the end I said to my husband we were going to have to open it up to the public,' she said.

Frances worked tirelessly to transform the castle into a place that would appeal to visitors who were looking for an authentic Scottish experience. The castle revealed both the rambunctious side of Highland history, with its battlements and dungeon, and its elegance, with the Edwardian furniture inside the turreted rooms. She rummaged through the attics and cellars to find items that had been hidden for centuries, bringing out artefacts which she felt would make interesting exhibition pieces. She put on display a piece of plaid that was given to Prince Charles Edward Stuart by 'Colonel Anne', Lady Mackintosh of Mackintosh, a medal belonging to the prince that commemorated his 1745 adventures and precious stones found in the area, including the world's largest cairngorm.

'We are very pleased with the number of visitors, and they all seemed to enjoy seeing the castle,' she told an Aberdeen reporter, soon after opening to the public:

> Of course, we've often shown friends round, and we're trying to keep everything as unorganised as possible – just as it used to be. I find people are always surprised how comfortable and homely the castle is inside, from the outside it does look rather bleak![8]

She elicited Charles Barron, a dramatist in Aberdeen, to write a history of the castle and put on a *son-et-lumière* performance, which was a type of sound and light show that had become fashionable in France. The world's first show, at the Château de Chambord in the Loire Valley, had only taken place in 1952, and so Frances was, once again, ahead of the curve. It ran every autumn for many years and, despite the unpredictable weather and the blight of midges, the castle came to life as it glowed with lights and a narrative told stories from its past.

It was one of several innovations Frances continued to bring to Braemar. The arts festival was still going strong in the sixties, and for the 1964 event, she encouraged Charles Barron to write an original play on the 1715 Jacobite Rebellion, which he called *The Earl of Mar*. It was performed over four nights at the Invercauld Theatre and Frances invited Barron, his actress wife, Margot, and the crew and performers to stay at Braemar Castle for the duration of the festival.[9]

With the royal family spending their summers in Royal Deeside, the Farquharsons were often invited to some of the social events, including the famous Ghillies Ball at Balmoral, a tradition begun by Queen Victoria and Prince Albert in 1852 to thank their staff for their hard work during their spell there. Queen Elizabeth II considered it one of the highlights of her calendar, and it was where the family celebrated the season by dancing eight-some reels with their estate staff, neighbours like the Farquharsons and the local community.

Ladies traditionally wore a tartan sash over their gowns (with the queen wearing the Royal Stuart tartan) and gentlemen donned black ties and kilts. It was here, in the late fifties, that Frances made a spectacular entrance in her extravagant tartan harem pants and turban, which had been custom-made by Aberdeen's Christie & Gregor. There would also be informal dinners each year with the royal family, either at Invercauld, Balmoral or Birkhall. As part of the 1957 season, for example, the Farquharsons were invited to attend the Queen Mother and Princess Margaret's party at Birkhall.

Frances and Alwyne would spend their summer and autumn at Invercauld, when they hosted the shooting parties, and over winter, when Royal Deeside was one of the coldest places in Scotland, they typically escaped the chill by travelling to warmer climates. Marybelle says:

> They'd go in the freezing winter when you couldn't get out of the house sometimes because of the snow drifts. But equally if they stayed there, she'd be covered in furs, going out for a walk in the garden.

Frances explained:

> We have between 20 and 30 people to stay at a time during the summer months and around 44 to dinner for the Braemar Games. We never go out to dinner except to Balmoral and Birkhall. We have a flat in London which we go to in the winter and spring. Fresh food from Invercauld is sent down once a week by train and I like to have the friends I don't see in Scotland to dinner.

They would spend several weeks in London each year, staying in their flat in Belgravia's Lowndes Square, because, she said, 'One is inclined to become too involved with one's own small world in Scotland'.

When she travelled down south to London or Newby Hall, Alwyne's family home, she would be armed with samples of wool and tartan to promote the local fabrics in any way she could. However, textiles weren't the only things that she exported from Invercauld. Game and salmon were transported to London to be served at their dinner parties, and Alwyne's father (his mother, Sylvia, died in 1950) at Newby Hall also received bountiful supplies. Betty Thornton, the cook there, described how the kitchen was endowed with grouse and venison from Invercauld, and the salmon would arrive in plaited fish baskets, because 'we were expected to be very self-sufficient'.[10] Frances' influence had rubbed off on the Comptons in more ways than one; by the 1960s, they had followed the example of other estates by opening Newby Hall to paying guests.

The Farquharsons shared a mutual love of travel, regularly going on exotic trips overseas, visiting friends in the United States or to Barbados. In 1962,

Alwyne bought a 1956 two-tone grey 'S' series Bentley, of which there were only 100 made, and which he would still be driving with care well into the 1980s.[11] They would pile their suitcases into the car and drive off on European road trips, taking in the sights as they whizzed along country roads with the top down. Their travels would take them through Germany, France, Italy and Spain, as they visited some of the places Frances had experienced as an adventurous twenty-something. They took the car ferry across the Gibraltar Strait to Tangiers, and in these trips to Spain and Morocco, or further afield to Mexico, Frances would pick up embroidered peasant tops, turquoise necklaces and espadrilles to add to her dressing-up box.

Frances may have taken to the skies with her first husband, but as she got older, she would find flying more terrifying, preferring to travel by land and sea where possible. As a teenager, Marybelle would sometimes go on these trips across the Continent.[12] 'She would drive the Bentley with an open top, and it was piled high with their luggage,' remembers Marybelle. 'By the time all the luggage was in, you couldn't see out of the car or see any of the views.'

★ ★ ★

For her first several years at Invercauld, Marybelle attended the local school and each morning cycled down the driveway, leaving her bike by the gates and catching the school bus into the village. Later, she was sent to boarding school in England, but in comparison to her life at Invercauld and the extensive open space that she could explore, she felt claustrophobic from being cooped up. Instead, she was given the opportunity to go to school in Switzerland, to study art in Florence and to spend time learning languages in Italy and Spain, where she stayed with friends of her mother in places like Rome and Turin.

In June 1961, Marybelle married the Hon. James Reginald Drummond, younger son of the Earl and Countess of Perth of Stobhall, Perthshire. As the son and stepdaughter of two of Scotland's clan chiefs, Drummond and Farquharson, it was hailed in the papers as 'Deeside's wedding of the year'.

After a ceremony at St Andrew's Church, Braemar, Marybelle, wearing a French white silk wedding dress, was piped from the church to a tune composed by Norman Meldrum – 'Miss Marybelle Gordon's Wedding March'.[13] The reception was held at Invercauld, and for Marybelle, it was a bittersweet moment to say goodbye to the place that had meant so much to her.

Chapter Twenty-Two

Royal Deeside was placed in the spotlight in August 1959, when President Eisenhower became the first American president to be entertained at Balmoral. His visit was marked by its informality, with the queen cooking drop scones, and barbecuing on the hillside, and he enjoyed drinks with the Queen Mother at Birkhall. The international headlines brought further attention to the region, with overseas visitors flocking to the moors to experience its charms for themselves.

The *Detroit Free Press* in August 1963 announced that 'The "in" place in August this year has shifted from the hot stretches of the Riviera, on the Continent, to the cool purple and gold reaches of Scotland'.[1] The article attributed the surge of interest to both the 1963 marriage of Princess Alexandra of Kent to Angus Ogilvy, who honeymooned at Balmoral, and to the 'glamorous, American-born Frances Farquharson'. It was in the Highlands that the smart set, they wrote, dressed in 'family tartans for the men, and plaid sashes below Rene hairdos for the girls', danced both 'lively Scottish reels and the Bossa Nova at hunt balls'.[2]

Just as she drove innovations on the estate, Frances led with exquisite style, always with an eye for bold new things to wear but keeping old favourites close to her. The polar bear coat that she had designed for her trade mission visit to New York in 1941 had come with her to Invercauld. It was known to have terrified unsuspecting workmen on the occasions that she wore it around the house.

'She just had an eye for fashion,' says Marybelle:

I never forgot, but I was about fifteen and she suddenly turned up in a tight skirt with slits up the side and the bottom was fringed. Well it looked like nothing on this earth to me, and it looked like a piece of old material that she'd found somewhere. I said, 'Mummy, you can't wear that,' and the next thing it was in fashion. That's how she was.

As well as throwing together vivid pinks, greens and yellows, or wearing a bright Farquharson tartan suit, she could still fit into many of the clothes she owned in the thirties, because she remained the same size throughout her life. Partly, this was down to the care she took over what she ate. She liked simple, good ingredients, and she never went on diets, choosing to indulge when appropriate, but otherwise sticking to healthy meals. She liked to eat wholesome food, insisting on homemade brown bread each day, vegetables that were cooked al dente and pearl barley water served at each meal.

Her friend Marcia Brocklebank remembers her wearing enormous tam-o'-shanters on her head which, she said, almost 'swamped her':

> It was put on her head on an angle, it was huge. It seemed to be half way across her shoulder. I believe she wore long skirts, she certainly didn't wear trousers. She wore capes. She was very sweet to me, because we went to buy some cardigans from her shop, and one was a Fair Isle design, and I liked that very much. I've still got it actually. And I remember, I said, 'I don't know whether to get this one', which was a normal length, or a long one, and she said, 'oh, you get the long one, because it makes you look thinner, and it hides your hips', so I got that one. And it survived all these years. Beautifully made. She really was a galvanising influence in the community, and her greatest strength was her positive attitude. She was a flamboyant, positive, charming, perceptive human being. She was very small, so she buzzed around, and was very dynamic. She was clever and smart.

She may have turned 60 in November 1962, but Frances always chose to defy her age. She was a believer that you are only as old as you feel and could connect easily with young people who found her to be such a bright spark. Someone described her flow of talk as being like a 'happy stream', and she often became close to the friends her daughter brought to Invercauld, who were awed by her vivacity, her wisdom and the way she encouraged them in their lives.

One of these visitors was Hugh Cantlie, who was formerly in the Scot's Guards. He remembers:

She was the most remarkable woman. Years ago in my young days in the army, I was friends with Marybelle and stayed at Invercauld. Frances was full of energy, full of ideas, full of drive, and she kept it up all the time. If you had a problem she was the first person you would go to. She was someone you felt at ease with, and when we spoke over dinner, she was obviously interested in what I had to say.[3]

She always liked to encourage people to do the things they were good at and passionate about, and when she found out that Hugh wished to be a writer, with a strong interest and knowledge of conserving historic buildings, she helped him realise the possibilities:

One of the times I was staying there, and she said, 'by the way I want you to write an article for [the magazine] Country Life on Braemar Castle. You will do it.' So I duly did it, and I went to see the editor, Ricky Compton, who was the Laird's nephew, and he was rather impressed with it, so I wrote another six articles.[4]

These pieces would later form a book, *Ancestral Castles of Scotland*, and Hugh went on to deliver lectures on these subjects, all thanks to Frances' positive encouragement.

What struck Hugh on his visits to Invercauld was the comfortable, lived-in feel of it:

There were geraniums on the windowsill, and it was really a family home. I didn't have grand dinners, rather we ate in the tartan room. She always seemed to have tartan around her. I think she felt like Scotland needed a bit of propping up and she was proud of being a Scot.[5]

Marcia Brocklebank was, like Frances, an American woman who had married a British man. The art historian moved to Sussex after marrying banker Charles Brocklebank, and they lived together in Giffords Hall, built in 1520 in the same style as Hampton Court. Marcia first met Frances through the Earl of Perth, Marybelle's father-in-law. 'The Earl of Perth's wife, Nancy, was an east coast American, from New York,' she says. 'And they were both very good friends of mine. They introduced me to Marybelle around 1962, when I wasn't married at this point.'

When Marcia came to Invercauld with Marybelle, she was immediately impressed by her mother, and the two struck up a close friendship. She spent many happy times at Invercauld, where she enjoyed being entertained by Frances and Alwyne. 'They were very much in love, despite the huge age difference,' she says:

> She didn't seem a lot older, although she was. I remember Alwyne was very congenial, and welcoming and very much the important senior, but in a gentle way. So they were wonderful foils to each other, because there she was being colourful and flamboyant, and he was this sensitive man, this very kind and gentle man. He was lovely.

Throughout the sixties and seventies, Frances continued to organise the Braemar Highland Festival every August and September, with a programme of new drama performances, music and dance. As well as the original plays by writers like Charles Barron, there were Highland flings led by Bobby Watson, Anne MacDearmid and Iain MacSween performing island and cradle songs, and ceilidhs and concerts of singing, fiddling, piping and dancing.[6]

In 1964, Frances made sure she highlighted to the local paper some of the fascinating things at the galleries that year, such as quality tweeds, mosaics 'to rival Italian works', and handwoven black sheep's wool tweed. One of the artists she championed was Colin Scott, from Dundee, who specialised in wood carvings of birds. When he visited Braemar in the early sixties to show his wood carvings to Frances at the Speciality Shop, she was quick to offer her encouragement. She arranged for him to stay at Braemar, while he used the workshop of a local joiner, and gave him a challenge to carve all the birds and animals found in the local area. They were then put on display in the galleries, and it was reported that she even took his carvings to the Queen's Garden Party in Edinburgh, to drum up more business for him.

'She puts tremendous efforts each year into projecting Scottish craft and culture to the tourists from all over the world,' wrote the *Aberdeen Press and Journal*:

> The tourist season in Braemar owes much to the laird's American wife, whose publicity background and dynamic drive makes her persistently to seek out and project the potential in the culture and crafts of the area … She is the 'impresario of the Invercauld Festival' and there are many small tourist resorts which must envy Braemar her zeal.[7]

In 1974, Frances invited the Aberdeen artist Eric Auld and his wife for dinner at Invercauld, and she asked him if he would create some artworks to be included in an exhibition in Invercauld Galleries featuring paintings and photographs of Deeside. She wrote a letter to him afterwards, in her big, looped handwriting, inviting him on a visit to the hills, where he could find the best views for painting and sketch some of the ghillies and gamekeepers:

> If it could include a really great picture of Invercauld itself, it would be marvellous as so many of our guests either want a painting or photograph of a painting to take away with them. As you know, all Keepers appear to be great characters and their stances, their clothes, their sticks and all the paraphernalia which goes with hill management seems to impress people from other countries.[8]

For an edition of *Tatler* in August 1965, which profiled life on the Invercauld Estate, Alwyne, who posed in the library in kilt, sporran and tweed jacket, said he was 'more Scots than most of the people hereabouts'. The article featured photographs of some of the workers on the land, including the chief gamekeeper, Donald McDonald, chief shepherd, Donald Campbell, who protected the black-faced sheep from birds of prey and wild cats, George Collie, in charge of forestry, and factor Derek Petrie, who was considered the laird's right-hand man.[9]

Frances described Deeside as:

> … like a huge family. I feel my husband belongs here. So I belong here. I fell in love with the place as everyone does. The people are so warm, so loyal and willing and content. They don't want to go abroad. They say they have the best here, why should they? Even though now I have travelled a great deal, I think there is nowhere on earth so beautiful and impressive. I think everyone in Scotland will say that it has a kind of allure for anybody who has one drop of Scottish blood.[10]

She adored championing the region's culture, and her Scottish Festival in Braemar continued to be a space for Scottish artists. Ahead of the 1967 festival, she wrote to the Oklahoma-based editor of the *Highlander*, Colonel Cliff MacLean Hansen, who was an occasional guest at Invercauld, to promote that year's plays and performers:

I have set my policy, and kept to it, of having everything Scottish. It seems to me there is no point of having a festival in the Highlands of plays and other performances coming from all over the world when audiences can see these things under other circumstances in the capitols of Europe and America.

She was particularly proud that year of the production of Charles Barron's especially written play, *Colonel Anne*, which told the story of the Jacobite heroine who rode on horseback with double pistols and protected Bonnie Prince Charlie at Moy Hall. It was the type of story, she knew, that would warm the blood of those Americans with Highland ancestry. 'These stirring Jacobite times always provide lovely music, haunting melodies and exciting incidents,' she wrote.[11]

Working for the estate as electrician, David Geddes was often recruited to pick up the important visitors from Prestwick Airport. A frequent guest in the late sixties and seventies was Willard Rockwell, founder of Rockwell International, integral to the American space programme, and his vice president, Frank Gard Jameson Sr. As David Geddes remembers, Jameson flew into Prestwick Airport on his own jet, bringing his accountant with him, as he preferred not to deal with money himself.

David was there to collect him and the many guests he brought with him. In the late seventies, he brought his wife, actress Eva Gabor, and another year, John Connally, the 39th Governor of Texas. Governor Connally gave a rattlesnake's tail as a gift to one of the secretaries of the Braemar Gathering, with the advice to shake the tail if the weather conditions for the day looked poor, as tradition stipulated that it would bring on the sunshine.[12]

Frances continued to build the reputation of Invercauld, with week-long parties and magical dinners that were steeped in Scottish tradition. As well as attracting some of the wealthiest people in America, guests included Jordanian and Lebanese families and groups of Scandinavians. Frances recounted the story of a grand group of Swedes who came to stay for a week, expensively dressed in jewels and Savile Row suits. Yet she struggled to work out who was married to whom, and later discovered that they took turns to share different beds. As she told Joy Billington at the *Washington Post*, 'They were all married but they all swapped about. I had a Swedish friend and she said to me, "Darling, you are so ingénue, it's incredible. I've told you for years what goes on in Sweden".'

Another of their guests was Joe Peeler, a renowned Los Angeles tax attorney, and his wife Elizabeth, who visited Invercauld in 1973 as part of an extensive motoring trip around Scotland. Joe had been, with his firm Peeler & Wilson, personal adviser to J. Paul Getty, overseeing his holdings including the Getty Estate and the Getty Trust. After staying with their friends, the Earl and Countess of Glasgow at Kelburn Castle on the west coast, they travelled north to Deeside for grouse shooting.[13]

In December 1977, *Town and Country* magazine profiled the best sporting estates in Scotland to visit for fishing. The author, Suzanne Wilding, highlighted Invercauld as the leading 'secret' destination for guests from the States, and named Mr and Mrs Farquharson as the best hosts, and Frances as 'a housekeeper par excellence'. Some sporting estates, she said, 'advertise widely, but be wary of the written word; if the fishing is inexpensive, it is sure to be no good'. She said that the Farquharsons, on the other hand, 'have never advertised – word of mouth recommendation has been more than enough'. One guest, a Mrs Sheffield Phelps from Seattle, had heard of her hometown's Francie Farquharson and travelled to Scotland in 1970 with a group of fourteen to celebrate her husband's fiftieth birthday. As Thora Qaddumi wrote in an article in the *Seattle Post Intelligencer*, 'Mrs Farquharson is remembered by several Seattleites who went to school with her here. They can't help but speak with a touch of awe about the Seattle woman who married a Laird.'

The article in *Town and Country* made special mention of Norman Meldrum and his pipes, highlighting how his 'strange, eerie music reverberates around the table, you can almost retreat in time to when Invercauld was a keep and the Farquharsons were busy fighting the neighbourhood clans'.[14] Wilding described Invercauld as having 'typically Highland interiors', with:

> … graceful furniture in the reception rooms and antlered heads of Scottish red deer looking down on miles of tartan-carpeted hallways. Over the years the bedrooms have been refurbished and the 16th century has been combined with the 20th. As the Farquharsons proudly explain, 'We try to make the past live today.'[15]

The past was an important part of the promotion of Invercauld, and Alwyne was constantly busy with Farquharsons dropping in from around the world. He told Hugh Mulligan, in a widely syndicated article to American newspapers across the country, that 'in summer we get Farquharsons from all over – Canada, New Zealand, America. People do like to visit the old family home, see where it all happened and pose for snaps with the clan chief.'[16]

Chapter Twenty-Three

Over the years, Alwyne Farquharson had developed a reputation as a thoughtful and kind landowner who dressed, and acted, the part of a Highland chief. As a laird who was actively involved in the farming on the estate, Alwyne was proud of his fold of Highland cattle which had won numerous prizes, but he was also conscious of the future of Invercauld and preserving its history, as hidden treasures were often uncovered in unexplored parts of the house.

When they found a work of art by Panini, he was depressed to find that similar pieces were kept in storage in the National Galleries. 'One is always worried,' he said, 'that if you push off these things to the Record Office, they simply get buried amongst the mass of other material.'[1] They kept some of the key finds on display in glass-fronted cabinets, such as the small box given to the Farquharsons by Mary, Queen of Scots, and weapons that were used in battle as a marker of Scotland's turbulent history.

He secretly hoped, when uranium prospectors were exploring upper Deeside, that they would go home empty handed as he didn't like the thought of the land being plundered. 'It's right and nice that the Scots themselves should have a say in the running of their country. There has to be some form of control over speculation in land,' he said:

I'm a bit conservative by nature. We are very limited in the kinds of things we can do here. We already have skiing and hang-gliding, maybe there'll be a caravan site before long, But there are so few really wild parts of countryside left in Europe that it would be a tragedy to turn this into some kind of Blackpool.[2]

The untamed beauty of the region and Frances' presence at Invercauld was endlessly fascinating, and so there were new opportunities to feature on television.

In 1975, they appeared on a programme for Thames TV called *A Place in Europe*, which focused on Braemar Castle, and spoke of the castle's chequered history.[3]

There had been another television programme made with them in the 1960s. Former US Air Force chief-of-staff, General Curtis LeMay was filmed shooting grouse at Invercauld in 1966 for a hunting and fishing series, *The American Sportsman*.[4]

Marcia Brocklebank remembers a time when Frances and Alwyne came to stay in her home in Suffolk for the weekend:

> We had a wonderful time, because we went to an island off the Suffolk coast, where a man was giving an oyster lunch, and was being photo-graphed for the BBC, and of course she just loved that, and came into her own, in this situation. And it was a surprise, because we knew we'd been invited to this island, and had to go out in a boat, and had to be carried in on the fisherman's shoulder, because it was low tide, but we didn't know that it was all going to be on BBC. She was very good at that.

Frances continued entertaining at Invercauld, while also running the theatre, the Galleries and the Speciality Shop alongside new businesses, including an antique shop, which opened in 1973, and a men's clothing shop. She was so busy that she was grateful for the help from young friends of the family. In the seventies and eighties, the three teenage daughters of Cherry, the 16th Baroness Strange, who lived at Megginch Castle in Kinross, were recruited to help at Invercauld and assist with the various businesses that Frances was running. They absolutely adored the wise and fascinating Frances, who perhaps thought of the older women who treated her with such kindness when she first arrived in Europe in the twenties.

'When I married, she didn't realise what I did for these great house parties, so a friend of hers sent someone to replace me,' says Marybelle:

> She was tremendously conscious of helping people. My stepfather would remember how young people would come to her and they were dying to do something for her, and she did everything in her power to give them a chance to do that. She was very interested in the young and doing things for them.

Firstly, Charlotte Drummond, the elder sister, helped out at Invercauld. 'She was a wonderful person, a great friend, and immeasurably kind to me,' she remembers. 'I loved my times spent at Invercauld, and worked there for several summers in the seventies.' After she left, the youngest daughter, Catherine Drummond-Herdman, then took over. Catherine remembered with fondness her time as Frances' assistant at Invercauld for several summers and autumns, when the castle was filled with visitors and family members, and where Frances was an effortless host and entertainer. She says:

Francie was indeed the most amazing, progressive and stylish woman. She was also brave and uncomplaining, spirited and witty. When I knew her, she was older and yet retained all these characteristics. She had an enquiring mind and was an incredibly gracious, thoughtful, diplomatic and welcoming hostess.

It was a little bit scary for a 17-year-old, but what an exceptional role model she was to me, of what you can achieve. Her handwriting was hugely flamboyant and covered the pages in confident black felt tipped writing pens, when you were lucky enough to receive a letter from her, there was no mistaking who was writing to you!

We had many fun hours organising a show in the Festival theatre in Braemar as well. She led on the character for the Braemar games, always appearing swathed in Farquharson tartan and she had this glorious tartan tam-o'-shanter to finish off her outfit. Her favourite colour was pink and she had all the doors, most of the buildings and many of the rooms at Invercauld painted this wonderful cheery shade of pink.

She was very elegant and I treasure the happy times spent chatting over the tea tray which consisted of freshly picked and brewed lime flowers and melt-in-the-mouth shortbread, or Keith's famous Lemon Drizzle cake – I can taste it even now! The china was delicate to match the tea, the steam from the freshly-poured tea rose up as the sun came in through the windows, either the Tartan Room if it was a bit cold, or the drawing room with its stylish pink striped furniture. You could look across the lawn, to the foaming and tumbling River Dee and up to the majestic, heather-covered purple mountains, where in the autumn the stags roared – and in fact they came down into the woods quite close to the castle. She was an inspirational woman who I still look back upon for guidance all these years later.

In 1977 Alwyne's father, Edward Compton, died and he left Torloisk House, on Mull, to his son. The grand Scots Baronial home, located on the isolated north-west of the island, was where his mother, Sylvia, stayed during the war. Here, as she fretted about the fate of her two sons, both fighting overseas, she took solace in making tapestries and by gazing at the incredible sea views from across their rolling lawn, where the white sands of Muick were just visible.

The house had passed to the Compton family following the 1814 marriage of Spencer Compton, 2nd Marquess of Northampton, to Margaret Douglas Maclean Clephane – a match secured by her godfather, Sir Walter Scott.

The house, with its bay windows and turrets, and set in an isolated corner of the island, was a favourite retreat of Frances, where she found that the idyllic sea views and the huge gardens with beech trees reminded her of her childhood in the Pacific Northwest. The ten-bedroom home dated back to 1770, but had been extended and renovated over the years. She redecorated it to her tastes, introducing her favourite colours and filling the rooms with antique furniture mixed together from different time periods.

Rather than travelling abroad, such as going to Mexico, as they had done in the 1970s, and which had inspired some of her fashions, Mull would now be their preferred place to visit, where there was much work needed to revitalise the house. She found it incredibly peaceful; she could walk in the gardens when it was sunny, enjoying the woodland that had been planned out by Sir Walter Scott in the 1800s. One of Frances' favourite rooms was the Chinese boudoir, a cosy sitting room with the walls covered in wooden panels that had been salvaged from a nearby shipwreck. Sitting in the bay window of the drawing room, wood crackling on the fire, she could see the islands of Gometra, Ulva and Islay in the distance.

As she told a reporter:

> Mull is slightly warmer, but much damper. It's built on peat, whereas Braemar and Invercauld are built on granite. It sits high over the sea in the west of Mull. I love it because it's very 'manana' there, almost Spanish. Nobody worries about anything ... Alwyne's family have always been there, and when you arrive they're always so smiling and welcoming.

The Braemar Gathering had once been described as 'one of the greatest shows on earth', and it made international headlines in 1981 with the first appearance of Princess Diana, following her fairy-tale wedding to Prince Charles. The newlyweds spent most of their honeymoon at Balmoral, and on 5 September, Diana stepped into the Royal Pavilion to watch the games for the first time. The crowds watched her with fascination, snapping pictures with their cameras of the princess wearing a maroon tartan wool dress by Caroline Charles, with a black Glengarry style bonnet.

While she received wide praise for her adoption of tartan when in Scotland, Diana was really following in the footsteps of Frances. It was Frances who had, since the late forties, been the forerunner of wearing Scottish textiles in novel ways. In footage from the event, Frances can be seen in a bright Farquharson tartan suit and a large red bonnet with black pom-pom on her head, as she curtsies and shakes hands with Diana and is greeted warmly by Prince Charles with a kiss on the cheek. She had been using the Games to bolster the tartan industry for years, and even into her seventies and eighties, she saw no reason to tone down her sense of style. Her capes still swept the ground and enveloped her, and her bonnets were big and bold, bobbing with every move.

Norma Sudworth's memories of Frances at this time were of her eye-catching sense of style, which made her appear larger than life:

She was the centre of attention, in a nice way. She was flamboyant in her character and in her dress, and she was a very attractive woman. She used to wear stockings with her Farquharson tartan. Great big mohair bonnets in red, green and gold, and she would wear it with her Farquharson tartan cloak, which she would swan about wearing. She was quite a sight, flapping about in her cape, bonnet and stockings.[5]

As she got older, Frances swapped her heels for flat shoes with thick tights or ankle socks to keep warm. She was suffering from problems with her kidneys, which impacted on her circulation, and the pain in her back became more pronounced. Yet she never revealed her discomfort to others. She thrived as a host of parties and entertainments, and there was so much she wanted to achieve in Braemar. She still had the sparkle in her eyes that defied her age, but she was also coming to terms with her body being unable to do the things it used to, and she was tiring out more quickly than before.

'She was in pain every day of her life,' says Marybelle:

She never complained, and some days were worse, and some days better, and she may have suffered from rheumatism. Unless you are someone who sits around and moans, you just go on with it. I don't know how she did it, but she just did.

She always loved parties. Even when she was older, she would be swept up with the crumbs. She was always the last to leave. She loved people. She loved all the shooting parties with all these different people. It was exhilarating. It was like having a glass of champagne to her.

Meeting new people, discussing goodness knows what. I'm the total opposite of it. But she thrived. There were times when she was very ill and she suffered with her back, but there'd be a party, and you'd think, oh she's not going to go. But she got up, she got into her ballgown, and she was there, and she was there until the end. Because the adrenaline would burst out, with all the people and fun and dancing, and even as an old woman she was like that. She never lost her joy of life.

The Invercauld Galleries and Speciality Shop continued to do good business with visitors to the village. Frances was passionate about every patchwork quilt or woven fabric, the pure Scottish silks and tweeds dyed with heather, the cashmere sweaters and brass kilt pins, and the silver christening spoons which she designed herself and which she gave as a gift to Prince William for his christening in August 1982.[6]

The number of her shops in the village grew, and in 1982, she opened a health and beauty shop in the old-fashioned chemist's, after it had closed. She said:

I was petrified the shop would be lost to the village for good, so I rented it from the estate just in case a chemist ever comes along. It just goes on and on. I have now become so involved with so many things that I just do what I can manage myself.[7]

She realised that despite her enthusiasm, there was a limit to what she could do. Rather than putting on performances, she began showing films in the theatre, 'only good films. I wouldn't have anything but good in a church', and organised weekly ceilidhs for locals and visitors.[8]

Even in her eighty-eighth year she was continuing to promote Braemar and arrange new events for the village. 'At the moment I'm organising a ceilidh where my husband's piper, Meldrum, will be providing the musical accompaniment,' she said in August 1990. She had plenty of ambition for the festival, introducing performances by the Scottish Ballet and Opera companies, which were enjoyed by the royal family. 'They all come over, but I never tell people they do, or if they are coming,' she said.[9]

One of the young designers she encouraged was Annie Stewart, who had established a Scottish textiles business, Anta, in 1984 with her husband, Lachlan – both former students of Edinburgh College of Art. Their beautiful handwoven tartan silks, with their unconventional use of colour, appealed to Frances' appreciation of real craftsmanship with a twist. She invited Annie to meet her at Invercauld in 1990, to discuss how she could help support Anta.

'I could tell immediately she was a woman of elegance and style,' says Annie:

> We had established our company a few years ago, and were in the process of restoring a castle ourselves, so she had either heard about us through that, or had come across some of our designs. She invited me to Invercauld for tea, which must have been in summer 1990, and we showed our textiles and ceramics and what we were doing. She showed us around the gardens, and I remember being struck by the unusual cabbage rose-patterned wallpaper. That was surprising, as was the tartan furniture, as it tended only to be used for clothing at that time. Tartan by its very nature is attention-grabbing and she realised the fun of tartan, particularly as she was married to a clan chieftain. It suited her position, and she always wore it and used it with incredible taste.
>
> She gave me great encouragement, and offered us space in the Invercauld Galleries. She loved all the colours in our tartans, because she preferred the unusual tartans over the conventional, and she admired the people who were doing it differently. I clicked with her right away as we had the same ethos.

Annie was so inspired by her meeting with Frances that she designed a special tartan, named in her honour. Annie met Frances a second time, this time with Ilse Crawford, founding editor of *Elle Decoration*. They had a notion to arrange a feature on the wonderful interiors of Invercauld, but it was not to be.

★ ★ ★

Frances had been reluctant to step back from her activities, and she and Alwyne continued to spend time at their home on the Isle of Mull, rather than going overseas. It was here, in Torloisk, that she died in her sleep on 19 April 1991, after a short illness. She was 89 years old. On news of her death, the *Aberdeen Press and Journal* described her as a 'fervent admirer of her adopted country'.[10] Her funeral service was held at Crathie Church on 26 April, and George Petty-Fitzmaurice, the 8th Marquess of Lansdowne, who lived at Meikleour House, Perthshire, delivered a eulogy that encapsulated her personality, as much as it was possible to pin it down. 'In trying to recapture a vision of her, let me try to tell you what I see,' he told the mourners:

I see an intensely dynamic, tiny and compelling lady of great beauty, with the most wonderful eyes from which shine a brilliant intelligence, humour so youthful, sometimes almost girlishly naughty, but with never a trace of unkindness and illuminating her utterly fascinating regard, there is an exceptional perspicacity which somehow combines merriment with a deeply human sympathy and an inextinguishable interest in everything and everybody that comes within the focus of those truly magical eyes. Oh! How we have all laughed with her. How we have valued her sympathy and understanding, how grateful we have been for her absolute loyalty in friendship and for her unerring sense of direction and of what was seemly and harmonious.[11]

She was buried at Crathie Old Kirk Yard, with one of her brightly coloured tam-o'-shanter hats adorning her casket.

The kirk yard was the final resting place for many other Farquharsons who had come before her, including Francis Farquharson, the 'Baron Ban' who had founded Ballater. And so, she took her place alongside them as influential figures in the history of the clan.

At the funeral, Marybelle was struck by the number of people who came to say goodbye to her:

There were all these young people, and people assumed they were my friends, but they were hers. She always said you are as young as you think. She was very open minded. She was interested in people and thrived on it.

In the over forty years she spent living in Deeside, her impact on it was immeasurable. She filled it with her uniquely colourful sense of style, her innovative spirit, and her ambition to always change and improve, helping the region enormously. As Norma Sudworth remembers:

I think the village took a little bit of getting used to her, but I was very fond of her, as I had known her since I was four. I found her to be always polite, prepared to listen, and she took advice, she didn't go barging ahead. She had so much energy and she created jobs, so the village has a lot to be thankful for with her. It was sad when she became too old to carry on with the theater. The Speciality shop continued on after she died, but everything else disappeared after her death, the craft shop and antique shop, and it was a loss.[12]

Chapter Twenty-Four

After her mother's death, Marybelle decided to try to keep open two of Frances' fashion boutiques in Braemar. She combined the running of the Invercauld Speciality Shop and the men's shop, Invercauld Sportsman, with her own painting and sculpting. 'Although it is a bit of a challenge, it is something I wanted to do,' she told a reporter at the *Press and Journal*:

> I was always interested in the shop when my mother was alive. There is a lot of wonderful knitwear being produced in Scotland if you look for it. Tourists are expecting to take something home that they can't get at home and I intend giving them that. Sadly, in a lot of shops today, so much is imported. Yet Scotland has a lot of good things to offer.[1]

There were ambitions to keep the Invercauld Theatre going, with Alwyne in 1992 agreeing to lease the theatre to the village's trust for a 'peppercorn rent' in memory of his wife. The group were enthusiastic in carrying out the repairs to make it active once more, and to start staging regular productions again, but ultimately, like her shops, it failed to find the enthusiasm after her death. The Auld Kirk was developed into flats and the murals that Frances had commissioned were covered up.

Marybelle was unsure what to do with her mother's extensive collection of clothing. She contacted the keeper of costumes at Aberdeen Art Gallery, who was amazed at the quality of the donation when she came to see it. Ultimately, Frances' wardrobe went to both Aberdeen Art Gallery and the National Museum of Scotland. A large exhibition showcasing her clothing entitled 'Sartorial Elegance' was held at Provost Skene's House in 1999, where visitors could see her life displayed before their eyes: the Schiaparelli suits and hats, the Marks & Spencer pieces and the extravagant tartan creations designed to champion Scottish heritage at the Braemar Gathering.

As Aberdeen Art Gallery and Museums noted, in the publicity for their collection:

> Her love of stylish dress and couture is evident from the marvellous costumes and accessories from this period of her life. Designs by Schiaparelli, Molyneux, Irene Dana and shoes from Saks and Delman fill her wardrobe. Mrs Farquharson also possessed that rare talent of successfully combining high street ready to wear with couture to create a unique blend of elegant dressing.

After his wife's death, Alwyne Farquharson lived for another thirty-two years, and when he died in 2021 at the age of 102, he was Scotland's longest-serving clan chieftain. Upon his decision to retire from being an active laird, he moved to Norfolk, where he lived with his second wife, Patricia de Winton, at Brancaster Staithe, and where he would sometimes meet with his friend, the Duke of Edinburgh, for coffee at Sandringham. He continued to attend the Braemar Gathering in his colourful Highland dress up until 2019, the year that also marked his centenary.

He was always appreciated for his kindness and his sense of duty to the region. In 2006, he handed over Braemar Castle to the community, where they built on the work of Frances in making it a vibrant tourist attraction for Royal Deeside.

★ ★ ★

She may have been Seattle-born and lived a varied and adventurous life in many different roles, but it was as chatelaine of Invercauld and Braemar that Frances Farquharson found contentment. She embraced Scotland and did what she could to help encourage artists and musicians and to change the fortunes of those who lived in the region. She may have dreamed of the European capitals as a child, but it was here that she felt she was destined to belong.

As Frances once said:

> In my summer bedroom at Invercauld, I can look at Braemar, and in Braemar I can see Invercauld. I really have never wanted to go anywhere else.

Notes

Introduction

1 'Looking at Life', *Daily Mail*, 11 December 1933, Onlooker.
2 'Millionaire's Guests in Blazing Mansion', *Sunday Times*, 10 December 1933.
3 'Duke and Officer Die in English Fire', *New York Times*, 10 December 1933.
4 Ibid.
5 *Associated Press*, 9 December 1933.
6 'The Lady Who Put Life into Braemar', Sheila Hamilton, *Evening Express*, 4 September 1982.
7 Author interview with Norma Sudworth.

Chapter One

1 'Mrs MB Oldham Dies', *Seattle Daily Times*, 23 January 1922.
2 H. James Boswell, American Blue Book: Western Washington, Seattle, Lowman and Hanford County (1922).
3 'Eggerman will Leave Law Firm', *Seattle Daily Times*, 25 March 1930.
4 *Seattle Sunday Times*, 26 February 1911.
5 'Society', *Seattle Sunday Times*, 16 May 1915.
6 'Hundreds Pay Last Tribute to Oldham at Simple Rites', *Seattle Times*, 11 December 1941.
7 Frances Farquharson memoir, Chapter One.
8 'Something to be Thankful For', Mrs James Rodney, *Daily Mail*, 26 November 1942.

Chapter Two

1 'Seattle to Honor Shakespeare: Girls Will Be Seen in Pageant', *Seattle Daily Times*, 11 April 1915.
2 'Allegorical Operetta at HW Treat Home', *Seattle Sunday Times*, 25 April 1915.

3   'Hundreds Pay Last Tribute to Oldham at Simple Rites', *Seattle Times*, 11 December 1941.
4   'Mrs MB Oldham Dies', *Seattle Daily Times*, 23 January 1922.
5   Cynthia Grey, *Seattle Star*, 5 May 1917.
6   Ibid.
7   'Bazaar to Aid Lighthouse for Blind', *Seattle Daily Times*, 19 November 1919.
8   'Society', *Seattle Sunday Times*, 7 May 1916.
9   'House Party', Betty Brainerd, *Seattle Star*, 26 July 1919.
10   'Red Cross Jumble Shop', Betty Brainerd, *Seattle Star*, 22 August 1919.
11   'The Hon. Mrs James Rodney On Her Allowance', *Harper's Bazaar*, April 1936.
12   *Seattle Star*, 15 February 1918.
13   'Whence the Flappers?', *Seattle Star*, 21 August 1919.
14   *Seattle Sunday Times*, 25 March 1917.
15   *Seattle Daily Times*, 30 July 1921.
16   'The Week in Society World', *Seattle Sunday Times*, 27 April 1919.
17   'Butler-Harrington Nuptials', Betty Brainerd, *Seattle Star*, 13 June 1919.
18   'Mrs MB Oldham Dies', *Seattle Daily Times*, 23 January 1922.
19   'Personal', *Seattle Star*, 14 April 1923.
20   Seattle Daily Times, 3 May 1925.

Chapter Three

1   Frances Farquharson, unpublished memoir.
2   'Personal', *Seattle Star*, 24 January 1925.
3   Frances Farquharson, unpublished memoir.
4   Ibid.
5   'Personal', *Seattle Star*, 24 January 1925.
6   Frances Farquharson, unpublished memoir.
7   Ibid.
8   Ibid.
9   Ibid.
10   Ibid.
11   *New York Herald*, 8 April 1925.
12   Oleg Cassini, *In My Own Fashion: An Autobiography* (Simon & Schuster, 1987).
13   Ibid.
14   Frances Farquharson, unpublished memoir.
15   'Seattle Girl in Royal Circles, Letter No.11, London', *Seattle Daily Times*, 26 July 1925.

Chapter Four

1   'Personal', *Seattle Star*, 11 May 1925.
2   *Ibid.*, 13 May 1925.
3   'Seattle Girl in Royal Circles, Letter No.11, London', *Seattle Daily Times*, 26 July 1925.
4   *The Sketch*, 21 December 1921.

5   'Seattle Girl in Royal Circles, Letter No.11, London', *Seattle Daily Times*, 26 July 1925.
6   'Titled Women Who Keep Society Dressed in Style', *The Ogden Standard-Examiner*, 20 March 1927.
7   'Seattle Girl in Royal Circles', Letter No.11, London', *Seattle Daily Times*, 26 July 1925.
8   Frances Farquharson, unpublished memoir.
9   Ibid.
10 'Frances Oldham of Seattle to Wed Son of British Lord', *Seattle Daily Times*, 29 July 1928.
11 Frances Farquharson, unpublished memoir.
12 Ibid.
13 'Seattle Girl Guest of Royalty: Frances Oldham at Luncheon in Marlborough House', *Seattle Daily Times*, 19 July 1925.
14 'Letter No. 1, London', *Seattle Daily Times*, 5 July 1925.
15 Ibid.
16 Ibid.
17 Ibid.
18 Ibid.
19 Frances Farquharson, unpublished memoir.
20 Ibid.
21 Ibid.
22 'Americans at Madrid', *Los Angeles Evening Express*, 26 July 1921.

Chapter Five

1   Frances Farquharson, unpublished memoir.
2   'Exiled Queen of Greece Marie's Most Beautiful Daughter, Her Own Cook', Marjorie Dorman, *Brooklyn Daily Eagle*, 19 July 1928.
3   'A Queen Who is King', Frances Lovell Oldham, *Seattle Daily Times*, 31 October 1926.
4   Frances Farquharson, unpublished memoir.
5   Ibid.
6   'Exiled Queen of Greece Marie's Most Beautiful Daughter, Her Own Cook', Marjorie Dorman, *Brooklyn Daily Eagle*, 19 July 1928.
7   'A Queen Who is King', Frances Lovell Oldham, *Seattle Daily Times*, 1 November 1926.
8   Ibid.
9   Frances Farquharson, unpublished memoir.
10 Ibid.
11 Ibid.

Chapter Six

1   'Things Feminine, People and Places', *Weekly Dispatch*, 21 March 1926.
2   'The Round of the Day', *Westminster Gazette*, 17 April 1926.

3   'Daughter of King George Fond of Americans. Frances Oldham presented to
     Princess Mary', *Seattle Daily Times*, 5 September 1926.
4   Ibid.
5   'Queen Charlotte's Birthday Cake', *Nottingham Evening Post*, 10 May 1928.
6   'Seattle Society Girl is Guest of Royalty', Frances Lovell-Oldham, *Seattle Daily
     Times*, 16 April 1928.
7   'Monte Blue and Seattle Wife are Happy in Paris', Frances Lovell Oldham, *Seattle
     Daily Times*, 5 August 1928.
8   Ibid.
9   Ibid.
10   First World War pension records.
11   'Frances Oldham is Wed to War Hero in London', *Seattle Daily Times*,
     25 August 1928.
12   'Miss Oldham is Honor Guest at Round of Parties', *Seattle Daily Times*,
     12 August 1928.
13   'Frances Oldham is Wed to War Hero in London', *Seattle Daily Times*,
     25 August 1928.
14   Ibid.
15   'Vanities for Women', *Daily Mirror*, 8 October 1926.
16   'Frances Oldham is Wed to War Hero in London', *Seattle Daily Times*,
     25 August 1928.

Chapter Seven

1   'Things We Remember About Cowes, By The Hon. Mrs James Rodney',
     Harper's Bazaar, September1932.
2   'Flying to the Party', *Dundee Courier*, 26 September 1929.
3   'Colour-mix Your Room', Mrs James Rodney, *Daily Mail*, 13 December 1930.
4   'A British Air Route in America', Captain C.E. Ward, *The Bystander*,
     24 September 1930.
5   'Fly Little Lady, Fly', The Hon. Mrs James Rodney, *Sunday Dispatch*,
     26 January 1930.
6   'Visitors at Marienbad Prepare for Golf Tourney on August 3', *New York Herald*,
     7 July 1929.
7   'When in Rome, do as Rome Does', Hon. Mrs James Rodney, *Daily Mirror*,
     25 November 1930.
8   'Xmas Puddings Can Be Different!', Hon. Mrs James Rodney, *Daily Mail*,
     11 December 1930.
9   'They All Eat at Different Times', *Daily Mail*, 19 June 1931.
10   'London Visitors Arrive', *Seattle Times*, 28 December 1928.
11   'Society', *The Province*, Vancouver, 20 January 1929.
12   'Rooms Follow the New Dress Fashions', Mrs James Rodney, *Daily Mail*,
     17 July 1931.
13   'Goodbye to the Bright Young People', The Hon. Mrs James Rodney, *John Bull*,
     21 December 1931.
14   'Girls Who Earn Their Livings', Mrs James Rodney, *Daily Mirror*,
     27 February 1931.
15   'The Next to Nothing a Year Girl', *Daily Mail*, 19 March 1931.

16 'Marriage is such fun!', Mrs James Rodney, *Daily Mail*, 6 July 1931.

17 Ibid.

18 'Hard Times' Snobs', Mrs James Rodney, *Daily Mail*, 28 May 1931.

19 'Diary of a Modern Young Man', *Birmingham Weekly Mercury*, 19 March 1933.

20 'A Gossipy Letter from Paris', The Hon. Mrs James Rodney, *Weekly Dispatch*, 1 8 May 1930.

21 'Modes and Manners', *Daily Mail*, 29 May 1930.

22 Ibid.

23 'Marriages Fail Through Bad Cooking', The Hon. Mrs James Rodney, *Daily Mail*, 30 October 1930.

24 'Bathrooms That Look Like Boudoirs', The Hon. Mrs James Rodney, *Daily Mail*, 5 January 1931.

25 'Colour-Mix Your Room', Mrs James Rodney, *Daily Mail*, 13 December 1930.

26 'How I choose my ideal dinner menu, colour means as much as selection of food', *Daily Mirror*, 3 December 1930.

27 Ibid.

28 'Why Not Think About Food?', Mrs James Rodney, *Daily Mail*, 28 November 1930.

29 'Reception', *Daily Telegraph*, 22 June 1932.

30 'London Social Notes', *New York Herald*, 1 May 1933.

31 'Men and Women of To-Day', *Dundee Courier*, 20 May 1930.

32 'The Hon Mrs James Rodney', *The Sphere*, 28 January 1933.

33 Penelope Rowlands, *A Dash of Daring: Carmel Snow and Her Life in Fashion, Art, and Letters* (Atria Books, 2010).

34 Ibid.

35 'A Name for all Seasons', Janice Turner, *The Times*, 31 December 2005.

36 Ibid.

37 'I Know a Place', The Hon. Mrs James Rodney, *Harper's Bazaar*, June 1933.

38 'Those Sporting Clothes', Mrs James Rodney, *Daily Mail*, 18 April 1931.

39 'Solent Sailors', The Hon. Mrs James Rodney, *Harper's Bazaar*, August 1933.

40 'Society Goes A-Snacking', The Hon. Mrs James Rodney, *Harper's Bazaar*, February 1932.

41 'Cinema Parties', The Hon. Mrs James Rodney, *Harper's Bazaar*, May 1932.

42 'Banquets and Parties', The Hon. Mrs James Rodney, *Harper's Bazaar*, July 1932.

Chapter Eight

1 'Looking at Life', Onlooker, *Daily Mail*, 11 December 1933.

2 'Mrs Rodney's Tragedy', *Daily Telegraph*, 11 December 1933.

3 Ibid.

4 'Mystery of Country House Fire Tragedy', *Daily Mail*, 11 December 1933.

5 'Millionaire's Guests in Blazing Mansion', *Sunday Times*, 10 December 1933.

6 'Mansion Fire Theory', *Daily Mail*, 11 December 1933.

7 'Mystery of Country House Fire Tragedy', *Daily Mail*, 11 December 1933.

8 'I Came to New York to See My Baby', The Hon. Mrs James Rodney, *Detroit Evening Times*, 30 March 1941.

9 'Good Progress after seven weeks in hospital, Mrs James Rodney', *Daily Mail*, 29 January 1934.

10 Ibid.

11 'Mrs James Rodney Leaves Hospital', *Dundee Courier*, 20 March 1934.

12 'Hon. Mrs James Rodney', *Aberdeen Journal*, 23 April 1934.

13 'Injured Widow has a Relapse', *The Ottawa Journal*, 12 May 1934.

14 'Recovering', *Evening Standard*, 18 June 1934.

15 'Reflections from Society's Mirror', *Seattle Star*, 7 August 1934.

16 'Looking at Life', *Daily Mail*, 20 August 1934.

17 'London Social Notes', *New York Herald*, 13 October 1934.

18 'Ann Whittingham, Lord Tennyson and Lady Back in the States', *Chicago Daily Tribune*, 4 November 1934.

19 'Mansion Fire Sensation', Weekly Dispatch, 25 March 1934.

20 Penelope Rowlands, *A Dash of Daring: Carmel Snow and Her Life in Fashion, Art, and Letters* (Atria Books, 2010).

21 Ibid.

22 Ibid.

23 Ibid.

24 'London Glimpses', The Hon. Mrs James Rodney, *Harper's Bazaar*, December 1934.

25 'Walk a Little Faster', *Seattle Times*, 20 January 1935.

26 Ibid.

Chapter Nine

1 'Happy New Year', The Hon. Mrs James Rodney, *Harper's Bazaar*, January 1935.

2 Penelope Rowlands, A Dash of Daring: Carmel Snow and Her Life in Fashion, Art, and Letters (Atria Books, 2010).

3 'A Name For All Seasons', Janice Turner, *The Times*, 31 December 2005.

4 'Walk a Little Faster', *Seattle Times*, 20 January 1935.

5 'London Glimpses', The Hon. Mrs James Rodney, *Harper's Bazaar*, December 1934.

6 'State Parties', The Hon. Mrs James Rodney, *Harper's Bazaar*, May 1935.

7 'London News', The Hon. Mrs James Rodney, *Harper's Bazaar*, February 1936.

8 'London Social Notes, *New York Herald*, 13 June 1935.

9 'Goings-On', *The Bystander*, 3 July 1935.

10 'Looking at Life', *Daily Mail*, 11 October 1934.

11 Frances Osborne, *The Bolter: Idina Sackville – The Woman Who Scandalised 1920s Society and Became White Mischief's Infamous Seductress* (Virago, 2009).

12 Ibid.

13 Ibid.

14 'Inquest on Scots Laird's Wife', *Dundee Evening Telegraph*, 10 April 2019.

Chapter Ten

1   'Social Faces', *The Bystander*, 28 August 1935.
2   'Paris, Autumn '35', The Hon. Mrs James Rodney, *Harper's Bazaar*, September 1935.
3   Ibid.
4   The Hon. Mrs James Rodney, *Harper's Bazaar*, September 1936.
5   'London Glimpses', The Hon. Mrs James Rodney, *Harper's Bazaar*, December 1934.
6   'Masquerade', The Hon. Mrs James Rodney, *Harper's Bazaar*, Christmas 1935.
7   'Entre Nous', *Seattle Daily Times*, 4 March 1936.
8   'Charming Visitor from London', *Seattle Daily Times*, 31 March 1936.
9   'The Postilion Hat as Part of the Tailored Suit Costume', *Women's Wear Daily*, 29 June 1936.
10 'Café Chantant, New Programme at the Ritz', *Tatler*, 13 October 1937.
11 'And This is What They Wore', *Daily Mirror*, 18 January 1936.
12 'Summer on your Mind', The Hon. Mrs James Rodney, *Harper's Bazaar*, June 1938.
13 Meryle Secrest, *Elsa Schiaparelli: A Biography* (Penguin, 2015).
14 'Court Circular', *The Times*, 3 June 1938.
15 'Court and Society', *The Observer*, 3 April 1938.
16 'What the Smart Set is Doing Abroad this Summer', June Rhodes, *The Kingston Whig-Standard*, 16 August 1938.
17 'The Opening Act', The Hon. Mrs James Rodney, *Harper's Bazaar*, July 1938.
18 'The Robin's Here Again', The Hon. Mrs James Rodney, *Harper's Bazaar*, September 1938.
19 'What Smart Women are Wearing, London Fashion News by Yvone', *Aberdeen Press and Journal*, 19 November 1938.
20 'I Came to New York to See My Baby', The Hon. Mrs James Rodney, *Detroit Evening Times*, 30 March 1941.

Chapter Eleven

1   France Farquharson, unpublished memoir.
2   'Cannibals are Kind', Elsa Schiaparelli, *Harper's Bazaar*, March 1939.
3   France Farquharson, unpublished memoir.
4   'Paris Openings', The Hon. Mrs James Rodney, *Harper's Bazaar*, September 1939.
5   Ibid.
6   Ibid.
7   Ibid.
8   *Ibid.*: chapter entitled 'Where I Dines, I Sleeps'.
9   Ibid.
10 Penelope Rowlands, A Dash of Daring: Carmel Snow and Her Life in Fashion, Art, and Letters (Atria Books, 2010).
11 Frances Farquharson memoir: chapter entitled 'Where I Dines, I Sleeps.
12 Ibid.
13 'I Came to New York to See My Baby', The Hon. Mrs James Rodney, *Detroit Evening Times*, 30 March 1941.

14   Ancestry records, Passenger Ships – sailed on SS *Washington* to New York via Galway, 7 July.
15   Frances Farquharson memoir: chapter entitled 'Where I Dines, I Sleeps'.
16   Ibid.
17   Frances Farquharson memoir: chapter entitled 'Where I Dines, I Sleeps'.
18   Ibid.
19   Ibid.
20   Ibid.
21   'The Thin Red Line', *Harper's Bazaar*, March 1941.
22   'Mobile Beauty', The Hon. Mrs James Rodney, *Harper's Bazaar*, November 1940.
23   'Ex-Seattleite Quits Britain to Visit NY', Miss Joan Younger, *Seattle Times*, 9 February 1941.
24   'At the National Gallery', *Harper's Bazaar*, September 1941.
25   Frances Farquharson memoir: chapter entitled 'Where I Dines, I Sleeps'.
26   Ibid.
27   Ibid.
28   Ibid.
29   Ibid.

Chapter Twelve

1   Board of Trade Export Council papers, 30 May 1940.
2   Penelope Rowlands, A Dash of Daring: Carmel Snow and Her Life in Fashion, Art, and Letters (Atria Books, 2010).
3   France Farquharson, unpublished memoir.
4   Ibid.
5   'Ex-Seattleite Quits Britain to Visit NY', Miss Joan Younger, *Seattle Times*, 9 February 1941.
6   Frances Farquharson memoir: chapter 'Where I Dines, I Sleeps'.
7   'Bon Voyage', *Harper's Bazaar*, February 1941.
8   'Britain Gallantly Delivers the Goods Despite War Perils', Dorothy Roe, *Fort Worth Star-Telegram*, 9 July 1941.
9   'To the Cities of North America from London', *Harper's Bazaar*, November 1941.
10   'Hon. Mrs Rodney Visits US for British Style Magazine', *Seattle Times*, 25 May 1941.
11   'Ex-Seattleite Quits Britain to Visit NY', Miss Joan Younger, *Seattle Times*, 9 February 1941.
12   Ibid.
13   'Hon. Mrs Rodney Visits US for British Style Magazine', *Seattle Times*, 25 May 1941.
14   'US Likes Lancashire Fabrics', *Manchester Evening News*, 3 October 1941.

Chapter Thirteen

1   France Farquharson, unpublished memoir.
2   Ibid.

3   'Hon. Mrs Rodney Visits US for British Style Magazine', *Seattle Times*,
    25 May 1941.
4   'It's the Fashion', *Harper's Bazaar*, June 1942.
5   *Harper's Bazaar*, March 1941.
6   'Hundreds Pay Last Tribute to Oldham at Simple Rites', *Seattle Times*,
    11 December 1941.
7   Ibid.

Chapter Fourteen

1   Frances Farquharson memoir: chapter entitled 'Rationing'.
2   Ibid.
3   'London Styles Trim, Says Former Frances Oldham', by LEF, *Seattle Times*,
    5 December 1943.
4   'Something to be Thankful For', Mrs James Rodney, *Daily Mail*,
    26 November 1942.
5   Frances Farquharson memoir: chapter entitled 'Where I Dines, I Sleeps'.
6   Ibid.

Chapter Fifteen

1   'Going Away', Myrtle d'Erlanger, *Harper's Bazaar*, July 1935.
2   'Invercauld Welcome Mrs Myrtle Farquharson', *The Scotsman*, 3 September 1937.
3   'The Deeside Lairds, He's heir to five hundred years of Invercauld history', Tim
    Power, *Evening Express*, 1 September 1978.
4   'MC for Laird of Invercauld', *Aberdeen Press and Journal*, 20 October 1944.

Chapter Sixteen

1   'The Deeside Lairds, He's heir to five hundred years of Invercauld history',
    Tim Power, *Evening Express*, 1 September 1978.
2   Ibid.

Chapter Seventeen

1   'The Lady Who Put Life into Braemar', *Aberdeen Evening Express*,
    4 September 1982.
2   'Farquharson Country Wedding Gift', *Aberdeen Press and Journal*, 16 May 1949.
3   Author interview with Marcia Brocklebank, October 2022.
4   'Dying King Shaped Gathering Day', Susy Macauley, *Aberdeen Press and Journal*,
    3 Sept 2022.
5   'Frances the Fabulous', *The Scotsman*, 25 April 2003.
6   'The Opening Act', The Hon. Mrs James Rodney, *Harper's Bazaar*, July 1938.

Chapter Eighteen

1   Robertson, Frances, 'Power in the landscape: Regenerating the Scottish Highlands after WWII', in *The Culture of Nature in the History of Design* (Routledge, 2009)
2   'Poor Outlook for the Twelfth', *The Times*, 11 August 1954.
3   'Hanalei Hideaway for Highlanders', *The Honolulu Advertiser*, 3 May 1953.
4   'The World's Most Famous Village', Sheila Hamilton, *Aberdeen Evening Express*, 8 July 1987.
5   'The Lady Who Put Life into Braemar', *Aberdeen Evening Express*, 4 September 1982.
6   Ibid.
7   Braemar Arranges a Festival, *Dundee Courier*, 7 March 1953.
8   'Braemar Centre of Scottish Culture', *Aberdeen Evening Express*, 17 July 1953.
9   'Looking Ahead', *Aberdeen Evening Express*, 30 November 1953.
10   'The World of Entertainment', *Aberdeen Evening Express*, 1 May 1954.
11   *Tatler & Bystander*, 21 September 1949.
12   'A Home on Deeside', *Tatler*, 18 August 1965.
13   Notes from meeting with Mrs Farquharson, London, 19.10.1955.
14   'Island Industry Leaps the Fashion Barrier', Jean Smith, *The Scotsman*, 6 September 1966.
15   'Queen Mother at Braemar', *Dundee Courier*, 6 October 1955.
16   'Royalty Calls to Congratulate', *Aberdeen Evening Express*, 16 October 1956.
17   Notes from meeting with Mrs Farquharson, London, 19.10.1955.
18   'Fashion Village' *Scottish Daily Mail*, 28 March 1964.

Chapter Nineteen

1   'The Londoner's Diary', *Evening Standard*, 9 September 1952.
2   'US Gal is Queen's Highland Neighbor', Nancy Randolph, *Daily News*, 7 September 1953.
3   'Hanalei Hideaway for Highlanders', *The Honolulu Advertiser*, 3 May 1953.
4   Ibid.
5   'Vast Scottish Estate will Lure Rod, Gun Fans for "the Season"', Susan Smith, *San Francisco Examiner*, 25 March 1953.
6   Ibid.
7   Ibid.
8   'Hanalei Hideaway for Highlanders', *The Honolulu Advertiser*, 3 May 1953.
9   'One-Month Visit Stretching Out to Four-Month Sojourn', Susan Smith, *San Francisco Examiner*, 16 August 1953.
10   'Americans Sail to Shoot Grouse', *New York Times*, 6 August 1939.
11   Virginia Safford, *The Minneapolis Star*, 31 October 1957.
12   William Shawcross, Queen Elizabeth the Queen Mother: The Official Biography (Macmillan 2009).

Chapter Twenty

1   'Scottish Castle Highlights Tour', Virginia Safford on Travel, *Star Tribune*, 3 November 1957.

2   Virginia Safford, *The Minneapolis Star*, 31 October 1957.
3   'Scottish Castle Highlights Tour', Virginia Safford on Travel, *Star Tribune*,
    3 November 1957.
4   Virginia Safford, *The Minneapolis Star*, 31 October 1957.
5   'Lives: Herself, Overcastled in Scotland: Hosting Royals, Paying the Piper,
    The Washington Post, 18 August 1985.
6   'Fishing Scotland's Classic Salmon Streams: The Dee, the Tay and the Spey',
    Suzanne Wilding, *Town and Country*, December 1977.
7   Ibid.
8   'Lives: Herself, Overcastled in Scotland: Hosting Royals, Paying the Piper,
    The Washington Post, 18 August 1985.
9   'Braemar Plaque Unveiled', *Brechin Advertiser*, 11 August 1953.
10 Author interview with Norma Sudworth.
11 Ibid.
12 Ibid.
13 Virginia Safford, *The Minneapolis Star*, 31 October 1957.
14 Ibid.
15 Ibid.
16 'Royal Neighbours', Dave Roberts, *The Cincinnati Enquirer*, 29 August 1962.
17 'World Beat: Invercauld Castle', Dave Roberts, *The Cincinnati Enquirer*,
    27 August 1962.
18 Ibid.
19 Author interview with Norma Sudworth.
20 'What the Smart Set is Doing Abroad this Summer', June Rhodes, *The Kingston
    Whig-Standard*, 16 August 1938.
21 'From A Woman's Viewpoint', Alison Settle, *The Observer*, 18 July 1954.

Chapter Twenty-One

1   'Scottish Castle Highlights Tour', Virginia Safford, *Star Tribune*,
    3 November 1957.
2   William Shawcross, Queen Elizabeth the Queen Mother: The Official Biography
    (Macmillan, 2009).
3   'Braemar Castle – from Fortress to Home', Hugh Montgomery, *The Field*,
    Vol. 266, 10 August 1985.
4   'The Marraige of Miss Frances Fleetwood Wilson', *Aberdeen Journal*, 12 July 1898.
5   'Round and About', *Dundee Courier*, 12 December 1952.
6   'The Lady Who Put Life into Braemar', *Aberdeen Evening Express*,
    4 September 1982.
7   'Blaze Ruins Rooms at Braemar Castle', *Aberdeen Evening Express*,
    3 September 1960.
8   'Speaking Personally', *The Courier and Advertiser*, 8 August 1961.
9   'Premiere for Jacobite Play on Braes o' Ma'r, *Aberdeen Press and Journal*,
    3 August 1964.
10 Betty Thornton, *Meet Me in the Kitchen* (Athena Press, 2009).
11 'King of the Road', Alan Hunter, *Daily Record*, 15 October 1988.
12 *Tatler & Bystander*, 7 September 1955.
13 'Deeside's Wedding of the Year', *Aberdeen Evening Express*, 24 June 1961.

Chapter Twenty-Two

1   'Riviera's Out; Scotland's In', *Detroit Free Press*, 6 August 1963.
2   Ibid.
3   Interview with Major Hugh Cantlie.
4   Ibid.
5   Ibid.
6   'Braemar Festival', *The Times*, 1 September 1964.
7   'Braemar Feast of Folklore is Ready', *Aberdeen Press and Journal*, 15 June 1964.
8   Letter from Frances Farquharson to Eric Auld, 1974, in the collection at Braemar Castle.
9   'A Home on Deeside', *Tatler*, 18 August 1965.
10 'The Lady Who Put Life into Braemar', *Aberdeen Evening Express*, 4 September 1982.
11 'About the All-Scottish Festival', Colonel Cliff H. MacLean Hanson, *The Highlander*, June 1967.
12 'Rattlesnake's Tail Keeps Sun Shining', *Dundee Courier*, 5 September 1987.
13 'Summer Activities Hither and Yon', Christy Fox, *Los Angeles Times*, 8 July 1973.
14 'Fishing Scotland's Classic Salmon Streams: The Dee, the Tay and the Spey', Suzanne Wilding, *Town and Country*, December 1977.
15 Ibid.
16 'Far-Flung Kin Knocking at Castle Doors', Hugh A. Mulligan, *Corpus Christi Caller*, 22 December 1972.

Chapter Twenty-Three

1   'The Deeside Lairds, He's heir to five hundred years of Invercauld history', Tim Power, *Evening Express*, 1 September 1978.
2   Ibid.
3   Television listings, *Cambridge Evening News*, 29 May 1975.
4   'Gen LeMay Shoots in Moors', *Journal and Courier*, 12 February 1966.
5   Author interview with Norma Sudworth.
6   'The Lady Who Put Life into Braemar', *Aberdeen Evening Express*, 4 September 1982.
7   Ibid.
8   Ibid.
9   'Londoner's Diary', *Evening Standard*, 13 August 1990.
10 Aberdeen Press and Journal, 22 April 1991.
11 'Society Loses Old Friends', *Highland Society* magazine.
12 Author interview with Norma Sudworth.

Chapter Twenty-Four

1   'Laird's Lass Takes Over Local Shops at Braemar', Gary Cooper, *Aberdeen Press and Journal*, 8 May 1993.

Bibliography

Betty Thornton, *Meet Me in the Kitchen* (Athena Press, 2009)

Brown, James, *The New Deeside Guide* (HardPress, 2018)

H. James Boswell, *American Blue Book: Western Washington, Seattle* (Lowman and Hanford, 1922)

Hastings, Clare, *Hold the Front Page! The Wit and Wisdom of Anne Scott-James* (Pimpernel Press, 2020)

Michie, John Grant, *The Records of Invercauld* (HardPress, 2018)

Oleg Cassini, *In My Own Fashion: An Autobiography* (Simon & Schuster, 1987)

Onderwater, Hans, *Gentlemen in Blue: 600 Squadron* (Pen & Sword, 1997)

Osborne, Frances, *The Bolter: Idina Sackville – The Woman Who Scandalised 1920s Society and Became White Mischief's Infamous Seductress* (Virago, 2009)

Penelope Rowlands, *A Dash of Daring: Carmel Snow and Her Life in Fashion, Art, and Letters* (Atria Books, 2010)

Schiaparelli, Elsa, *Shocking Life: The Autobiography* (V&A, 2018)

Secrest, Meryle, *Elsa Schiaparelli: A Biography* (Penguin, 2014)

Sweet, Matthew, The West End Front: The Wartime Secrets of London's Grand Hotels (Faber & Faber, 2012)

Taylor, Elizabeth, *The Braemar Highlands: Their Tales, Traditions and Evil* (HardPress, 2018)

Tinniswood, Adrian, *Noble Ambitions: The Fall and Rise of the Post-War Country House* (Vintage, 2021)

Tinniswood, Adrian, *The Long Weekend: Life in the English Countryside* (Vintage, 2016)

Vreeland, Alexander, *Diana Vreeland: The Modern Woman: The Bazaar Years 1936–1962* (Rizzoli, 2015)

William Shawcross, *Queen Elizabeth the Queen Mother: The Official Biography* (Macmillan 2009)

Index

The destination for history
www.thehistorypress.co.uk